Transcripts
From the
Master K H

Andrew Carter

authorHOUSE®

AuthorHouse™ UK
1663 Liberty Drive
Bloomington, IN 47403 USA
www.authorhouse.co.uk
Phone: 0800.197.4150

Published by AuthorHouse 09/20/2016

ISBN: 978-1-5246-6184-7 (sc)
ISBN: 978-1-5246-6185-4 (hc)
ISBN: 978-1-5246-6186-1 (e)

Print information available on the last page.

This book is printed on acid-free paper.

Contents

Contents

Introduction

By Andrew Carter

When producing a work like this, the flow of words is more important than the punctuation. It is the words that carry the vibration of what they represent and can only be done in a hand written way of working. The pen becomes an extension of the work, it flows. To intellectually edit this work would destroy its essence and purpose. So it has been left exactly as it was written. It could have been presented so it was easier for the reader to work through it, but that would then have been a logical approach, whereas some of the purpose of this work is to engage in a more abstract approach thereby expanding the consciousness of the reader. This is the new approach and requires the stimulation of the intuition as against the intellect. There are blank pages for you to make notes, if you engage in this way then you will be engaging with the work itself and you will find you will make remarkable progress.

All work starts with an idea which is then built upon. Most work is based upon existing ideas therefore they can be classed as commercial and marketable. New ideas have no existing following which existing ideas have built up. So a new book based upon existing ideas, that have been presented by others, have a better chance of doing well. The idea for this work was simply its title: The Transcripts from the Master K H, that was all. The idea also identified with a Master of the Wisdom as being the source of the idea and the contents of the book. Not something I have ever done before but I went with it anyway.

I have come to realise that the identification with the Master K H was for a specific purpose. And that was to enable a new style of writing, that without the identification, couldn't have been done. Words flowed into the mind without effort due to this identification. Whether the Master K H was the source of the idea or not, doesn't matter. What matters is the work itself. It has been presented, prior to the release of the book, as a course, with great effect upon those who attended. Expanding their consciousness and developing their intuition. It contains: Meditations and insights, with reflections and offers a way of integrating meditation with everyday life. So there is no separation between the two. The concepts and approach are based upon the three aspects of man, those being, for this work: the Earthly man, the Spiritual Man and the Divine Man. It is well worth devoting time to reading this book and engaging in the concepts and meditations.

Consciousness has no boundaries, it is infinite.

From an atom to a Universe, nothing is separate, and
yet, the smallest of life is a part of a greater life.

Life is eternal and consciousness never dies.

TRANSCRIPTS FROM THE

MASTER K H

BOOK ONE

NOTES

NOTES

Transcripts from the Master KH

There is a life that goes beyond the boundaries of human life as you understand it, this life encompasses love. Can you conceive that life and love are so intertwined that the difference for you could hardly be perceived, and yet in your perception you separate both according to your physical plane existence? What does life mean to you? What does love mean to you?

You see life as the life you are living with all the confines that it represents, the imprisonment of life is the imprisonment of your soul. Go beyond the boundaries of the life as yourself within your physical life, your mind dwells so much upon your physical life, I bet it is immersed within in.

You see life from your understanding as a struggle, continually struggling for its existence and for its identity. Your identity is not your struggle for life, for life is not a struggle, your senses perceive your life as a misconception of the reality of the One Life. You see yourself as a separatist identity and your life proceeds in that way as a separatist identity. Therefore, your experiences will occur as the result of being a separatist identity.

Now, you cannot rationalise this because misconception will be the result, your identity on one hand is individual, meaning you have the ability to think and feel in the present, and you have the ability to vision the future, and it is the present always where your thinking should be, and it is at that moment in the present when all your forces are aligned, we can say that everything that is separate ceases to be separate because all vibration is aligned, each note within each sphere resonates within the harmonic note of the One Life.

This you can bring about by being in the present, and to be in the present is to realise the present as a condition of silence, the quiet awakening will then occur.

The silence I have mentioned is not outer physical plane silence, but an inner silence.

Your relationship to this is the soul.

Now this inner silence recognises the perpetual existence of life, the energy of silence plays upon the substance of form, brothers you will alleviate much of what you suffer if you stop mentally trying to work out your suffering, and as a separatist identity, this could be the case. Now when you enter more fully into the One Life, you will realise many lives exist within One Life. Now if your world has no meaning for you, then you have not come to understand it, you have not recognised the life that exists as being part of One Life.

There is no cohesion to your thoughts and feelings, they are mixed up, so to speak, you have not arrived at the fact of your existence, and where does that existence take you? Is it just walking horizontally across the face of the planet? Does your thinking only exist within this particular reality? Do you only feel within this reality? If so there will exist confusion, although your imprisonment will not understand your confusion. In that moment within the present, there exists an immortality and you can become magnetically drawn into that place, because love binds all things together even though they may appear separate.

Now if you look at a circle and place a horizontal line through its centre point, and that line ends at the edge of the circle, you will see that circle now has two halves, two halves of one whole. It is still a whole in its own circumference, and this circumference depends on many things. But there it is, you see a top half and a bottom half, the circle has been separated, and this is true for many people, they are separated. In fact, a barrier has been placed between the top half of the circle and the bottom half of the circle.

Now think about the bottom half of this circle as being your physical plane life and the three aspects that concern it - your thought, your feeling, and your physical actions. The horizontal line separates your thought as you understand it concerning your physical life, contemplate what that physical thought may contain and how much of it concerns your physical life. How much of this thought is just a reaction?

You have to be thinking to do something your eyes perceive, then an instant thought produces either a feeling and action, or you may just feel, or you may not feel at all, you may just act, and let us not just place this action as a bodily action, it may be an expression of sound which you identify as speech.

So my brothers, can you conceive that all your actions, whether mental, emotional, or physical, produce a reaction? Mostly in your minds a reaction can be a negative exchange because a reaction denotes a lack of thinking. We can look at this from two levels of experience. The first we are discussing, the second we have to go back to the circle - remember it has a horizontal line through it. Now the top half of this circle represents a higher version of what we are discussing, the lower half is a distorted reflection of the top half. If you realise that, or try to understand that even though the top half is a mystery, then a reaction, again subconsciously expressed, will be of a different vibration.

If you can understand everything is a vibration, a higher vibration contains love, a lower vibration, and this lower vibration we are concerned with is the human vibration in relationship to the lower half of the circle, contains a lack or an absence of love, it will be of a selfish nature.

'Why would this be so? My reactions are not of a selfish nature.'

Do they contain desire, my brother?

Desire that concerns the self, the 'I' identity, the separatist identity, the identity that only sees through the self that only looks upon the world with self-interest? Is that not the lower circle?

I will diverse slightly. The circle is capable of becoming the sphere, you are living on the earth which is a spherical shape, what holds all together within this sphere is gravity. The edge of the earth is the place high above its surface and the distance between the surface, and where you enter into space beyond the earth is known as its atmosphere. That is as far as you can go physically, now if you are just inside this edge you will fall back down to earth. If you are just the other side, you will float off into space, you will become weightless. So there is a something that holds all upon the earth as a part of the earth.

The Law of Attraction does this and in the case of the earth, it is a one whole, everything that makes it up, everything growing out of it, everything that walks upon it and everything that moves through its skies. That one fact will prove to you everything that is physical is a part of one thing, the earth and its life forms. Nature is balanced, humanity is balance, it fights itself because it sees itself as separate.

Belief is a very strange thing.

Philosophies govern belief, belief comes from philosophy, whether that is purely a living philosophy of good or bad values, or a more complex philosophy that transmits certain values, all philosophy that is contained within the lower circle is limited only to be separate. As with values, those that do not abide are not part of its circle.

Everything is circumscribed by a circle, this denotes the radiation of its energy, the vibration within the circle depends upon what that circle contains. If that circle is separatist from other circles, then from our perspective it will emit force, not energy - two different things.

Force is a vibration that carries an aspect of control. It carries the consciousness of that control, it seeks to render that which it is impacting upon, in line with the particular consciousness that the force seeks to achieve.

Energy is something quite different. It has a multitude of different vibrations, examples of this are life and love. Energy also carries, and is a transmitter of, consciousness. The energy of life, for example, contains a certain quality that is then transmitted into the various planes. Through each level of life there is a centre, a vortex of energy of the life stream that emits its vibrations across the horizontal aspect of that plane.

Love, by comparison, underlies all existence, an aspect or particle of love exists within all states of being, therefore, ponder upon whether love holds all things together, or does active intelligence hold all things together?

The answer is, from a human perspective, intelligence bring things into manifestation in ordered sequence, and love overlays intelligence from the centre point of intelligence, where there is nought but divine intelligence.

Visualise now the circle with the horizontal line, now place a centre point in the circle. You will find the centre point will not stay at the centre of the circle, it will move along the horizontal line, and if you identify yourself as the centre point within the lower worlds, you will see what is happening. As your life circumstance moves to the right or the left, so will your centre point, because it is not fixed at the centre, it is fluid just like a bubble of water upon a shiny plate.

What does this signify to you?

The movement to the left or to the right of the circle means your thinking and feeling will be according to the position of your centre point.

One thing I have to say to you here is that any movement left or right is then dependent upon the force that is directed to you, or how your inner force is relating to the external force that you are being affected by.

Let us assume when your centre point moves to the left you become passive, and let us assume when it moves to the right, you become forceful. Upon this horizontal line you may not be one or the other, you are daily both, as you could extend that time frame to weeks or months or years. Now if that is the case, that you have been passive for years, what will happen if your centre point suddenly changed and moved horizontally to the right? Also, what would happen if your centre point was forceful for years and moved horizontally to the left?

Most people fluctuate between the two in very short time frames.

There is nothing upon the horizontal line that is holding the centre point at the centre of the circle.

Now if you relate that to your consciousness you can easily see how your thinking and feeling changes according to the position of your centre point upon the horizontal line.

This is life upon the horizontal line and this also is love upon the horizontal line, because love upon the lower aspect of the circle is desire, the desire according to need, and your need is in relationship to your centre point.

Now life and love also exist upon the vertical line, so now imagine your circle, take away the horizontal line, and place a vertical line which passes through the centre point of the circle, and then touches the top and bottom of the circle.

What does that tell you?

Again the circle is two halves, but slightly different from the previous circle, there is a right and a left section. Firstly, what creates the vertical line? It is those moments when your centre point on the horizontal line can actually stop at the centre of the circle, you can visualise this centre point, firstly upon the horizontal line, see this in relationship to your life, your outer life and inner life, notice how it moves.

Now image if that centre point moves so far as to collide with the periphery of your circle, then your centre point will be stuck upon the periphery, it would be very hard from this position to pull it back to the centre. This place upon the periphery is a total immersion within the lower worlds, and depending upon which direction will be the result, one is symbolic of an astral condition, the other is symbolic of a mental condition, both reflect on physical conditions.

So now bring into your experience a short period of stillness.

You can imagine your centre point gradually taking its place at the centre of the circle. Depending upon your condition at this time will depend upon the length of time it will take to bring your point upon the horizontal line to the centre.

If this is proving difficult for you, bring your intention into your head centre, the centre of Spiritual Man, above that will be a centre for the Divine Man, this you can imagine as a sphere of light.

Remember the 'as if' principle. If you are not familiar with that, it is a principle that assumes you are what you are striving to become.

This my brothers, I give to you with the first statement, 'I am the spiritual'.

You fully assume that fact within the head centre.

Approach the second statement, 'I am the Divine Man'.

Assume your identification with that statement with the sphere above the head centre. Visualise once more the circle with the horizontal line.

You see your centre point, it will now be placed at the centre, and because it is at the centre, a line will be going upwards from it, and a line will be going down from it, until both lines come to rest upon the edge of your circle.

Bring now the light from the Divine Man into your circle, its entrance is at the top of the vertical line, down to the centre point, the light continues to the bottom, but also travels along the horizontal line in both directions. When this light reaches the periphery, it activates your circle and your circle radiates energy, the energy of light, into humanity.

Relax your focus, your work is done.

I just wish to project a little more understanding regarding the circle. Imagine once more the circle with the vertical line, with no horizontal line, and your centre point.

Where does it lie upon this vertical line?

Is it in the top of the circle or the bottom? If it is in the centre, your horizontal line will appear. How strong is your vertical line? Is the top as strong as the bottom? Is your point moving or fixed? You will find your point will not be moving so much as it did upon the horizontal line, in fact it will become fixed. If it is at the centre, all well and good. If not, it will be in one half or the other; if it is above the centre you will be influenced by the right half of the centre; if it is below the centre you will be influences by the left hand side of the circle. Identify with Spiritual Man (head centre) and Divine Man (sphere above).

To bring your point to the centre, create another point exactly the same distance from the centre, in other words, if your point is just below the centre, create a point above the centre. When you bring your created point to the centre through an act of the will, the other point will automatically be drawn to the centre. Achieve this now by an act of the will and the horizontal line will appear once more. Identify with the flow of energy from the Divine Man that radiates out from your circle to humanity.

Two actions you have achieved with this visualisation, you have placed your centre point upon the horizontal line, and you have also created your vertical line. You, as an individual within the One Life, can now start to work from your centre point. The integration of spirit and matter is depicted by the horizontal line (matter) the vertical line (spirit), but do not forget all this is from the centre point, that point of inner balance, that point of receptivity and also distribution, you cannot co-create without the horizontal line.

But also the potentialities of the horizontal line cannot be fulfilled without the vertical, and what you have learnt from the point upon this line, is that it has to be placed at the only place of convergence, at the centre. Aspire by all means towards that which lies above, but do it from that immovable centre.

Let me now present the possibility of expansion through identification.

Firstly, there is a need to understand what is meant by identification. What is your identification regarding yourself? Where do you identify yourself? Do you identify with love and life? You can identify with many things through recognition, but do you understand them? Are they a living thing for you? Do you recognise yourself within the One Life or do you see yourself as self-contained? The principle of love is not self-contained, so become identified with the principle of love, recognise this principle as the underlying principle of the solar system and this plane, of which we are all concerned with.

So, you recognise it, you identify with it, then you need to seek to understand it, but you will not understand it from an intellectual level, so do not strain your head about it. You understand it as the Spiritual Man in the head centre, not the head itself, you can start to embody it through the heart centre. The Christ holds the principle of love for humanity within the Buddhic sphere.

Your simple relationship to the point and the circle, the horizontal and vertical lines, is so powerful that it will create for you a sphere, the Spiritual Man lies within the Buddhic sphere, the man on earth lies within four planes, that is the sphere that he creates, and it is through this sphere that the principle of love flows outward and the sphere expands. Eventually two spheres meet, the Spiritual Man and the man on earth meet at the midway point, through love the life of the soul is known.

This is now the process: recognition, identification, understanding, embodiment, expansion.

How do you recognise the principle of love?

Love is an attractive force, love is essential for unity, first this is seen acting out within the lower worlds bringing about unity in mind, emotion and the physical body, the energy here is the etheric body, the ethers underlie all three aspects, so you have mental ether, emotional ether and physical ether. This is the substance for their relativity, so when there is a reference to these three states, you can conclude they are not separate from each other, each one depends upon the other, there is a balance here, an energetic balance that relies upon energy transference from one to the other.

We go back now to the identification with the Spiritual Man, the Spiritual Man is the controlling factor for the energy flow, and the unity of these three states of being for their existence and their co-ordination upon the Physical Manifest plane. So to recognise each aspect as one aspect brings about a realisation how each one affects the other. You need to take a very sure approach to this recognition regarding the principle of love.

What part of the body is not receiving this love?

What part of the body cannot accept this principle, although this principle lies within the body in every cell and atom?

Do you work with the body to resolve this issue?

In one respect there needs to be a recognition of where love is absent, because where there is love there is no break in communication from one part of the body to the other. Look towards the condition of the Spiritual Man as it resides within the body, because love is, and comes from, the Spiritual Man. Each part of the body is governed by consciousness, a lack of love lies within whichever aspect of consciousness that governs whichever part of the body, will reveal to you where there is a lack of recognition of love.

I seek to bring healing to you for the physical body via your recognition of the Spiritual Man.

So identify the Spiritual Man first aspect, with the principle of love second aspect, and the physical body third aspect, primarily you can bring healing through the relationship of this triangle.

If there is any difficulty in any part of your physical body, then there will be a depletion of the principle of love present, as love is an essential part of the physical body for its continuation of appearance, then this principle needs to be reinstated with the consciousness and directed to the specific area of the body for its regeneration through the application of the principle of love. Now I am going to give a method for the reestablishment of this principle, but also be aware another person might be needed to help with this process, but only if they themselves are conscious of the principle of love.

Meditation

Firstly, you need to render yourself free from any harmful thoughts or feeling, do this with open eyes, blending object and space into one continuity of consciousness.

Now become abundantly aware of your heart centre as a vessel for the outpouring and expression of love.

Now become acquainted with the Spiritual Man, the centre above your head, the eyes closed would be better now.

There are three streams of energy that come to the Spiritual Man from the Divine Man, the love stream is the second aspect.

Now we have many things to consider here, you can use this aspect to bring comfort to any physical distress, if that does not exist then the second aspect will relay its consciousness to those areas that are indeed immersed within a negative state, so you can assume the energy of love is the positive pole, and will enlighten and alleviate what I will call the negative pole which relates to form substance.

You, at this stage, ponder upon what has been said whilst fully retaining your identification with the Spiritual Man.

When you are ready to make an attempt to bring through the energy of love, make a request to the Spiritual Man for the healing energy of love to enter your auric field.

This energy will be blue-white in colour, this is the colour pathway of the Christ which you now identify with, as he represents the highest principle of love and holds this principle for when humanity is ready to receive it.

Now breathe in this energy now present in your auric field into your body and to the areas that require it to be present.

There can now occur a washing through of the emotional vehicle, use this as a releasing process, any problems offer them up to the Spiritual Man.

Pause and take yourself into the higher aspects of this vehicle and try to gain an experience from this. It will represent a higher order of love, experiences at this point will vary, the strength and versatility of your creative imagination will govern the result you gain from this. If you achieve a degree of success you will integrate aspects of your emotional vehicle with the Spiritual Man.

Your concentration and focus for this stage needs to be acute as you focus the love stream into your mental vehicle and bring your mental vehicle into its highest aspects, all this is like climbing a ladder, offer any mental problems to the Spiritual Man above the head.

You will know when you have reached the highest aspect because momentarily your mental vehicle will stop thinking.

You can now request a recognition from the Spiritual Man and open up to a communication.

Seek to understand the energy of love, seek to understand the second aspect of the Divine Man

Seek to relate the Divine Man to your existence within the One Life.

I realise I am asking a lot from you, but enter into a place of recognition, acknowledge to yourself that this is a possibility, and then relax with this intention.

Become consciously aware now of your physical presence, it would be advisable to record any impressions.

All this of which we are concerned with, is the recognition of the second aspect of love, but love is not complete within itself without wisdom and it is wisdom that discriminates, and discrimination in itself has a very close relationship to recognition. Recognition is attained through many levels, it is no good placing the concept of recognition upon one or two levels of experience, although your level of experience may be limited as such to only so many levels. But that is a good place to start, it is no good trying to recognise the higher levels such as Buddhic, as is stated the Buddhic plane, without recognising the lower planes on which you live and move and have your being. So within your quiet moments, if you can consciously recognise the need to acquire such moments, and within maybe that short time you are given, you will become free from your outside, and I will use the word 'experience', and all that is associated with that, for example your responsibility and stress. Then you will come to know yourself, and through this release, in that short time of burdens, you then become yourself within time.

This space releases your commitments; can you be without commitments? You may argue this fact, and of course your identification is to responsibility and commitment. But how do you take them upon yourself? Have you joy of living? Have you embodied the previous meditations and alignments? Or are they burdens? These are carried and they are the result of your negativity towards what you deem as responsibility which leads to commitment. You commit yourself to whatever the task is, and a task is not a joyful act. Certainly not all that we enter into through the Spiritual Man is joyful as you would understand that word, but it is fulfilling and that, if you can relate it as such, is joyful. Now if you are committed to the One Life, then you have no need to, if I can use the word, moan about this that or the other because everything is part of the One Life, then whatever you encounter is but a part of yourself, as you yourself are part of the One Life.

Consider the fact that the mind is a link between the consciousness of experience and the Spiritual Man. Your life experience is something that needs, and is required to be, recognised because from the progression of the five aspects, you will see identification. Identification places the consciousness upon a certain plane and all that resides within that plane. Now on the physical plane there is much that will emotionally attract you, and there is much that will mentally stimulate you, if you are seeking that avenue for mental stimulation, but what type of mental stimulation?

Bringing all things into balance, and I am not talking just about the physical plane, but also within that statement the spiritual planes, and your recognition and identification for that is the Spiritual Man. Your Spiritual Man needs to be part of your life just as much as your physical, emotional, and mental counterparts of the Spiritual Man.

Thus you can see recognition and identification need to be applied to the Spiritual Man, but also to the physical world from a centre of consciousness within the Spiritual Man.

What does this statement mean to you?

Quite often the connection between the two cannot be comprehended. If we now place our point of identification within the Spiritual Man, what upon the physical plane are you identifying with, which is not of the Spiritual Man, but of the Physical Man within the consciousness of that man?

Now there are many things that need to be identified with the Physical Man on a purely living basis, but there are many others that will lead you upon the wrong path, and that will not be the path of 'love' and 'life', maybe much 'life', but not in the correct form for its existence within the physical plane from the aspect of the Spiritual Man and your identification with it, then you can experience the physical planes in all their diversity and there will be no problem because your identification is the Spiritual Man. Do you understand the meaning of this?

I wish to bring an example into your mind. Let us say you go to a football match and you are a supporter of the home team and you shout and cheer just the same as everyone else. Now, if your identification is with the Spiritual Man you will enjoy the game even if your home team loses. You may be disappointed, but that will be as far as it goes. Now, if you are the Physical Man in this situation, it would be quite different because you may get aggressive and shout abuse at the so-called opposition, and that could lead to many things, and everyone is quite aware of that from past happenings concerning this particular identification. So you see, you can move within all the different circumstances of the physical plane if your identification is not upon its duality, and one thing you need to understand is that if you have a presence within it, and your identification is the Spiritual

Man, then you will be transforming the effect of the Physical Man by just being there.

So, recognise the aspects of your life from your identification with the Spiritual Man, which will reveal where your present identifications lie from the aspect of the Physical Man, you don't have to relinquish anything, unless it truly is not serving you and is definitely harming you. Because from this comes understanding, such a vastness encompasses this word, to understand, this is something everyone seeks in whatever degree it takes.

Let us now consider understanding comes from thinking. Yes, there is another higher aspect to this which is called 'knowing', but to get to that state, to be in knowing, requires the thinker to be present, it depends on the degree of activity of the thinker. There are two aspects of thinking. There is the thinking upon knowledge and this is what you have retained as memory, so the degree of thinking will depend upon the degree of knowledge. Ponder for a moment what that means. It means your degree of thinking is limited to your retained knowledge, and here we see the problem. Is thinking contained within knowledge and also, what has love and life to do with thinking? Thinking is not contained within the field of knowledge at all, thinking can go beyond that which is called a boundary. This boundary exists in terms of the knowledge you possess.

How do you go beyond that?

You realise, and you need to realise in the state of silence, that there is a vast overshadowing wisdom that you can leap into, to then transpose this wisdom into knowledge, but it may not be a conformity of knowledge, but a diversity of knowledge.

Let us now discuss the faculty of common sense. This, would you believe, is also part of the Spiritual Man. It retains a place that can distinguish and discriminate the truth, it is a mediator, it relates to the Physical Man and also the Spiritual Man. You have created many values that in essence are just common sense. If everyone identified with the Spiritual Man and applied common sense, most of the rules as you know them would disappear, and why? Because there would be no need for them.

Rules create standards that people are supposed to live up to. They confine you within their limitations. Obviously there are certain rules for living, but then the Spiritual Man knows these rules and doesn't need to be informed of them. There are many that are living up to certain rules and standards that are so separative in nature that they unfortunately have no recognition of the Spiritual Man, and their identification is upon the rules, but of course man-made rules have a duality, they have a positive and negative, the negative being what the rules do not allow you to do, even if it is quite obvious what the action should be.

Now relate this to understanding. I wish to inform you that understanding has its roots and accomplishment through love. How can you understand something, anything, if you have no love within your heart? Yes, you could understand the mechanics of things, how they work, but could you understand their purpose, the underlying principle from their manifestation?

Consider the purpose of the internet. "Oh, that's easy", people would say. Instant communication, instant knowledge, and many other things concerning what it appears on the surface and what it means to you. Why this instant communication? One reason, the purpose of which is to shrink the boundaries that exist between people, organisations, countries, to bring humanity together to lift humanity into the Spiritual Man.

But, of course, the internet also has the darkness as well as the light, and many things in between. There are viruses, as you call them, that can infect your computer, and there are also many viruses that can infect, and these you easily understand, the physical body. It has become a well-used term when they don't really know what it is. "You have a virus." That may well be true because there are viruses that infect the emotional vehicle with glamour, and the mental vehicle with illusion. These need to be recognised and identified so they can be cleaned out of the system. You talk about removing toxins from the physical body, this philosophy requires the removal of toxins from the emotional and mental bodies, this is where it can all start.

This is where you seek to understand now yourself, this third stage is very important, you need to understand what is polluting the emotional and mental bodies. Only the Spiritual Man can inform you, so first you have to recognise the Spiritual Man by aligning the Physical Man.

Can you now find time to make this recognition and identification?

Meditation

The mind will make the connection, consider the Physical Man, but first you are required to become present within the space. To be present means no physical emotion or mental action, you just become the space. There is no need at this point for any visualisation or breathing exercise to achieve this, if you focus calmly upon the space and object as being non separatist, then you will be receptive. There is no need to recognise the physical body as mostly you identify too much with it. Consider it is the means by which the Spiritual Man expresses itself in the manifest world and is not a principle, you also need not identify with it as it can take care of itself, if your recognition and identification is lifted higher into the Spiritual Man.

Now at this point bring yourself in focus into the centre above the head, which you identify as the Spiritual Man. Use your mind to make this connection, let the Spiritual Man into your emotions by means of love and light, which comes from the centre above the head.

Bring your emotional body in resonance with this centre, imagine two tuning forks. One is the Spiritual Man which now sends out a note, the second is the emotional body which seeks to respond. Imagine that note as waves of energy coming through the aura into your emotional body. Is it responding and resonating in tune with the Spiritual Man?

Imagine now two points of light, one is the Spiritual Man above the head, the other is the emotional body, which may well locate itself upon the body in the region of the solar plexus and sacral centre, a line of energy occurs between the two, you continue until both are in resonance.

Proceed into the mental body and enter into the mind. Allow your mind to bring about an absence of intellectual thought, of everyday thought, that can precipitate because of the fact of your stillness.

Realise the mental body is closer to the Spiritual Man than your emotional body, retain your focus upon the Spiritual Man and you bring to mind the two tuning forks, one is the Spiritual Man and the other the mental body.

The Spiritual Man sounds out a note towards the mental body, you imagine waves of energy passing through the auric field into the mental body and then you visualise two points of light, the first is the Spiritual Man, and the second represents the mental body.

You imagine them both in resonance.

The point of light for the mental body you may locate upon the physical body, a line of energy occurs between the two, you proceed until both points are in resonance. Assume your alignment has been achieved.

Now you are identified with the Spiritual Man, you bring your mind to bear upon any understanding you need to gain from your alignment. So, from this point of focus within the Spiritual Man, bring your attention to the mental body. Is there anything you need to understand? Bring light into your mental body from the Spiritual Man to help bring illumination.

Proceed now to the emotional body, allow the light to flow through from the mental body into the emotional body. Is there anything you need to understand about your emotions in the world of emotions? Continue, bring added light into the physical body, imagine this light as healing light from the Spiritual Man. Now there is a complete flow of energy through the lower bodies, you will find whatever you have understood from the mental body will also be reflected within the emotional body, and will have maybe manifested within the physical body.

So the next stage is to bring in the positive pole of your understanding, if it is something that has been shown to you as being damaging to yourself in manifestation, then the opposite needs to be sought after. If you have received from the alignment, then you can bring in more illumination.

Focus once more, but very directly into the Spiritual Man above the head, stay within its radiance, start to sense another energy above the Spiritual Man through a tentative line of mind energy up from the Spiritual Man into the Divine Man above the Spiritual Man.

The Divine Man is pure illumination, pure love, and pure purpose. This is represented to you as a sphere of intense light, maybe colour, if so a blue may be present as the Divine Man also possesses the Christ Light of consciousness.

Bring now this energy into your mental body, release any opposing forces there, place one word of illumination into your mental body "I am Truth". State that with deliberation.

The light proceeds into your emotional body, ejecting any opposing forces there, and you place a word of illumination there, "I am able to Trust." This you do purposefully.

We approach the physical body in a different manner. Re-establish the flow of energy from the Divine Man. As it enters the physical body it brings in a complete harmony and you place a word within it, into the heart centre, "I am Love". Embody this love from the Divine Man as you enter into his presence.

Many things have been accomplished here, much of which you will be unaware of, but I can say the energy within the substance of your bodies will have changed, their structures will have become more orderly.

Persistent use of the three words, Truth, Trust, and Love will bring you many rewards. According to the Spiritual Man you live your life with, and in, truth. Trust comes from the truth that you register, and love encompasses all your deeds and actions.

What is required here is the breaking through of barriers, from the present state of consciousness that is present upon the horizontal line. This statement may not be understood, "What barriers?" There is no awareness or recognition of any barriers. What will present this recognition into the mind, as the mind has two aspects, the mind related to the brain consciousness and the mind related to the consciousness coming from the Spiritual Man? Barriers bring a limitation. How many of you feel a restlessness, an un-fulfilment in life, but do not know why? The worse it gets the more you are approaching the barrier, until there is a recognition of something that lies beyond your present consciousness and you do not need to know what it is, that is the dilemma that is a part of the release of your logical mind.

How can you recognise something that you don't know, that hasn't been presented to you in word form? It is a dilemma that the mind has to transcend from your present realities into an expanded reality. This barrier exists in many levels, so when the mind becomes the enquiring mind, not in the respect of seeking existing knowledge, although there may be a need for this when it is appropriate to do so. Let me explain further.

Your present consciousness is presenting a barrier, and realise that it always will. The mind enables you to break through the barrier when it is in resonance with the Spiritual Man, who has access to an unbelievable amount of knowledge and wisdom. But the Spiritual Man, in the first instance, identifies with you through love. It can through intelligence (common sense), but it is the love that creates the channel for the knowledge and wisdom. The mind is of an active intelligent nature, but the mind that is love does not seek the knowledge and wisdom for itself, because what is the point of that and what use would it be? It will have achieved nothing for humanity, or indeed the Divine Plan.

Now the mind that has the love aspect missing is but the logical mind, and worse than that, our unconscious mind, a surface mind, a mind that will not elevate the present consciousness out of its imprisonment. Now the mind that is love blends with the mind that is active intelligence.

There are no barriers for the mind that is of love because it will also be of the heart, the human mind that has been developed through the human experience is the barrier. It is initially also possessed of emotion, when the emotion has no control as such, the mind is intellect, that is when the real barrier is presented because it is intellect, it also identifies itself with itself. It is self-satisfied with itself in many ways, it convinces itself it is right, it is impressed by communication and knowledge of a superficial nature, it sets itself up within its own house and locks the door.

Consciousness is not cleverness. Do you wish to become clever to impress people with your abilities, to deceive people, to avoid the truth, to gain recognition, to reap the rewards of your cleverness? Eventually time catches up and all that you have wished for in the material world cannot be retained as cleverness, with age, declines. Free your mind up from everything you understand, you will not lose your present understanding, but you must realise there is a greater understanding you can achieve, because you place a limitation upon your understanding, you believe your understanding is what you read and what is communicated to you.

Meditation

Why do you not try to understand more? Empty your head now at this present moment, what do you find? Is there nothing? If so, that is good.

Now focus rapidly upon the Spiritual Man above the head, allow for a resonance to occur, retain your empty mind.

Now while empty become expectant of some sort of communication from the Spiritual Man, the Spiritual Man relays abstract realities.

If you are in some way already starting to embody the Spiritual Man, then there will be a channel of communication already available to you, because you will be manifesting some aspect of the Divine Plan into humanity. Do not put yourself down with the thoughts of 'it is not very much', that does not matter because no matter how small you think it is, you are part of all other people who are also manifesting the Divine Plan, therefore you are the Divine Plan in incarnation.

This is important for you to understand, so the Spiritual Man will relay into your consciousness another portion of the Divine Plan that you are able to manifest into the physical world.

Again do not expect momentous things because they may not be what they would appear to be. Momentous things normally have a glamour attached to them as they satisfy the self. This type of thing needs to be reflected upon as they will blot out the light from the Spiritual Man.

If you are aspiring, then whilst in alignment silently wish to understand your purpose.

Finish this contemplative meditation by sounding the OM towards the Spiritual Man above your head.

Reflect upon the Spiritual Man as being a part of your life, it is the essence of the true man. Become acquainted with the Spiritual Man during the day by, at times, emptying the mind and focussing above the head. You need not be in meditation, how you would separate that from everyday life, so it can be with eyes open. This aspect of meditation needs to be clarified somewhat. The way you have been impressed from birth, taught and learnt, places your mind in a separate state of reasoning, you compartmentalise everything as being a separate activity. Now you can reflect upon this by thinking about your activities, meditation is assumed to be done when one has time, and mostly there is a clear need for this to happen, but it tends to be down the pecking order somewhat. At some point your will realise the need for it, you will have an inner urge towards it, and initially it will be to gain some sort of control over life and, in particular, yourself within life, and you will see it as a separate part of your life in the way you think about it. It is something not dissimilar to going to the gym, you adopt the same attitudes, also you could separate the activity of meditation and going to the gym as being separate from each other, other than you are the one participating in both. How far from the truth this could be?

Take, for example, your meditation. People can take this so seriously and also so naively. If you just got on with it just like any other task you perform during the day, it would alleviate your stress concerning it. If you believe that stress doesn't exist, well think about how you approach it. Firstly, is the time factor - how to create the time. Think of all the reasons why not, I am not here to list them all for you, you are clever enough to work them out, unless of course your identification is so elsewhere other than meditation, then your consciousness will not see the obstacles, in fact they will not appear as obstacles at all. This is the first thing that sees it as separate.

Secondly, you will require in your mind to have a suitable place to perform your meditation - another obstacle you will place in your mind because, to you, it has to have certain requirements. A separate space, it has to be my space, it needs to be quiet, and I need not to be disturbed. Also certain adornments need to be present to enable me to meditate.

The third obstacle is - what meditation do I do? No doubt the meditation that will produce results for you is the one you may find boring and repetitive and you will get nothing from it. You will then decide very quickly to stop doing it.

The meditation format I am referring to is one that will effect an alignment with the Spiritual Man, aligning with the Spiritual Man will create a line of light that pierces through the planes of glamour and illusion. I refer to this as being the emotional astral plane and the lower mental plane. You will not, due to this, receive any impressions from those planes.

Let me elucidate upon the astral plane. There, if your identification becomes fixed within, and that is quite easy to do as the astral plane will reflect to you whatever you are wishing for, this can be the result of a meditation that takes your mind into the astral plane.

For example, if you wish desperately to contact an angel, you most definitely will upon the astral plane, but it will be only as a result of your wishes and desires, and there is much more to be found upon the astral plane, in particular if you are seeking the afterlife.

Results for you if your meditation is focussed upon this, they will be dreamy and incomprehensible and may send you to sleep. If your meditation incorporates the lower mental plane, then there would occur a powerful interaction between the two, resulting in a belief that is based upon glamour and illusion. This will have stimulated your solar plexus and therein lies your ego. Can you imagine the result of this? Everything that you experience will be the result of what you wish for, and also what has been attracted to you, as a result of this. Your ego will then tell you, and impregnate your mind that this is the truth.

Notice how the word 'truth' does not resonate with what I have spoken of, because truth comes from two aspects - the higher mind and the aspect of love upon the plane of Buddhi. The intuition relays truth, the intuition comes from the Spiritual Man. Most of what is spoken of concerning the intuition is not of the intuition, it is from what has been spoken of, glamour and illusion.

A common statement at this point of evolution is "I prefer to work with the intuition".

What is this saying?

It is saying that they are not working with the intuition in any understanding of the intuition, they are working with fragments of the intuition, but these fragments give an easy option to the long process of becoming conscious upon the plane of intuition. You may have grasped some aspects of intuition and then you believe, because it has excited you, that you have obtained something beyond what you had always believed to be impossible, that you now know what the intuition is, and you proceed to embody it according to your fragment of experience. You then become fixed in your fragment of experience. This presents a barrier to your consciousness and because many have reached this stage, they then affirm to you their belief, and because it is so similar to what you have experienced, you then become excited about it and therein lies the problem. In the first place, you have to become separatist towards those that have not had your experience, and then become identified with those that have.

What you really have here is a fragment of the intuition with a portion of your consciousness placed within the lower mind and astral plane, so your fragment of intuition identifies with illusion and glamour, and as you know no different to your experiences, you then become unable to accept any other. You may read these words or the words may be relayed to you and you will not be able to understand them. In fact, you may well say, "I am above these words, they do not apply to me".

Before we go back to my original proposal on meditation, and yet all that has been said has a reference to it, I wish to bring to your attention firstly, that if you have understood all that has been said, then it will be useful for you to relay it to others. If you have interpreted your own version of what has been said, then you can confirm to yourself that you are on the right track. If you believe your version is better, then you are not so enlightened and need to read further in the light of this.

Secondly, I need to make reference to what is known today as Lightworkers, 'today' being towards the end of 2014. This identification has come about through the transition from one age to another, known as the New Age, and as such is now in respect of the energies present for the transformation in consciousness of humanity, are very different from the previous age.

Let me now define the word 'Lightworker' and see if it can bring you a greater understanding and recognition in terms of the Spiritual Man. The word 'lightworker' means a worker in the light, a worker with light that is in service to the Divine Plan.

Light comes from three aspects. The light you are familiar with is the light of the physical sun, it is the light of life as you know it. There is the light of the soul and the light of spirit. To define it further, all light blends with the light of the soul, the light of spirit and the light of matter blended with the light of the soul. So if you are what people now refer to as 'Lightworkers', you will be working with the lights previously mentioned, you will display this light emotionally and mentally and physically, you will be acting upon the Divine Plan, you will not be dwelling unduly upon your personality, as the light of spirit will take your attention away from it naturally, as you will, as a result, expand your consciousness into the three aspects of light, you will not separate spirit from matter.

If you are a Lightworker you will engage upon all levels and you will bring the light into manifestation upon the physical plane, you will be serving the good of the whole, the One Life. Be assured if you are only seeking an escape from the physical environment, you will wander endlessly upon the astral plane, you will be deluded, and many are. We will come back to this subject, as that is enough to digest and to stimulate your thinking.

As you live in time, you sequence time as events within time. These events, to you, are separate happenings. We have discussed this, but now realise that all your events are but one event, each event links to another through the Law of Attraction, hence I am seeking to show you the importance of meditation, and how it carries through life as a sequence of events. I have outlined some meditations already; I will be presenting more for your use.

Let us suppose you have not meditated this morning, your day yesterday was busy and there was some emotion and worry present, and today is very busy, there was not time to meditate. This, as previously mentioned, is one of the obstacles that needs to be overcome, so today you have not created the space and silence, you have not aligned, your mind is full of the day, you have your schedule and you have many things to do, you are immersed in your tasks, you have identified your thoughts and feelings with the tasks, the tasks have become part of yourself within the three worlds, so your tasks then become coloured by your emotions and thoughts connected with the tasks. The result being, the tasks will become harder, especially if also you have a worry concerning them within time and space.

Along comes the Law of Attraction, and I should say that it is always present.

Think again what I have said, your thoughts and actions have identified themselves with what lies in front of you for that day.

I could expand that further than the one day we are considering. You end up in a traffic jam, can you conceive that could be the result of your identification with the day's tasks? You may well say, "That's ridiculous, I haven't caused the traffic jam". That's true, you haven't, but do you remember just before you left, in your haste you knocked a cup onto the floor and had to clear it up? Also, the phone rang and you answered it, you then left half an hour later and ended up in a traffic jam. Your response may be, "I understand about the cup, but not the phone call". You may consider these two things here, if you had meditated, your power of discrimination would have suggested to you not to answer the phone, secondly the person who phoned you was someone that you were meeting in the afternoon. Remember that you have identified your thoughts and feelings with your tasks in, I may say, a negative way. That person had received the energy of your identification as, upon those levels, all is connected so they, in their turn, according to their own state of consciousness, found themselves in a little trouble with the Law of Attraction and were informing you that they would be an hour later. Can you see now how your day could escalate with problems all because you didn't meditate?

It is obviously not quite as simple as that, because you have to meditate in the appropriate way that will attract the good into your day, so that it will flow and attract other beneficial things as it progresses. For this to happen you have to acquire the realisation that there is no difference between sitting down for meditation and continuing an awakened sense of receptivity and alignment throughout the day.

Consider this when you meditate specifically to align to these higher states of consciousness, then those higher states of consciousness can be present during your day if you do not separate your meditation from your daily living experience, and realise your daily living experience will be the result of your continuity of meditation.

This is quite a dilemma to your intellect that I present to you, whereby you experience very little from your meditation from a feeling nature, and that is no different, I might say, from the astral nature, although there is a higher feeling nature that is established within the heart, but that does not feed the emotional body in a way that would feed your ego, because the heart centre and the Spiritual Man are so connected you will not go wrong in your identifications.

That you can achieve a state of meditation during the day, and this is without trying, all concerns the quietening of the intellectual mind, but this aspect of your mind becomes receptive which means it is active and because of its identification with the Spiritual Man, it is not active with personality thought, and if it is, which it has to be as you are living your life upon the physical plane, then your mind is capable of going into one state for life circumstance, then into the other state that is of the Spiritual Man. You will know this as the silence that you can experience, but it is not just the silence of the mind you will experience, it is the silence that you feel within the space of your environment. This can be active throughout the day, then your day will not produce all those things through the Law of Attraction that will turn your day into a nightmare.

As the Spiritual Man relays consciousness, then your consciousness will know what the Law of Cause and Effect is trying to tell you. You may ask, "Why does all this happen? Why cannot life just be an easy flow from one thing to another without any obstacles? Why do I have to meditate without any apparent results?"

I have mentioned the obstacles of the world in which you live and a recognition of yourself within that world. You have to recognise where your identifications lie and your thoughts and feelings towards them, and how they affect you. You have to understand what is happening, all the interactions upon the physical plane produce energy if the interactions are productive of a spiritual nature, or they produce force if they are of a personality nature. Both affect you in different ways. Your personality, which is that specific aspect of you that is of the physical world, is, in many ways, related to force. Force is something that is applied to whatever that particular force is focussed upon, so consider this in your three activities - mental, emotional, and physical. You apply force all the time in one direction or the other because of your identifications upon those levels. If you do not understand this, look towards a family relationship, mother to child. What does the mother apply to the child, but force? I will explain this. If the mother is governed by these three states previously mentioned, and any of them could be dominant, then, for example the mother's emotional state of, we can say self, is applied to the child.

This is force, the force of wanting the child to comply with the mother's demands.

What are those demands? Well, if they are emotional then the mother wants the child to be exactly how the mother wishes it to be, and on that level, well behaved and respond to the mother as the mother desires it to be.

Where is the truth in this?

So, you can conceive force does not relay truth, it relays a consciousness related to the desire nature of the person that is projecting the force.

This is the problem faced at the time of breaking the patterns of human consciousness, or I should say, lack of consciousness, as consciousness would perceive the situations from your identification with the Spiritual Man. Many emotional and mental reactions in what I am presenting with the mother and child are patterned reactions to when the mother was a child with the additional stress of situation and environment. This just doesn't involve the mother as regards the child, but the father and grandparents and other family members.

Do any of them listen to the child? You may say, "All the time".

You may hear what the child is saying only from your negative identification for your own peace and quiet, or you will not hear the child at all and talk over the child if you are in the company of your friends. The child then becomes an inconvenience to your desire to communicate with your friends, but forget not, the child has a link with the mother for at least seven years. They also present a challenge to you, not a physical challenge, but a soul challenge because the child has not developed the personality that you have, it is still governed by the soul until the personality develops. The child will reflect to you in its behaviour the patterns of personality that you possess that needs to be addressed. To understand the child is to understand yourself, because the child will tell you the truth. It can do no other as its mental reasoning within the manifest world has not become patterned by it, until, of course you apply your force upon the child, then it will change. It will give up its simplicity of truth and will become the product of the force applied upon it. This is very sad because the child is very creative and the force of negative suggestion will extinguish this creativity. But this creativity is the creativity of the soul and the child is relaying to you what you are lacking in yourself that is of the soul.

The mother-father-child relationship goes much deeper than that, but it is not wise for me to bring to your attention anything beyond this lifetime.

What characteristics of the child affect you? Is it the fact you require them to behave?

What a strange word, as that word will be related to your own level of consciousness. What do you deem as correct behaviour?

I would advise that you review this, and also meditate upon these two words - behave and correct. The word 'correct' also relates to a correct answer to a question, therefore, you would give a tick in the box as against a cross. The tick you could see as green and the cross as red, very much like traffic lights. Conformity suggests to you a means whereby there is a certain way to behave. Here you have placed two other words, right and wrong, so you then have a positive or negative identification. So you influence your child, your partner, and all people you come across, with an expression of what you deem as correct in your consciousness, and also how to behave, whether that complies with the rules or otherwise. I seek to inform you that everyone is affected by positive or negative suggestion.

Within the three worlds, the negative suggestion blots out the truth. How limited is the belief about right and wrong? There is no right or wrong, there is just experience and learning. The Spiritual Man watches and waits for you to understand this, and not continue to live this principle of right and wrong. Then you will understand there lies the concept of love as the balance for what you have manifested in the consciousness. Love extinguishes right and wrong on the level of what you understand, as it pertains to knowledge, as it pertains to behaviour, or as it pertains to governments in the many aspects of society.

So, truth lies beyond the principle of right and wrong. Truth is the essence of wisdom so you look toward the Spiritual Man, and the Spiritual Man in others.

That is your common bond on a group consciousness level, not upon your personality level, although your spiritual may well be resident via a thread of consciousness into your mental and emotional bodies, the Spiritual Man may well be influencing your physical body and this thread of consciousness is light.

Light has an analogy to colour.

Regarding the Spiritual Man in relationship to colour. Do not assume to start with that, if you were in a room with many people all of whom had identified, and to varying degrees, embodied the Spiritual Man into their mental and emotional bodies, that you would all agree with each other. Now to agree with something someone is saying is to validate what they are saying, and to take upon yourself the energy of what they are saying by agreeing with it, you will have identified with that they are saying. What does this mean? If you do truly agree in this respect it will have a similarity of resonance with your own aspects of consciousness.

What would happen if you agreed, but actually didn't?

Then the energy of what is being said will come into conflict with the vibration of existing consciousness. Then your internal dialogue would criticise and judge what had been said, it will then destroy your own truth.

Because truth has to be embodied and lived.

Do not agree with something that you do not believe in, but on the other hand, if you expressed your opinion regarding what they were saying in truth, even though you disagreed, then you might learn something from the encounter. Always look towards learning because this person may be displaying wisdom, but you do not understand it, so in the end you will never disagree with anything because to disagree is to identify with the negative polarity of its meaning, you will find other words more fitting, and they will be a derivative of the word, Truth, for example, "That sounds true" or, "That's true", rather than, "I agree". When you agree, you give the person power in their personality whereas, "That's true" relates to the Spiritual Man. The Spiritual Man has far more expanded vocabulary than the personality man, far more creative, far more expressive.

Do not inhibit the Spiritual Man from your expression, you may make mistakes, but are they because you will come across many personalities, many aspect of concretised thought, but then when the light of the spiritual then radiates outwards, are you not trying to bring a spark of light into their consciousness, even though they will not realise it, and this spark will not be a high spiritual concept. It will be something that will break their pattern to expand their consciousness into, even if only in a small sentence of thought that, for them, is enquiring thought. To enquire is to make an attempt to go beyond your mental thought concerning what it knows and of course you can enquire towards the Spiritual Man.

What will you enquire about?

You could enquire about Truth, the truth of what you may ask, the truth of yourself is a good start for you. Do you want to stay the same, even if you do possess a certain amount of wisdom and knowledge? There is a point when you realise that you're never meant to stay the same, no matter how far you have progressed. This is what the urge towards, and the call of the Spiritual Man creates within the light of the mind, and that light has a point of light that the Spiritual Man has placed there within your consciousness, and because it has, you are becoming the Spiritual Man. The Physical Man will know something is changing and in some cases, or I should say, many cases, the Physical Man will want to extinguish the light, this presence that is of the Spiritual Man.

This will not occur at the start, at the time that the light has been created, because it is all very new to you and you are getting from it, the mental aspect of the Physical Man is interested in the knowledge, the emotional aspect of the Physical Man is experiencing all the sensations, the psychic ability to sense the colours, the different encounters, so you may say the Physical Man is aspiring and he will encounter many things to aspire to, many avenues, many philosophies.

Every so often a part of the One Life will inform you of a truth or a partial truth, at this point, through a teacher. Whatever that represents as a part of the wisdom of the One Life, then the point of light within the brain consciousness will light up and become a little brighter. You may not be aware of this as the mental aspect of the Physical Man is still seeking knowledge.

There is much that will confuse you, there is much that is not truth at all, and you may well be thinking it is, as you continue to meditate with the Spiritual Man, as you focus, you will start to be impressed yourself with truth. You will start to discriminate truth, and then as you are approaching a major realisation, the Physical Man which is you that lives within the manifest world, will rebel and start to place more importance upon those physical things in life, you will turn your back upon the Spiritual Man because you are being confronted with choice.

The spiritual, as yet, is not strong enough a light to have given you a purpose and because of that, it is not in any sort of manifestation upon the physical plane. The light of the Spiritual Man has not attracted to you all those coincidences that you deem as coincidences, for you to mentally realise what your destiny holds.

I have mentioned the light of spirit and the light of matter, both are one of the same, just a different vibration, so it is when you consider the Spiritual Man and the Physical Man. Only one thing that is the problem here, the Physical Man does not comprehend the Spiritual Man, and at a certain place where you find yourself, you will start to reject the Spiritual Man. You will be outside of your comfort zone, you will have to confront commitments to other people, you will have to break away from existing behaviour patterns and much more, because you will have to confront truth and therein will lie your difficulty.

Do you commit to the Spiritual Man, the unknowable?

Or do you stay with the commitments of the Physical Man that you have built up over your lifetime?

Your identification has started to change, but are you aware enough to make the transition, are you capable of seeing through the veils that the Physical Man is blinded by? Can you dedicate your time towards the Spiritual Man?

I have mentioned meditation; this you have incorporated into your life. It may be sporadic or it may be daily, you may consider that is enough for you to do, you have friends of like mind, as you call it, who you meet up with, and maybe you have embarked upon a course. Can you go further than this, when you will be confronted by the Physical Man and all it represents in the people, circumstances, and environment that it is associated with? That is a leap of faith into the unknown whereby all that I have mentioned is in some way your security. Security for the physical relies upon familiarity, and in some respects identifying with physical actions as routine, a pattern which is performed within a time scale.

You have three words there - familiarity, routine, pattern.

Let me now add the previous word - security.

If you ponder and think about this, and pondering is but relaxed thinking, you will identify these words within your life. This is what the Physical Man has come to know and he feels safe within this structure, with the occasional breaking away to then fall back into it, and as time goes by, this structure becomes more deep seated within the consciousness.

The Spiritual Man also relates to these aspects in quite a different way in that it sets up a rhythm and all else revolves around this rhythm. The first analogy that the Physical Man creates, concretisation in all its aspects, a fixed position in thought and also feeling, there is no leeway as it becomes more condensed into time, whereas the second identification with the Spiritual Man leads to expression. You leave behind your fixed opinions, your right and wrong, because truth does not relay to you one answer to a question. It can give you many answers which will lead to more questions, you will enquire about truth, you will want to know more. This you can do in meditation any time of the day that you can give your mind over to the subject, because there is a truth to everything. This you will come to understand.

What is the truth you seek to know at this given time?

Ponder upon that, no matter how absurd it seems to you.

What is the truth of your existence?

If you can realise that first, then anything else you wish to know will unfold into your brain consciousness, through an identification. This will then attract to you a specific vibration from the One Life, as this is where your truth lies.

Meditation

If you can now find time to enter into meditation, become cognisant upon the fact of your existence within a vast field of life, you take your silent space wherever you are located, you can recognise all the life-forms that you are aware of from the human to the animal, plant and mineral.

You take yourself into a place of unity by identifying with the Spiritual Man above the head, and from that point of identification the idea will come to you that all these kingdoms of nature are part of one thing. They seem separate and they are, in only one way - in a physical way, in the aspect of form.

Realise you have been taught through all the knowledge that you have received in life, that you are a separate individual, thinking, feeling and moving within life.

Throw this concept away.

You become aware of the light from the Spiritual Man is intensifying.

You ask the question, "Why does everything then behave in a separate way?"

You wish to establish in your mind some sort of truth.

The Spiritual Man addresses you and informs you that, firstly, the mineral kingdom is not separate like the human being, and you can understand that the mineral kingdom has formed within one being. The earth. Not only that, you recognise that there is a geometric structure that governs the minerals and crystals, and there also is an etheric geometric structure, and through this fact, all is part of one thing through geometry.

You realise a consciousness is present, the same consciousness that is present, and that has created a piece of quartz crystal that has emerged in Brazil to a piece of quartz crystal that has emerged in Madagascar.

Do not limit your truth just to quartz, think about other crystals and minerals that are present within the earth, and that have been born out of the earth. Realise the planet contains a consciousness and is a part of the consciousness of the One Life in manifested form, and that fragment of the greater consciousness lives inside the outer manifest form.

At some point you may wish to surface your mind consciousness back into your location, but first realise that this consciousness you have been expanding your mind into, is also life. It is physical life and yet realise too, it is also love, because love binds all things together.

The One Life has created all these forms through love and an evolving wisdom that is far beyond our comprehension.

If you have chosen to surface, and there may be much you need to write down and assimilate into your brain consciousness, realise the precipitation of truth concerning the subject that you have expanded into will take, for your understanding time, and so you will work with time concerning this. Expectation is a human condition that requires time to instantly give results, do not lose expectation, but realise that the result of your expectation is a future occurrence and that all depends upon our dedication towards the Spiritual Man.

I am going to continue with this meditation. It is up to you whether you do so or not.

You are required to enter into the previous preliminary alignment, so you have established your truth concerning the crystals and minerals. Do not see them as separate, as they are a part of you.

Now see the surface of the planet.

You now take your consciousness from the womb of the planet, you may identify this as inner earth, and what you see now is the sun rising upon its surface.

You identify with the light of the sun and that light falls upon the plants and flowers, they have grown out of the earth from a seed. Within, the seed contains the plant and flower.

By analogy the Spiritual Man plants a seed within the Physical Man (earth) and what does that need to grow and mature into the flower, a symbol of perfection? It is light, but in the case of the flower it also requires water, which is also a life-giving substance. We see water is related to the emotions, and do not identify this in a negative way because the emotions are highly energetic for sustaining life in a joyful way.

So, now in your meditation, identify the energy of the earth and the geometrics of the crystal within the geometrics of the plants and flowers, see their perfect symmetry.

The same light, water, earth and the energy of the crystals and minerals have produced a perfect form. All this is part of the One Life, as is truth, as are the plants and flowers, as is yourself.

Identify yourself with the plants and flowers through expanding your consciousness into their geometries and also their colour.

You see also the colours of the crystals and minerals and you realise both kingdoms are part of the One Life.

You do this by realising you, yourself are part of the One Life, and the Three Kingdoms of nature are also found within you.

At this point you seek to understand this more fully.

This will be through a further expansion into the animal kingdom, but first bring to mind a flower, see the perfection of the geometrics in its symmetry, how the petals are arranged and unfolded in a spiral motion.

Now realise the geometrics of the crystals, being a stable form regarding growth, have manifested a perfection within the plants and flowers, geometry carries a language which you now associate with symbols.

The cube, the triangle, the pentagram, the six sided star. Can you see how all this is part of one thing - creation - and the vast creative processes that have taken place? You realise this is happening on other levels than the physical, expand your mind out into these levels from the Spiritual Man to the Divine Man.

Identify once more with the Spiritual Man and embody in your consciousness that the sphere of the Spiritual Man encompasses all that lies below it, and the Divine Man encompasses the Spiritual Man and all else that lies below it, so from your place within the physical worlds, you can, if you wish, incorporate into your consciousness the intangible worlds that lie beyond time in which the Spiritual Man walks.

Through the spiral movement created by the plants and flowers, the creative process continued and there occurred the animals, who walked the earth. They have the ability to feed themselves unlike the plants who rely upon the earth and do not move. The animals reveal much to you, in the form of instinct, sensitivity, highly attuned senses to the environment, developed because of the need to survive.

You understand the words 'fight' and 'flight'. The human being still possesses this instinct, the animals feed off the plants and also themselves.

Realise from the perfection of plants that are unable to move, the animals have evolved and then you yourself have evolved, as a result of this you come into appearance, each kingdom is the result of the one below it, and so it is that there is a kingdom represented by the Spiritual Man and this is what you are evolving towards.

So you have realised your movement has come from the animals, so where does your intellect come from? Has this just happened or was there something that created that spark?

Focus upon the Spiritual Man for the answer.

The evolution required from the Spiritual Man created the human, every human is the result of the Spiritual Man. The Spiritual Man seeks to be embodied by the human, hence the point of light that is created within the consciousness, and here is where the balance lies.

If you live with the concept of truth, then an expansion of consciousness will be the result.

Now you are starting to embody the principle of non-separation and unity, not just with your human brothers, but all the lower kingdoms.

So the Spiritual Man has created a point of light and it is light you now seek to understand and recognise. Light is vibration, light is colour, light carries sounds. Take the silent space into your consciousness and identify with the Spiritual Man above the head. There is a connection with the Spiritual Man and a light within the centre of the head, experience both vibrating together in resonance.

You imagine a line of light between the two, not that you have to because they are in essence inseparable, but from your point of evolution, you need to identify in that way. There will come a time when it is not necessary, but do not assume that now otherwise the Physical Man will put your light out.

Sound the OM into the light that is within the head.

Now sound the OM from that light into the Spiritual Man above the head.

Identify with the Spiritual Man, understand that he carries a vast amount of wisdom, this wisdom overshadows you, and can be accessed through light.

The vibration above the head increases and above the Spiritual Man you see three spheres of light. These spheres in their totality represent the Divine Man. The three spheres are interlocking; each one has a unique sound.

Choose a sphere, the one that has been chosen represents divine mind, bring this sphere into the Spiritual Man and as it merges with the Spiritual Man, a ray of light comes into the head and surrounds the point of light that has been placed there by the Spiritual Man.

State, 'I am as one with the divine mind'.

Choose a second sphere, this sphere is divine love. Integrate this sphere with the Spiritual Man, you imagine it merging, and a ray of light enters the head and surrounds the point of light that is there.

State, 'I am as one with divine love'.

The third and last sphere awaits your receptivity, you merge this sphere with the Spiritual Man, a ray of light enters the head and surrounds the point of light.

State, 'I am as one with divine will'.

Now, from your point of light you send a line of light to a centre just about six inches outside of your physical brow, and from that centre the blending three lights from above integrate and await their manifestation.

This you will do by sounding the OM and at the same time project divine mind, divine love, and divine will out towards the consciousness of humanity.

You pause and realise the three aspects of the Divine Man that now surround your point of light have their own unique sound, so bring the vibratory sound of the divine mind into your aura.

Can you perceive this sound as a symbol?

Its symbol will be the five pointed star and this you will visualise above the head where you have identified with the Spiritual Man.

Assimilate the experience then turn your attention to the aspect of divine love that surrounds your point of light. This vibrating sound will resonate through your entire being, but first bring its sound into your aura.

Love integrates and brings everything together in harmony. Its symbol you imagine within the Spiritual Man above the head. It is a six pointed star.

Can you perceive the sound of divine love?

Can you feel the vibration of divine love? Assimilate it into the very cells of your body.

Divine love heals, understand this, and embody its principles.

You do not have to think about this, you just have to identify with it. This is not an intellectual process, just go with it, so to speak, and enter into synthesis and harmony, feel yourself in harmony with divine love, then many of your inner conflicts will disappear.

Become aware of the aspect of divine will that surrounds your point of light, pause at this place of silence before you bring the sound of the divine will into your aura, you may use the sound of the OM to do this.

Realise that the divine will relays to you your purpose. You have a purpose other than your personality life.

Whilst sounding the OM, also wish that your purpose become known within your consciousness. Do not think about what your purpose is or may be, as this will stop the process.

Relax your attention when ready.

Let us now consider love.

What actually does that mean to you?

Is this love for your intimate partner and your family, or does this go beyond that to be more inclusive? And with the consideration of love is also an undeniable relationship with life. In our consideration today, love, as is commonly known, relates to the sense of trust. Physical love is not inclusive love, and so you may well be seeking a higher understanding with this, and by identifying that physical love is not what the second aspect of divinity represents, you will seek to inhibit that part of your nature that is a desire, by becoming more mentally orientated. The problem here lies in that the mental application upon the emotional body leads to a suppression of the natural course of energy exchange between the centres of consciousness.

Now you need also to consider the aspect of the reference to the word 'control'. This is of a mental nature, it cannot be any other, and in this situation control becomes a limitation.

Realise that a control over the emotional body is not really giving yourself a response to it.

If you respond to your emotional body, and by that I mean from an identification with the Spiritual Man, then you will come to understand it. Many see the emotional body as a major problem for them and yet this is feeling, and feeling has a higher correspondence, so inhibit this feeling, then you will not be receptive to the higher feeling nature.

You will not be creative.

I seek to relay to you the emotional body is more important than your intellectual body, which you may understand as mental thought. Mental thought is quite interesting as it concerns your level of consciousness and also your identifications concerning your level of consciousness, and your emotional body will be supporting your identifications and leading you more into those area of concretised thought.

A change of vibration is now necessary to bring about an understanding, this I seek to do though an alignment to the Master J.

Now consider the fact that the emotional body is made up of seven levels known as sub planes, your senses as such, also extend from the purely physical sense as you understand it, into a more psychic sense on the certain levels of the emotional body. The possibility exists that this could sub-divide further whereby you would finally reach the number forty-nine, a very mystical number for transmutation. Recognition of these levels is a major aspect for understanding them. When I refer to recognition, I refer to the divine energy of love, also you cannot recognise something from your intellectual mind, it cannot possibly conceive what lies behind the appearance. All that appears to you as separate, desirable or undesirable, has the ability to be brought into synthesis with the second aspect of love.

Do not seek to do this from your personality, because that is distinctly separate when it comes to love, and love is also truth, because if you align to truth then you come to understand love through wisdom.

There are greater things that you can do, and there are greater things that you can become.

Throw away the burdens of your responsibility, you carry so much weight upon your shoulders, so many worries that do not concern you, so many impressions you take upon yourself.

Your intellect can perceive the rights and the wrongs and forms judgements, it separates people into groups that have the same identifications and beliefs, and then your love will only extend to those that believe in the same as you. Many troubled individuals know not what they do, they see themselves through others and their physical group identity, and then justify their actions. If they but only realised they are hurting themselves.

They are creating their future challenges, suffer not the little children. Do you and others uphold that with your actions?

You may say you do and treat children with this in mind, but have you ever thought that whatever undesirable action, not just physical, will have an effect upon the children, and do not just restrict what this means to your own area of influence. Your influence upon others, upon yourself, your inability to love, to even try to understand the concept, becomes a mass state of consciousness.

You think that your thinking is individual to yourself, you think that love is individual to yourself and your immediate family - not so. Many of your humankind are not of the heart, their emotional body continues to expect to be satisfied with results, the results of your thoughts and actions, now is a time of great change. Your thinking needs to be inclusive, watch your children, see how they behave when you are exerting your will upon them.

And what is your will? Is it spiritual will? Because, think on this, that spiritual will leads to cosmic love where all is as one.

And where does love identify with money? It is not for me to relay that to you, because, for many, their identification with money leads to what I have said - 'suffer not the little children'. These children hold the future of humanity within their tiny hands. Think on this, that you, because your heart centres are closed, will close the heart centres of the little children. If you do not agree with that, how many children are sent crying to school? How many children are given the responsibility to succeed with exams? With their ability to socialise? To say the right thing?

Do you care what happens?

What is happening within your family unit will be happening elsewhere in the world in possibly more severe ways, and you will be feeding that, because where there is the least love will be the worst conditions. All is relevant to everything else, so if you change then that will affect everything. Your conditioning is the problem, this is not your fault, it is nobody's fault, it is all part of evolution, but now is the time for change.

Do you understand the fact of your conditioning, the patterns, the routine, the separation?

Love does not exist in many areas, such as your conversations, be aware of your identifications.

Do you Judge? This is other than love, it prevents love.

Do not forget that love is healing and love is all inclusive, it creates a unity. Recognise your judgements have no basis, to judge another is to judge yourself because if love was present, you would understand certain laws are present that bring about a balance. You will attract to yourself even more reasons to judge and it will be of the same substance as to what you are judging. So, realise now there is no reason to judge, one does this because you see yourself as the most important person and what does not conform to your way of thinking is then judged and, of course, a judge gives a verdict.

So, now if you find yourself judging another, realise there is no point in the big equation for this, and leave behind what you have been thinking by bringing through into your crown centre the second ray energy of love. See this vast expanse of energy above your head. This is the overshadowing energy of love, identify with this love aspect by purely recognising its existence, and imagine it entering your head centre and covering your aura.

You will find you will not bother any more with the judgement.

This archaic way of judging people will be transcended when your heart opens to the whole. This will be a natural result of alleviating the stress you suffer through the lack of love and yes, it is very stressful to judge someone or something. It creates a tension in your body because of its nature. You only have to observe by being aligned to the energy of love, and notice those that judge.

I also wish to bring to your attention to the effect of criticism.

Two words that are of the same vibration - judge and criticise. Notice the faces of those that do this. Are they relaxed or are they frustrated? Notice their movements as they communicate this energy, their rapid speech, their unhappiness. All this creates a tension in your body and your body as a whole is many bodies and levels of interaction.

Love resides upon the causal level.

Shift in alignment to Master K.H.

So see then, that to reach out and embody this love, you have directed your thinking upon life, and the life I am bringing your attention to, is your physical life of thought and feeling. There is too much of it, communication should be creative and realise it can only be creative when you are using your creative mind.

The mind is a wonderful way of receiving creative concepts. You can achieve this by expanding your thinking into a different state or way of thinking. Firstly, you have to recognise the two aspects of mind. The brain consciousness is one, and that is what most people use, bring love into your brain consciousness. Then the second aspect, I have mentioned the higher mind, you will automatically attract into your brain consciousness, to achieve this you have to understand that you need to trust that this is so.

Now you realise the relationship of your brain consciousness with your heart centre, because if love is present, so is the Spiritual Man.

You need to be aware of your lateral thinking and your limitation of truth, because once you place an understanding and identification on something, then it can be nothing else other than what you have identified and understood. Straight away you have limited yourself within the brain consciousness, then all actions with any reference to the subject of your understanding and identification will be limited within a certain sphere, for example, and I am relaying this as it is a physical example of your limitation.

You are asked to explain and describe a chair.

Your response would be according to your limitation - what would it be?

Find a chair and see if you can expand your thinking upon it. What is the purpose of a chair? It enables you to sit as against standing. What is the reason for this? How does a chair serve you? What is its design? What is it made from? Its base is of a cubic formation and it has a vertical back. How does the chair relate to the table? All these things are but a way of attempting to expand your consciousness beyond the normal scope of vision.

A chair is taken for granted, just like many other things that have a significance, because from what and why did a chair manifest? Was that an isolated event, or was it a group event? Because a chair, when sat upon brings the physical body to a standstill and when there is more than one chair, for example at a dining table where the family are brought together for the purpose of eating, then you may conclude a chair is the result of the aspect of love, the bringing together through the Law of Attraction for a purpose.

Now the table itself is symbolic, for example, it is round, square, or a rectangle, it matters not what it is, it is just the fact that it is geometric, it has a design just like the chair. When you come together around a table, your auras are intermingled and there then will be the result of your interactions, is it in harmony, or is it in conflict? There are many people who suffer from digestive problems, have you ever thought about your thoughts and feelings whilst you are eating, the energy of the conversation, and the things that are said or unsaid, or the stress of eating correctly.

Another thing, my brothers, if you get together of a night, then your day will be clinging to your aura, all the interactions, thoughts and feelings will be colouring your aura, and your auras will be mingling. Now, if your day has been full of light and love, your aura will reflect this, it is well to look after your aura and tend to your thoughts and feelings.

The Spiritual Man commands the position of possessing enough light to transform your aura, use him when you are required to do so. Just simply invoke the energies from the Spiritual Man above the head, and imagine them coming down and cleansing your aura, especially before you sit down and eat together, you will find you will suffer less with digestive problems.

Whatever you do is affected by your aura and your aura is the result of the Inner Man, the Inner Man can be spoken of in relationship with the Spiritual Man, but also the Inner Man is the product of a point of light within the heart from the Spiritual Man and an essence of the Divine Man, therefore, the Inner Man can be representative of both these. If this is so, then the Physical Man will embody many principles of the Spiritual Man; one has been spoken of, and that is Truth. The Inner Man then will expand itself creatively and bring into manifestation those qualities concerning truth. The Inner Man expresses itself through all the centres of consciousness and this is true if the Inner Man is governed by the Physical Man, although I have to tell you that the higher centres will be but a dim light, they will only be functioning with the light of the Physical Man, on the level of the Physical Man.

Now much of what I have said may seem abstract and have no meaning, but just think upon this. If your thinking, feeling and action all concerns yourself, and the goals of the Physical Man are represented by acquisition, then the Inner Man will only concern the physical, it will be cut off from the Spiritual Man.

Consciousness, therefore, technically, will lie below the diaphragm and doesn't that all concern digestion, and food can be a major preoccupation of the Physical Man. Try to understand the terms 'quality, not quantity', and there you will find the difference, and I am not just talking about food, in fact that is probably the result of other actions. The actions of thought, the brain consciousness, is it capable of being selective in itself, or is it just a response to memory, knowledge and outer happenings? Does it see the truth behind all this? The Inner Man that is of the Spiritual Man doesn't even have to try because it knows the truth. The reality of it all is - can the thought processes switch off and not analyse and not think of this situation or that situation, or that person, or other person, and all this will be from where your consciousness is identified upon.

This is a problem with the new age teachings, that they present to you the need to work upon yourself, that is good if it is from the Spiritual Man, but an over-emphasis upon the self leads to an over-identification on others whereby you will then start to analyse them according to what you are working upon within yourself. Then you will become absorbed in the mental processes regarding yourself and others, you may well end up with a headache because the energy will become over-active within the brain consciousness.

Your close relationships provide the battleground for the discrimination between the brain consciousness (Physical Man) and the soul consciousness (Spiritual Man). You have to differentiate between the two. When you lift your consciousness into the Spiritual Man, then there will be no tension and you may wonder why, at times, you will experience no thinking at all, well, not thinking as you know it, because your brain consciousness will be released from its activity, therefore, it will not be the governing factor for thinking.

The Spiritual Man will render the activity of lower mind to as little as possible from its present state of consciousness, and will activate it when required. It will still function within the physical worlds with the necessities of life within that framework, but you will find, if you have not already found out, that your identifications with certain lower mind conversations will become less and less, you will find you have nothing to say upon the subject of conversation because your consciousness is such that there is no need to engage.

You also notice it will be quite different if the conversation is based upon truth, you may well have a lot to say on this subject, because this subject covers a vast over-shadowing of Wisdom. Therefore, be prepared to be abstract, be prepared to be joyful, the Spiritual Man is not serious or commanding, it is a teacher, but not how you understand a teacher who teaches from books and requires you to memorise the subject matter. The Spiritual Man is your true teacher and will not teach you from books, it seeks to bring the soul of man into the Inner Man so that the Inner Man embodies the Spiritual Man, then the Divine Man comes closer, and your relationship then will be with the Divine Plan. Here you can conceive all this relates to alignment.

I wish to relay to you that a quiet mind on your level is an active mind on another level, so when your mind is quiet, realise this, then your mind will receive quickly, with no fuss or strain, the Over-shadowing Wisdom that will transform your thinking and expand it into the Over-shadowing Wisdom when you are required to do so, because the Over-shadowing Wisdom then becomes a magnet for the brain consciousness and the Inner Man will use the mind as a receiving apparatus for this wisdom to then instil the brain consciousness.

If you have an over-active mind that cannot find answers to the questions it is presenting to you, then your mind is absorbed in the Physical Man who seeks to understand everything and anything within its mind circumference, and as that circumference is very small indeed, so it will end up full of thought and each thought will end up as part of every other thought you are thinking. You will then not resolve your thoughts and, as your thoughts will be tinged with emotion, then that too will be full and, of course, chaos will spill out to other people.

There is a need, Brethren, to discriminate your thought as to whether it is worthwhile at all. Where does it stand in the big scheme of things? Is it petty and incidental?

"Oh but," you may say, that person has said something to you that you disagree with, or they have criticised you as a person, and they need to apologise for it.

You obviously take this very seriously, your reputation is at stake. Respond if you need to, but not by talking to your friends about it, or attack the person verbally; you will only be defending your Physical Man. Sometimes it is necessary to correct a situation, but do it without any sense of hurt, do it joyfully, they have made a mistake.

If you live in truth these things will happen, but if you live in truth it will not bother you because your Inner Man is securely embodying the Spiritual Man.

With this subject in mind, I would like you to take this now into meditation.

Meditation

Focus yourself in the Anja centre.

Bring all to silence by realising silence exists within the space that is surrounding, realise also within the space is the presence, this is also surrounding you.

In this instance, relate this presence to consciousness, so consciousness itself is surrounding you.

Your Anja centre starts to become attuned to this consciousness that is the presence.

Now align your Anja centre to the Spiritual Man by taking a line of light from the Anja centre some inches outside of your brow.

Bring it into the centre of the head and up into the Spiritual Man, now you are aligned to the Spiritual Man and consciousness.

From the Spiritual Man, which is consciousness aligned to the Over-shadowing Wisdom, you identify with the Inner Man.

As I have mentioned the Inner Man is within the heart centre, but it may also be elsewhere, if you sense your Inner Man is in a centre lower than the heart centre, use the magnetic attracting energies of the Spiritual Man to lift the Inner Man into the heart centre, releasing anything that is of the Physical Man by projecting energies of light upon the situation from the Spiritual Man.

This is a clearing process prior to the identification with truth, take an attitude that it doesn't matter anymore because why should it? What purpose does it really serve?

You realise that you cannot expand consciousness if you hang on to any grievances, and also if you have any worries, ask for the light of illumination, but do not try to work anything out, as the answers will automatically come - this you need to trust.

You only have to want to do this for things to be accomplished.

When you are at a point of quiet, align now to the Divine Man.

Perceive a thread of light connecting the three aspects of man - the inner, the spiritual and the divine.

Request that you are a seeker of truth and wish that truth governs your life.

You perceive a cloud of blue-white light above your head, your aura vibrates in harmony with this light.

Your mental body is lifted into higher frequency.

Next your emotional body is also lifted into a higher frequency, this frequency now stimulates your etheric body and physical body.

You hear the words *"I am one in truth with the One Life"*.

Relax your focus back to its normal frequency.

Now truth is wisdom and this you have to understand if you are to expand your consciousness, because to do this requires no mental striving at all, no ability to memorise. If you imagine your brain consciousness possesses a library and you can relate also the Over-shadowing Wisdom to a library, now realise that wisdom cannot be learnt, it has to be embodied. You do not possess wisdom, you cannot acquire it as you would understand, you just need to align with it, then you will receive it when it is necessary to do so.

This is a different way of thinking and to understand this you are required to place your consciousness within the Over-shadowing Wisdom, by knowing it is there, and exists upon a different plane on a higher frequency. Therefore, any response will come via the Over-shadowing Wisdom, if you wish it to be so, realise you are also human so you may fall at the first hurdle by using the energy of control.

By this I mean you preconceive your method according to the patterns instilled within your memory and they are so familiar to you, even if you are not conscious of them all as many live within your subconscious, so you plan your route to enlightenment, set a goal, and then expect to live up to yourself.

Which self? This, you must realise, is your personality self. Yes, you need a goal, or shall we say a vision, but be sure my brother you cannot possibly know what that will be, not from your present limitations. So don't expect to become the wise guru, the enlightened man, where you will become a library of knowledge, and all this because you may see this condition as having no problems, you will solve everything and people will be nice to you, and the universe will look after you in every situation, and one of the biggest things that you will expect to be is healthy. So, with all the meditation, the strict diet, and the large amount of study, this is what you will expect and of course you wish people to look up to you.

Maybe I am being a little unfair and whoever heeds these words and has already understood what I am saying, then I congratulate you for your wisdom.

All that I have said is far from the truth of the reality because most of this has to do with you. You cannot expect to enter into the higher realms of consciousness as an individual identity.

The Spiritual Man, which over-shadows you, knows this and waits for you to extend yourself to others, it waits for you to do something worthwhile.

Instantly that statement will stimulate in your mind: you have to be famous and influence many people.

Not so. One small gesture of kindness is all it takes, so every time this occurs, something happens to you, you are becoming a part of the One Life, because you are contacting people through the heart centre and the Spiritual Man works through the heart centre, not the solar plexus. He recognises your compassion, and incidentally this is not a forced process, you don't think about being kind, well, in the first instance you have to recognise kindness and then identify with it, and then understand it. Your acts of kindness are not limited to the act itself and the people involved, that act will join itself in resonance of vibration with all the other acts of kindness, allowing their combined energy to dissipate a thought form that is contrary to kindness.

Can you now appreciate what one act of kindness can achieve?

Can you now appreciate that whatever you do that is in line with the Divine Plan will help to manifest that Divine Plan into the consciousness of humanity?

Now, kindness is something that is a response to the energy of love, desire doesn't come into it, unless of course you are being kind for a reason of gain, then you will not be in line with the energy of love. You will be in line with the materialistic forces, and that is not material goods, although that may be the desire.

There are forces that seek to imprison you in the three worlds and manipulation is one of its ways of imprisoning you and will lead you upon a slippery slope. The act of kindness will become a material thing for you to do, so do not try to seek avenues for you to display kindness, rest assured they will appear because the Spiritual Man will be seeking you to come closer to him.

Much that is taught requires of you a mental control, you understand what is said and then set about achieving what you perceive you should be, by inhibiting all those things that you shouldn't be doing. What you should be doing is to keep clearing the mind to allow the wisdom to enter, the wisdom will naturally transform you.

So, stop thinking about what you should be or shouldn't be, and become receptive to the energy of love and manifest these small acts of kindness, then you will be able to think about other things than the triviality of the little self.

One thing you can do when you display an act of kindness is to then align that act to the energy of love. Two things will occur here. One, you will by offering up your kindness be allowing the energy of love to enter the etheric network of the planet, the implications of this are vast.

If everyone did this there would be such a surge of the energy of love into the etheric network that it would impress the consciousness of humanity and transform many acts into acts of kindness.

The second is that you will then gain access to the wisdom because love and wisdom is a combined energy of the second aspect, you walk through the subjective all the time, but are unaware of it.

Now, believe you are capable of making a difference, because what is subjective will become eventually manifest. Ponder upon that because the causes lie within the subjective and the effects are seen playing out in the world, whether within your life or humanity as a whole. The unrest you see now is the result of what has occurred subjectively, you see, thought forms are built around conscious unrest which then feeds the astral aura and results in action and reaction. So, be aware of your own unrest and dissatisfaction, you become dissatisfied with what you have or have not, but you are the one who is responsible for your condition, and so are the many that create a thought form upon the mental plane, and so with any entity of thought substance that is fed and is contained with desire, so will it precipitate upon the physical plane.

It is well to look for causes, dissatisfaction is a cause.

Humanity always wants more. Are you in this position of wanting more? Not enough money, too much stress? Are you not loved? And it's the last statement you need to think seriously about, where there is a lack of love, there is dissatisfaction and mainly your life brothers, lacks love because you are all too busy to love.

What does this mean? It means you take more notice of people.

You become aware of when you need to give a kind word, and if you have accessed the wisdom, it will be the right word that will make all the difference. It could spark a light from their soul and their soul is the love that they require. It is good to receive love from others on the physical plane in compassion and understanding, but the soul can bring a different kind of love that, in those quiet moments of consciousness, can alleviate so much suffering, particularly of an emotional nature

Your feelings are so strange to me, you act upon them and if you cannot act, you stuff them down, so to speak, and what could happen then is your life force energy will dwindle and you will become very sad.

Your soul is eternal love and that comes into your heart centre, then you can smile at whoever you meet because you will not evaluate them, it will not matter because you are living in truth. You will know all things come to pass and everyone you pass also has a soul, but maybe they are not in communication with the Spiritual Man. That is OK, but be aware brothers, at times there is a need to discriminate yourself within circumstances, as you need to understand that consciousness is not so present.

Discrimination also produces versatility and that is creativity, so discrimination is a creative act that is the positive pole of discrimination; the negative pole is avoidance.

If you discriminate from the embodiment of the Spiritual Man, right action will follow, then the other esoteric statement, detachment, will automatically come into play. It is not wise to practice detachment if the Spiritual Man is not present because your memory contains a lot of what that word means from the aspect of the Spiritual Man, and you will judge another. It is wise to always be the Spiritual Man as you will move within life as you know it without having to strain the mind as to what you will engage with, you will know what to engage with and the amount of time for that interaction, as you will have expanded your perception from your point of total unity at the centre of your circle, and your circle will grow.

If you have to think too much about what you should do or not do, you are best to do nothing and allow the Spiritual Man to sort it out, because the more you think about things where, for you, there appears no apparent answer and you are stuck, you will disconnect from the Spiritual Man and you will not understand it. But all that has happened is that your intellectual mind, or I should say your logical mind, has become over-active thus is it producing force upon your bodies, every thought produces a vibration, most are fleeting, but if you condense your thought by overthinking something, to then have no conclusion, or you may arrive at the wrong conclusion, all those vibrations of thought will blot out the truth, and as you can only come to the realisation of truth from the Spiritual Man, you will be truly stuck within your thought. You will go round and round, increasing in vibration and then you will wonder why you have a headache.

The Spiritual Man can change everything for you, but you will need to acquire patience and keep striving towards him, and then, when you least expect it, the answers will come and your circumstances will change.

But you are required to relay what the Spiritual Man is telling you to others in many diverse ways, so even that requires you to drop the logical mind and not to work out why, just that you are available for something far greater than the work you do upon the physical plane, which you call a job. But do not give your job up, thinking that the Spiritual Man will give you a higher job, you may have a glimmer of this as you may be pursuing what you might think is your destiny. It is, but the first few steps you have taken, so do not concretise your thought regarding this, and leave room for the new and the creative to enter, and believe this can happen, but don't try to think it out.

Many people are wandering around in that state. "There's something I need to do, but I don't know what it is." This is what is said by many people.

What is happening is that you are sensing the Over-shadowing Wisdom, and the Spiritual Man is getting stronger, so you are sensing this, it is there above your head and part of you, your mind and emotions and your senses are feeling this. The problem is you then become obsessed by this and start to seek the answers, a lot of people will seek the answers by going for a reading, and there you will have it. The reading will tell you what you are sensing and confirm this to you, but it won't tell you what it is, or it may do and lead you off track, or you may not be able to wait.

Then, after a short amount of time when nothing has happened, you seek another reading and if you seek too much, you will find the opposition, the Reader will tune into your negative thought pattern that is stopping you from being aware of the next step and will project to you something totally contrary to what you should be doing.

They are predicting your future from your negative thought pattern, and that could well happen. There could be a possibility of some insight into the future, but therein a problem is presented - the time factor. People expect instant results, six months is still an instant result, so you are not going to walk away from a reading, and things will happen.

A word of warning: readings can be focussed upon emotion and physical problems, this is wrong and inappropriate as they cannot know, but it is a form of glamour when they predict a physical problem, all it does is boost their ego and put fear into you. That level of psychism is of the lowest order and should be taken no notice of and avoided. And, of course, there are messages. This is an area of amusement to us at times, if it makes people feel good, that is fine, otherwise it is misplaced, and of course you must remember nobody can tell you what to do, if this is the case - ignore it completely.

There are some of the forms of guidance, your guidance is the Spiritual Man, but guidance can come from books, or a teacher, because there are certain things worth knowing, as that can lead to expansion. We understand a certain book can give a wealth of knowledge for your circumstances, but never fix yourself upon any book, the Spiritual Man may present you with the right book at the right time. The Divine Man will present you with your purpose. Believe you me, these two states do exist, to recognise them is to realise that they present to you a progressive state of consciousness, you will not know perhaps what these are, but just keep identifying with them, then you will come to some sort of understanding and then, when you find yourself, you will start to embody them and your expansion will leave you amazed.

A change of vibration to The Master D.K.

Meditation

Prepare yourself to enter into the consciousness of the soul, this you will do by aligning your centres of consciousness with the three planetary centres: humanity, hierarchy, and Shamballa.

Bring yourself into resonance with your etheric physical, emotional, and mental vehicles by sounding the OM, firstly for the physical etheric, then the emotional, then the mental.

Extend a line of light from the heart centre towards the soul above the head, extend this line into the great ashramic group upon the Buddhic plane.

You see humanity as a sphere and the hierarchy as a sphere, both spheres are joined, one from the lower part of the sphere, (the hierarchy) and the other the top part of the sphere (humanity), the area they are locked together represents a group of workers, of which you are one; this group is the group of world's servers, incarnate or otherwise.

Realise you are a channel for the energies from the Buddhic plane, which you will relate to the Divine Plan.

You visualise an interplay between the two spheres, extend your line of light further into Shamballa and visualise this as a sphere that is connected to the sphere representing the hierarchy. They overlap and where they overlap there resides another group, this group channels the energy from Shamballa into hierarchy.

Can you now imagine they are working with love and life?

You see an interplay of energies between the three spheres.

Now realise the soul experiences all these energies, it relays to you the consciousness of all these spheres, it tells you. Also, they are all connected and consciousness from the soul is experienced on all these levels, be receptive now to the consciousness of the soul.

Extend yourself to the possibilities of something different and state:

I am the consciousness of the soul,

Imagine this consciousness as lighted energy, your causal body is the light body of the soul, you are surrounded by this light body.

Let it illuminate your mental body and experience an expansion from your focus in the head centre.

Anchor the energies into your brain consciousness with the sound of the OM.

Relax your attention.

To experience this consciousness, which is consciousness that at the moment is not present in your brain consciousness, the brain consciousness is required to relegate itself into second place, so to speak. In fact, its true position is in third place, although essentially neither state of consciousness is not a part of the One Life. So I am relaying to you a method that you will then reverse by including those states that you are seeking to go beyond, if you do manage to do this, those lower states will embody the consciousness from the higher states. Consciousness is inclusive, consciousness in all-encompassing, nothing lies outside of consciousness so you are fully present within the entire state of consciousness. To be present is to bring some sort of understanding of the eternal now, the aspect of love brings from out of the eternal now the wisdom of the all-pervading consciousness.

Your recognition of time, and your identification with time, is concerned with your lifetime, the eternal now, and the cosmic love continues through into all the states of time, where time is but an extension of the One Life. Conceive that you are part of the One Life, therefore, you continue your journey of evolution as part of the One Life. Your soul is the instrument for this journey and its consciousness will take you into the eternal now to sit in time and become timeless, by that I mean time passes you by and yet still you remain.

The Master K.H.

You have experienced some of this state and condition in meditation, and we have spoken about the continuation of this during the day, this is achieved through consciousness. The more you let go of your personal identification, the more you enter into the consciousness of the One Life, you then will simply drop into the eternal now, you will be absorbed into the centre point and there will lie all consciousness, and yet it cannot be defined because it contains everything. But it is also ever expanding within itself as it absorbs within itself more information, all things are reciprocate, so think now that a small portion of consciousness which is love and also wisdom, but also other vibrational aspects of life relayed through light, is available within this solar system and as a portion of that consciousness is embodied, then consciousness has expanded itself by receiving back the experience contained within the life that has embodied that consciousness. All that lies below that life also receives this consciousness, so that the life then receives from what lies below it and then expands its consciousness by the fact that what lies below it is a part of the One Life. So think now that the One Life expands itself by the many points of it that are in interplay with each other, this interplay enriches the whole until it becomes a synthesis of the whole, the whole then gives access into higher levels of consciousness.

So consciousness is contained within the One Life, but it is also apart from the One Life in the fact that it goes beyond the One

Life, as we understand the concept of the One Life. There is always another One Life that contains what we understand as the One Life. Consciousness lies within all these primary solar and cosmic lives, so go back to the understanding that consciousness is ever expanding, by this we identify expansion as "Being". An eternal state of oneness.

This in reference to a human being is very hard to explain, a state of knowing brings about being, but then knowing is not a state, it just is. There is nothing that cannot be achieved through knowing and yet knowing also can expand into more inclusive states of knowing. The all-encompassing state of knowing is beyond being itself, it is everything and yet it is nothing, because the individuality of everything is not perceived, everything is one thing, therefore, it is not selective, it has no need for the Law of Attraction within itself as it created the Law of Attraction, it is a communication and effect of the one aura and creative thought.

Now take this concept down to the human being and identify a human being with the state of being and knowing already the same word has an attractive quality between the two.

Where does the human place its being?

It places its subjective identification with the manifested form, the physical world that is the world of the human being, the glamour and illusion is all too evident.

I feel it not necessary, my brothers, to list these glamours and illusions as I will not be giving you due credit for your ability to discriminate these, also I cannot go so far into those levels to spell it out that basically, as this is not the way and it will not help you. You have to come to your own conclusions. You have free will so there is a certain line I cannot cross, but I will say certain centres of consciousness are concerned with this.

Meditation

Now, if you are unsure as to what is being presented to you, focus your consciousness from the heart centre into the head centre, use the physical eyes as a vehicle for the third eye and become still, you will be looking into the space. Now your awareness will be drawn towards, and I shall use the term the Spiritual Man as this is a common identification for the soul in this presentation, which over-shadows your head centre, so there you are, transfixed in this state.

Now you can address any questions you have.

Firstly, project a line of light down from the Spiritual Man into the head centre, down into the head itself, and out from the Ajna centre (brow centre) to a distance from it, where you will create a sphere of light.

This sphere will impress the brain consciousness with the answers to any questions, if the questions require at this time an answer.

For example, 'what part of my life and living is a glamour?' This could be substituted with the word 'illusion', you could ask for the energy of truth to be present from the Spiritual Man.

Start with simple things and bear in mind the complete abstraction away from the emotional, physical, and mental states, trust from out of this abstraction, which you will feel as not being anything, something will enter.

What does your heart tell you?

Are you living in line with what your heart is telling you and where does your heart identify with?

Is it with the well-being of others from a state of heart thinking? Again the word 'being', all is being revealed, as being part of the one being.

The Heart Transmission

The all-seeing eye sees beyond the superficial substance of manifestation, it sees a purpose behind what exists, whilst the fire of the heart burns a pathway of light beyond the confines of the attraction of substance within the manifest world and its forms. The heart knows the truth of being, the heart needs not to discriminate, as an open heart imbued with the fire of spirit, contains truth as its home. The voice of the silence enters through the heart in waves.

Can you conceive that all the failings of the past are the result of a closed heart? The heart cannot be contained within the form, the heart seeks expansion, do not restrict the heart to purely matters concerning the heart, let the heart take you into the higher realms of consciousness. The heart will reflect to you the soul, it will reflect to you the soul in others. You will know others from the heart if you are open to its possibilities, the strength of the heart comes to those who sit within the eternal now. Release the past and come into the bosom of the heart, you will find there love, you will find your place within the eternal realms. This transmission would prove of benefit to you if it was received in a meditative, receptive state, making sure the mind is clear to receive it.

Master K.H.

I have spoken about the void, the state between thinking and not thinking is raised up into the intuitive place whilst not thinking, so do not view my statement concerning thinking or not thinking from a linear position, for you might well say, "OK, now I am thinking", and you stop thinking and say, "now I am not thinking, what is supposed to happen?"

What might happen is that you start thinking again, so you need to recognise that your normal thinking processes concern your life and affairs and what goes on there, how you identify with them and their importance to you, and that importance will vary according to where you place your identification, if it is upon yourself then all manner of things will upset you, causing you to think more upon that level. Your train of thought will concern that level and I have used the word 'train' because that will be the speed of your thought, in that state of being it will be very difficult to come to no thinking.

Now, if you realise through an understanding concerning this, that the place of no thinking creates a space within your brain consciousness whereby another higher level of thinking can enter, you have to create the space. This will stimulate the pineal gland into activity, therefore, your brain consciousness will become receptive.

You wish not to become receptive to physical mind stuff, or your own past mind stuff accumulated within the subconscious. So the difference is from the linear aspect concerning thinking or not thinking, which you will understand that the not thinking is just an aspect of your thinking whereby you will struggle to not think as you have nothing to replace your present thinking.

Now, when the pineal gland is active, then it will be a different matter because to go from thinking to not thinking will be very easy, your not thinking state will be an active state and you will know the difference because then you will have attuned yourself to the Spiritual Man.

Your concerns with your personal affairs will have diminished, you will naturally then flow through time without carrying the burdens of the past. Now in that statement, the human mind thinks that the past is in years, Yes, you do accumulate the years, but then think upon this: if your present is a reflection of the past, then you are living the past every minute, every hour, every day, every year. So look a little closer to home and see what yesterday has given you - that is the past. What has the morning given you? That is the past. What has five minutes ago given you? That is the past. What are you thinking and feeling now, in the present? And while you have been reading this, it has become the past.

Now you have created time to read this, but from this place you are aware of the future, again, you tend to think in years, maybe before you started reading this you were aware of your next task, so whilst you are reading this you are aware of the future, so you are experiencing past and future, that which has happened and that which you have arranged to happen.

When you are not thinking and the pineal gland is active, your mind is elevated to a higher place, past and future then drop away.

It doesn't mean it changes, although change will eventuate, it just means that past or future is not actively affecting the mind, you are constantly in the present, and this is when there is a stillness and an immortality.

You know what your past has been and you know what arrangements you have made for the future, but they do not concern you, as when you once more become active upon the lower worlds, you will be able to then perform them. But the thing is now the future becomes very flexible and can change and transform, because your organisation and expectations will have been from a point that is now the past, but at the time the present, and you will have arrived at another present point.

If you have stabilised your present point within the eternal now, or it is fluctuating in varying degrees, occasionally entering into the eternal now, which is more than likely the case, then the future will also hold potentiality, spiritual potentiality.

It is worth considering that you have created space and this space is available within your mind, your thinking processes have become selective, you will naturally acquire this state of being.

How can the creative thought currents be made available to you if your mind is full of yourself and everyone else that you encounter?

This space you have created is not 'a nothing', it is a potential space, it will hold a magnetic attractive force that will then be in resonance with the Over-shadowing Wisdom, the creating thought processes of other, more advanced lives, and then thoughts will enter.

Their nature will be variable according to the plane they are required to manifest upon, be aware of this, there is no separation between spirit and matter.

Wherever you live and move and have your being, is where the light can penetrate the darkness, I refer to darkness as lack of consciousness. Now, if you have a purpose for these thoughts, and when you are consciously active as a disciple in the world of affairs, be open to the Over-shadowing Wisdom regarding your work, or I could say, your future work, because if you are active then your activity will attract the wisdom in line with your purpose potentiality and the Divine Plan. Do not under-estimate yourself in this respect, and herein lies a problem which I will address.

Do you believe in the subjective worlds and the Divine Plan? You cannot see it, or touch it, no advanced being is going to appear before you telling you your pathway - we cannot do that. Do not also underestimate your contribution, no matter how small you perceive it to be, because you will be perceiving it as an individual identity and from a place of separateness. Your contribution will be connected to many other contributions that are upon a similar vibrational tone, for example, love has its own tone. I have talked about this concerning kindness, now it is to bring the same understanding to your place within the Divine Plan, do not perceive yourself to be greater or lesser. If you wish to use those terms, realise that the greater is made up of the lesser, therefore, in essence, you are part of the greater, you are not separate, therefore, my brothers, you can receive wisdom and many of the other benefits from the greater, and from your created space these will enter into your thought, in fact, they will become your thoughts.

You then need to expand upon this thought that is the greater and then allow it to lower its vibration for use within the lower worlds, then you will be bringing in the greater consciousness into the lower consciousness, the greater notes will overlay the lower notes and bring them into harmony.

You can apply this concept to yourself, because the space you have created has its magnetic quality and because, through this space, the Spiritual Man relays its wisdom, this will of course produce a vibration, an inner vibration that will be creating harmony.

Now, to create harmony through vibration, there sometimes occurs a disharmony, this is how you will perceive it. It may well shake you up and you will think, "I was in harmony and now I'm not, my thoughts and feelings are all over the place and I am physically tired. I was all right before." Well, you perceived you were all right before because you felt comfortable.

Let us explore the meaning of being comfortable. Comfort can be viewed from many different perspectives; having a good economy is one of them, meaning enough money to be comfortable. We are not exploring that avenue, we are talking about an inner comfort, certain centres of the body have a relationship to this comfort, they function according to your psychological make-up and are conditioned by it, also they are susceptible to outer influences, they are the interface between the aura and the physical body. Their function is according to their vibration, now when you are comfortable they will be functioning in a very lazy way and will have adopted a fixed vibration, passive in comfort and forceful in trying to attain comfort, certain higher centres will only be functioning upon the lower levels.

The Spiritual Man in this case will not even be perceived as a shadow and, of course, in your search for comfort, your centres will adopt a specific vibration that will either inform the brain consciousness, or they will block their channels so that the brain consciousness is not informed at all.

You will, therefore, believe that you are comfortable, but in reality it will be an illusion, you will have created a system of vibration that has supressed those aspects of your life that are certainly not comfortable, and you will believe you are fine, and you will feel fine. You will also not listen to anybody's opinion of your situation as you will have shut off the reality of it from the brain consciousness, and then in your comfort you wonder why you have many minor complaints. This also you will reason out from your place of comfort and place the reason why upon the physical, hence you could say this is a fixed rigid position and will be reflected in the body as a limitation of movement.

So, comfort has not the ability for movement when the Spiritual Man starts to enter, you will then be impacted by energies of a higher vibration which will start to open certain chambers of the centres upon the body that have been closed, and because they are closed, they contain within them the problems of why they are closed and the energy consciousness of this.

So you see now how you will perceive it as disharmony. Quite right. It is on a lower level, but it presents itself as an opportunity to achieve a higher harmony.

Your brain consciousness will then start to receive the energy consciousness that has been locked up in the centres on the body and, of course, all the feelings concerning this. But the Spiritual Man is not separate from you, he will bring you insight, he will allow you to recognise these things in the light of his wisdom, and you will make certain adjustments, you could say I am talking about a transformation process, and when you are starting to realise this, you will start to think creatively.

That is the dilemma you face from a horizontal level of comfort, where time just ticks away and everything stays the same, and if this is where you are then so be it, your journey is a long one so do not pursue this path if it is not right timing for you, the time will come in another lifetime. You then find yourself at times above the horizontal level and you will wonder at the insight you are receiving and then during the same day, you are plunged below the horizontal level of comfort into disharmony.

Realise this is just a process of reclaiming your identity within the manifest world to then identify yourself with the spiritual worlds. The disharmony you had will pass. Do not take it and yourself seriously, you may need to work some things out and they will be indicating to you the need for change, and certain situations and things you do will feel so uncomfortable, whereas before you didn't take any notice of that, you will have to transform your beliefs about them and adjust accordingly.

It's not the fact that you are becoming more sensitive as such generally, it is just you will become more sensitive, or I may say 'aware', of what is not of the soul as the Spiritual Man before you had blocked both things, the impact of the events and your connection to the Spiritual Man.

But also you are becoming more sensitive to the Spiritual Man, you now need to realise what does not serve you, you have to recognise the essentials and non-essentials, all too often you create one thing after another, one responsibility after the other, and that takes all your time. You have created the space in your mind and you have now understood what no thinking means, now is the time to create the space within the physical worlds, much of what you do is not essential, if you really think about it.

You could argue otherwise, but what part of you will be arguing? It certainly will not be the Spiritual Man, because he is in contact with the Divine Man and the Divine Plan, and he knows what your purpose is, and you are not fully aware of this.

Your destiny is not in doing lots of non-essential things to clutter up the mind, to fill up the emotions and tire yourself out running here and there. You can run here and there, but have a purpose for it other than your comfort, your commitment, you can balance out the Spiritual Man with the Physical Man.

Mostly the Physical Man dominates, he runs along the horizontal line quite happily, even if he is moaning all the time, even about things half way across the world. Will that help? In fact, it will make matters worse. The power of negative thought, when it is of a massed intent, is very powerful and will manifest, given time. Do not seek the same methods of approach as you do with the Physical Man, it is not the same for the Spiritual Man.

Let us meditate upon this.

Come to realise your existence within the manifest world, and you recognise yourself as the Physical Man, you also realise you are receptive to the physical world through your senses.

They are the way you register it, so focus on the first sense, the sense of hearing, all the sounds that enter you through that sense.

Now, decipher the sounds you have been hearing as the Physical Man, all the sounds of the world, all the sounds of other people.

What does it say to you?

Has some of this served you?

Centre within the Spiritual Man, lift your consciousness above the head, this is the higher consciousness, enter into a state of no thought.

Before you do, present to the Spiritual Man your conclusions on your sense of hearing and what you have heard, then allow the Spiritual Man to inform you of the reality or non-reality of these sounds, and maybe you will recognise sounds that you have forgotten.

Discriminate those sounds and identify with the sounds that serve you, these are from the Spiritual Man, try to understand what, after a due period of silence, the Spiritual Man will now be relaying into your consciousness.

Observe also the reactions of the Physical Man as he may well want to interrupt.

Yes, believe these two aspects of you are part of you, but can be in conflict with the other, as I have spoken of.

Can you understand the Spiritual Man knows more than your Physical Man?

He will give you truth, the Physical Man does not like truth, if takes him out of his comfort zone, so what are you hearing that is not truth?

Is the Physical Man telling you that you cannot do that, you are not capable of it?

It scares you too much, or it will upset other people.

If other people are entrenched within their Physical Man, then you will find no understanding there unless you are very diplomatic, but then if they are going to lose something from you, they will not be very happy.

I will pause in this dialogue for you to connect fully with the Spiritual Man and the Over-shadowing Wisdom, so you may touch upon this wisdom and see the truth.

Now relax your attention upon this subject, find the time to evaluate your results of meditation with what I have presented: 'the essentials or the non-essentials', and with this statement you have the means whereby you can evaluate your consciousness.

Firstly you have to recognise the word 'essential', it means what is necessary and needs to be there, needs to be acted upon and needs to be part of life. So, when you start to think very deeply about this, and I suggest a state of waking meditation, the next stage is to identify what is essential and what is non-essential, and there you see a duality, a place of division. One aspect you need to consider is responsibility, and another is that you are living upon more than the physical plane, with that you just had to think about the physical body, but I will incorporate also your emotional and intellectual bodies, and it is within these three states that you are confronted with what I have proposed - the essentials or non-essentials.

Carrying this further, what is essential or non-essential, first to the Physical Man and then to the Spiritual Man? We can take this further and take into account the objective and subjective worlds of your being, and so you could also take this word 'being' as representative of a state that is reflective of our true self.

Yes, mainly this word 'being' represents a higher state that just is, and beyond all that I have mentioned, but I wish to propose this word as an achievement for each of your levels of consciousness that are essentially one consciousness, the consciousness of being is beyond consciousness as you understand it.

Your physical body represents activity in third dimensional reality, what is essential or non-essential for your form aspect needs to be of a balanced nature, a whole book could be written about it, and do not forget a lot of identification with the physical body is subject to glamour (emotional) and illusion (intellectual) and this seeks to imprison your soul within the form by your identification with it, and over-emphasis upon it.

All I have to say concerning this, which is basically common sense, and yet many of you do not apply it as many other things, emotionally or mentally, take control and affect your brain consciousness. For example, if you sit down all day at a job and then go home and sit down all night, well, it is quite obvious what will happen. On top of this, if you eat more than you burn up, then it also is quite obvious what will happen. Since life for you has become more comfortable, and all that it has to offer, then concerning the true well-being of the physical body, the brain consciousness can side step the issues.

Now if you stand in the light of the Spiritual Man and seek the truth, and that truth is your function within the Divine Man who holds the Plan, the Plan for yourself and humanity, there are many individual planes that relate in vibratory unison to others, which you will consider as a group, and the many groups become the One Group within the One Life, therefore, you are required to be able to perform the task that you require your physical body to carry out in line with the Plan, so the importance is the plan and that carries your purpose, and if your purpose is being manifested, then your physical body will help create the purpose and carry it out, all other concerns will drop below the threshold of consciousness as they will not interrupt you by giving your brain consciousness a headache concerning them.

The one word that holds you back from distinguishing the essentials from the non-essentials is 'control', to hold the power according to what your brain consciousness required for the physical, emotional, and intellectual bodies, and yet all the time you are seeking to be liked and also loved.

How can your thought control be seeking love? Well, control is a way of overcoming fear, fear of many things: success, loss, money, relationships.

Even the person who appears to be so self-contained as to not require to be liked at all as they have become cold, still is seeking inwardly love, although on the outside they are displaying the opposite. So control is a non-essential, you cannot move your consciousness at all if you are exerting control, your world will be confined within that control, and control is on many levels. The essentials contained within the spiritual contain truth, and truth is the substance for expression for the consciousness to release itself from its prison.

Love upon the lower level of being relates to the emotions and feelings, it has there its duality, and desire is one of them. Mentally the control of desire is according to the strength of the will of the mental body to inhibit that desire, if it is deemed undesirable, as mentioned the emotions will become cold, it is a non-essential to inhibit the emotional body as this is a creative agent, but it is desirable to understand it from the perspective of the Spiritual Man, and so is the mental body specifically the intellectual aspect, as this is the main factor that makes decisions or lack of decisions, as it has attachments, and that can be to outcomes and the success of them according to what your expectations are. Here again you exert your control in this respect. The answer to this non-essential is time, and that from the aspect of the Spiritual Man, outcomes cannot be perceived by the Physical Man and his intellect.

Can you not see, now, the restrictions you are placing upon yourself? Think these things and you attract their opposite, because you have fixed your identification on outcomes for everything you do, rather than allow it to flow and creatively adapt yourself to the changing situations as they unfold.

This is the positive polarity that moves on an upward spiral due to the balance of the negative polarity and is receptivity. Be prepared to change course, but be aware at some point there will present a barrier to you, and your recognition of this barrier will be according to your consciousness, if your consciousness is based upon a negative world, then you will see this barrier as an obstacle, rather than an opportunity to understand something that the barrier is withholding from you.

You will perceive this barrier as a difficulty, this is an illusion, it may feel uncomfortable as it may be testing you - and it will be - it will be testing your ability to think abstractly, it will be testing you on an emotional level as that is your sensitive area and affects your brain consciousness. In fact, this sensitive nature surrounds your brain consciousness, as does your mental nature, and yet all the time you are seeking an expansion of yourself into the infinite worlds of the Spiritual Man and the Over-shadowing Wisdom and truth whereby the Divine Man can light up your consciousness into the wonders of its kingdom.

Each realisation brings its opposition, that which has inhibited and restricted your consciousness to where it is. Now you may have a realisation about what is non-essential and then the opposition will appear as to why you cannot do anything about it, and remember this non-essential will have a connectivity on three levels: mental, emotional, and physical. Seek the answer upon the emotional level first, feel what it pertains to, then evaluate your thoughts concerning this, then realise that the truth of this non-essential is an illusion.

Place this problem to the Spiritual Man as you cannot resolve anything from these levels, not in the appropriate way, as you may see only light and dark, yes or no.

Attempt to expand your consciousness into the realms of reason, see if the non-essential is serving you and what aspect of you it is serving. Will you be releasing yourself the necessary time to create the space for the Spiritual Man to inspire as to your purpose?

Now place all your non-essentials out of your consciousness and focus upon your essentials as you think about these, and there will be some that you are not yet aware of.

If any create a feeling of negativity, they may well be non-essentials that you feel emotionally you have to do, that you are committed to, and have a responsibility for.

Then think as to whether it is your responsibility or whether this responsibility has been created by the limitations of your consciousness, then bring the light of truth from the Spiritual Man above the head into your thinking consciousness, do not be afraid as to repercussions, you do not have to act upon it, just identify with it and understand it.

You then stand at a point of silence and enter deeper into the abstraction of time, and then relinquish your responsibility emotionally and mentally, realising the transformation that will occur, then your consciousness will solve the problem without doing anything. Relax your attention,

Now, we will explain these last words, '*without doing anything*'. An understanding of this concept will alleviate much stress and expand your consciousness into the workings of substance upon the mental plane.

Now, understand your non-essentials are held within your mental and emotional bodies through the power of the Law of Attraction. You can understand attraction upon the physical plane, the same exists upon the emotional and mental planes, only to you it is intangible, so put all three together, then the Law of Attraction holds you in its magnetic field according to your identification of the non-essential.

Where is your identification?

If it is all three, then these ties need to be released, so working downwards from the mental plane, that is why I have suggested relinquishing your responsibility, and that will create the circumstances connected with my statement '*without doing anything*'.

You have to prepare the ground, so to speak, so after I have finished this concept you may well want/wish to repeat the previous exercise with a deeper understanding, when you mentally withdraw away from the non-essentials, then that substance upon the mental plane that held you within them via the Law of Attraction, will transform and be used more fully, and appropriated towards the essentials.

In fact this released substance, because it is then fluid, has the ability to be creative, so once the release, be aware that you then possess this mental substance for use to expand your essentials and bear in mind essentials are not responsibilities.

Can you understand that word? If we use the word, it is well to identify it with the Spiritual Man. The Spiritual Man may wish you to create a new avenue for this mental substance.

If you identify with the Divine Man above the Spiritual Man through a space, third eye alignment casting up above the Spiritual Man to the Over-shadowing Wisdom, a sea of vibrant light ever changing with a blue-white sphere at its centre, connect this sphere into the Spiritual Man, then into your head centre, then outward from the Ajna centre into the world of humanity, projecting this energy into its consciousness.

A selfless act you will be performing, but in essence you will be creating a channel and as you do so, that energy will be automatically stimulating this mental substance that you have released into a purposeful direction, remember, *'without doing anything'*. Things will be set in motion and through the Law of Attraction, more mental substance will be attracted and enter the brain consciousness, from out of the blue, so to speak, but keep your rational mind at bay, otherwise it will present a barrier. Your success will lie in transforming the feelings of your emotional body that has identified with the non-essential, if the Spiritual Man has started to become a part of your life, then they could well be in turmoil.

You will start to be feeling what is reality or non-reality, so you will have a duality with the non-essentials, parts of your emotions, through the Law of Attraction, identifies with the non-essentials and feels their need whatever the mind may be now thinking, otherwise there is an attachment to them.

Another part of your emotions will be wanting to release them as you will be feeling uncomfortable. Identifying with them, that is the dilemma. Both situations feel uncomfortable from the duality of your emotions and there would appear to be no answer, and nowhere to turn.

What you have to allow to happen is let the non-essentials gradually drop away, now if you can transfer that part of your emotions away from them and place their focus upon what I might term as the product of your creative mental substance, then the consciousness of the non-essentials that is within your emotional body will disappear and so will the non-essentials, all this because they cannot exist without the mental and emotional energy that is held within them by the Law of Attraction.

So the *'without doing anything'*, I am referring to is the physical participation in them, now if you don't mentally and emotionally participate with them, then the physical participation will fall away naturally, and so will the people concerned with them, if that is the case, therefore, you *'do without doing'*.

So, it is time to transfer your emotions away from the non-essentials, if you are ready to do that, as I do appreciate there is some kind of security for you in these non-essentials, because they may be a diversion away from the truth, and the truth can be very difficult to live with, so there is a need for you to build your emotional security, your own trust in yourself, this the Spiritual Man will do whereby others' opinions will be immediately sensed by the Spiritual Man. Opinions very rarely carry truth as they are an opinion which is limited to the consciousness of those expressing an opinion, which is usually inadequate and is probably not their opinion at all, it has been registered by the brain consciousness elsewhere, from another, from the media, etc. Now, emotionally you become attached to people on a personal level and through this attachment, energetically are formed interconnecting ties. To realise what I have said is to only register how you feel in certain people's company and you will know what I am saying. You seek, via the Spiritual Man, to become free from these attachments, free to make your own decisions and in that freedom, you will find security, you will be above the crowd.

Meditation

So, pause at this point and silently and slowly enter into the abstraction of physical objects and allow your focus to be on what you perceive as an empty space, it is not.

Its vibration brings you to a centre point of consciousness, the centre of the circle, that point of identification with the spiritual and physical worlds where they both converge and where they both become a balance within your consciousness.

From that centre point you attain a focus with the Spiritual Man.

When happy you have realised his presence, elevate again your consciousness into the Divine Man, see the Divine Man above the Spiritual Man as a crescent of energy blue-white in appearance.

This crescent now expands around you upon the level of the causal plane, the plane of souls.

You now place your emotional attachments to your non-essentials above your head with the Spiritual Man.

The Spiritual Man will evaluate the solution, then, one after the other, the light of the Spiritual Man will enter the head and out through the brow centre as a beam of light, dissolving each of these attachments until you stand fee.

Now you need to trust in your own guidance concerning these non-essentials and substitute a deeper understanding.

Now relax your attention upon this subject.

I wish now to move the instruction into the manifestation of purpose and to what is the purpose for your presence here upon earth. Is this a random event due to the procreation of your parents? And then how are you to live your life out without any true meaning, other than what is expected of you and your integration within society?

Well, that is not it, because that represents a separation from the Spiritual Man, time and time again the Spiritual Man conceives a new form within the manifest world, your parents are the physical means of your Spiritual Man taking a body.

There is no random coincidence to this and people have related this to the lessons that you need to learn, and experiences in this lifetime. I now wish to present otherwise; the former might be true, but also your presence has been born for a purpose. So many souls are lost without a purpose, and so many souls are trapped within what lessons they are here to learn, the only lesson you really need is the one that will motivate your purpose. And now think on this, your purpose is not an individual one, there are many that have a similarity of purpose, but the extent that you can express this purpose will be the extent of your radiatory influences, and the extent of your expression will be according to your alignment with the purpose that is held in substance within the Divine Plan.

Everyone has manifested a physical body for a purpose and as you would perceive it, great or small, the Over-shadowing Wisdom will light up the consciousness as to your purpose and we see an analogy here to purpose with the Monad and direction, many things that surround you as you move through the manifest world are there as signposts, but they may be very subtle in nature, look for the clues in what people say, whether directly to you or in a conversation you overhear. It matters not whether the person or persons are of a spiritual nature regarding their conversation, but they are all of the soul and their conversation could be stimulated in that way, and as all souls are in communication, then you are being given a clue indirectly from soul levels.

One could say you will pick this up more easily if your sixth sense is somewhat developed and is capable of impressing the other five senses and the brain consciousness.

Never ignore anything, never judge a book by its cover, your insight regarding your purpose may come in very strange ways, although to us it is not strange at all, it is just a way of communication.

Ask yourself what is your field of service and normally that is the one that excites you the most, and the one that will drag up your fears and lack of confidence, the one that will test and challenge you, but know this, it is the one that you are meant to engage with for your greatest amount of growth and usefulness towards humanity.

If you are afraid of speaking to groups, rest assured that this is part of your purpose. What you really wish to become will give you the most self-doubt. The enigma of this is presented to you with regards to the veils that surround humanity, there are three which imprison the soul and do not allow your Spiritual Man access to you. These veils are in direct opposition to your purpose so until that purpose starts to illuminate your mind, the energy consciousness of the veils will impregnate your brain consciousness with all the negative opposition. And of course, brothers, this opposition will create a seriousness within you, playing out as right or wrong, in short the fear of getting it wrong, the worry of not being liked, and ultimately the criticism that you may suffer.

If you are serious with your purpose and your identification with it, then your seriousness will go before as a form of control. You may have a degree of success, but you will also suffer the stress of this success. You cannot seek perfection with your purpose because you will misconceive this perfection, the secret is to enjoy your purpose, and what will happen then is you will be motivated towards and within it, attaching to you beneficial forces for its construction.

Look at what you have suffered in this life and there will lie your purpose as it will direct you to it, and realise that what you have gained during your life up to this point when I am addressing you, is part of the future manifestation of your purpose, nothing is wasted and nothing has been a waste of time, no matter how you feel about it. I understand that some things have been very upsetting, but you can alleviate your difficulty concerning this, your sadness, your grief, your hurts, by seeing them as part of your pathway to your purpose, and that when that purpose is starting to manifest then you gain strength from them, and know this - they will be left behind and will not be repeated.

You will have closed the gap in consciousness between the Physical Man and the Spiritual Man, no more will you experience the great divide that separates the two, this divide holds all consciousness within the confines of the Physical Man, and the Physical Man has many facets and possesses opposition forces, and one which will dominate is the Dweller on the Threshold, all the power and force of the self-contained ego through many lifetimes, the one that is the present manifestation which you relate to the surface mind, the conscious working mind, the mind that sees horizontally, then you have the rest of many incarnations within the sub-conscious mind.

Now when the Spiritual Man is approaching and another part of your mind recognises this and shouts to open the door to him, the Dweller will gather his forces and counter this approach, impregnating the mind with self-doubt, disrupting your emotions with guilt, and devitalising your etheric body with delusionary activity, it is the battleground of the self. Take heart and realise that all the good also has its forces, all those kind things that you have done also over many lifetimes, and that will start to counter the opposition from the Dweller, because all these kind acts have activated your heart centre and the heart centre communicates with the Spiritual Man. Realise also that the Spiritual Man has impregnated your brain consciousness and has placed a light there, so the Dweller might initially knock you off course, but it cannot win, you cannot go back whilst your heart has opened to the Spiritual Man, the Dweller may well cause you disruption in the centres below the heart, but because of that, other forces will come into play that are connected to the Spiritual Man and come to your aid, your insight will become clear and concise as to your distinctions, open up to this identification of the higher powers.

Meditation

Now, you will visualise, if you please, you are standing near the edge of a gorge and as you look out to try to see the other side, there is a fog veiling your vision, you cannot see more than ten feet in front of you, so you know that you could fall into this gorge.

Behind you are many people calling you back, you can hear them very clearly and it is quite deafening They are offering you many things that are appealing to you, they wish to save you so that you can live with them in the houses they have built to keep you within their confines.

You are tempted, but then an inner voice informs you to gaze out into the fog and listen for the voice of the Spiritual Man.

You feel a magnetic pull towards those behind you and yet something is urging you to listen, you battle with yourself until you gaze into the fog and start to listen, the noise behind starts to fade.

You hear a voice in your head, it is your voice, but not your thinking. It says "Do you want to live your truth, or do you want to live a lie? Do you want to release your burdens or do you want to carry them into your future and, of course, you can only carry them for so long?"

You ponder upon this, a thought then comes to mind, you realise you need to transgress this gorge and stand on the other side.

Then a voice enters your head, it is from the Spiritual Man from within the fog, this voice is calling you towards your true spiritual home.

You realise the truth and the fog starts to dissipate and reveals to you a rainbow bridge which spans the gorge, in fact the gorge is just an illusion, realising this the bridge turns into a golden pathway, and in the distance a disc of electric-blue light, and within this disc you see the image of the Divine Man.

You move down the path towards the disc, those that are behind you have perceived that you have disappeared into the gorge, for them the gorge and the fog are still there.

You stand in front of the disc, you pause and sound your note, this may be the OM, and then enter.

Everything becomes one, you see a continuity of consciousness, the higher planes open up to you.

Perceive the beauty of all that is above and all that is below, everything becomes aligned.

Now relax your attention.

There are certain aspects of this that need to be considered, from the aspect of consciousness, the gorge represents the gap in consciousness that exists between the Physical Man and the Divine Man, the fog represents the illusions of the physical material plane that clouds our thoughts and feelings, returning you then within their limited circumferences. As you can see all around you, those that were behind you are absorbed within this consciousness that is not consciousness, but a fixation of mental and emotional substance that is made up of all past thought and emotion, that becomes a fog that then clouds the brain consciousness to conceive itself as to what it is. There can be no other than this and for many, to realise there is a vaster consciousness that can be embodied, will not understand within their brain consciousness as that consciousness is elsewhere, other than the Spiritual Man and the Divine Man. In other words, it is just what it is and will not possess movement.

Can you imagine life without progressive thought, without creative thought, without abstract thought? I have posed these questions for you to try to recognise what they mean and identify with them.

Practice your creative thought with your imagination; the child imagines, the adult may dream, but has lost his imagination, unless of course it is stimulated by undesirable activities. Start with a nature walk around the garden, or in the woods, study the leaves, the flowers, the trees, just by noticing their shape, their colour, look at how they are formed, and then sit down anywhere you feel comfortable, and do not limit that to a quiet place, and then write a poem or verse about what you have seen, bring your experience into your mind, imagine the forms you have gazed upon and write just what comes into your head, be expressive, go beyond your normal boundaries of expression.

Add your feelings to this, be abstract and creative, you may well be surprised, you can bring this creative imagination to all aspects of life and, of course, you will be creating movement out of the mundane, and enliven your consciousness, which will then attract further creativity. When you enter more fully into this creative consciousness, other aspects of consciousness will enter and you will then turn back across the gorge, realising that what you have experienced and have embodied you need to relay to others.

So now look into the space and find the eternal point of stillness and you find yourself back in the disc of electric-blue light that represents the Divine Man.

Realise you are absorbing particles of light from the Divine Man and, at some point, you will wish to retrace your journey.

Leave the disc now and travel back down the golden pathway, heading back into the manifest world.

You are half way back when suddenly, out of nowhere, a figure approaches you. It has your likeness and is surrounded by light, the figure is ethereal in nature, you realise it is the Spiritual Man.

You pause on the pathway, the figure keeps moving towards you, then you realise the Spiritual Man is going to enter fully into your consciousness.

You wait, the Spiritual Man comes closer and then enters into you, you feel a shudder of energy and continue, you reach the end of the pathway and step off, and find yourself back on the other side, the crowd is still there.

You look back towards the Divine Man, the gorge has appeared once more, but for you the fog has cleared and spanning the gorge is the rainbow bridge.

You know you can travel back across any time when the need arises, but you also realise there is now a direct communication with the Divine Man.

You may be thinking "What was that all about?" Well, understand that the crowd can still see the gorge and the fog, you can see the gorge with a rainbow bridge and no fog.

It is not your place to be on the other side, your place is with those who only perceive the fog, you are there to teach them, to uplift them, to relay the consciousness to them, to inform them of the Spiritual Man and the Divine Man, and the more you do this in whatever way your presence requires, the more will be the communication with the Divine Man.

So now move back towards the crowd, do not worry, they will see you in a different light, they will have no pull over you as they will be seeking something different now, and they will realise this. Unconsciously maybe, but they will not place any demands upon you, as you and the Spiritual Man are one and you are aligned with the Divine Man.

Now, you have to live within those worlds spiritually, and also amongst the crowd physically, so you greet the crowd and you may recognise some of them.

What will you say to them?

Proceed to relay the consciousness of the Over-shadowing Wisdom to them, remember, you can imagine your alignment via the rainbow bridge to the Divine Man.

Do not hold back, you are here to extend the consciousness of truth.

Relax your focus on this when you are ready.

I will leave you with the last stanza of the Affirmation of the Disciple:

> And standing thus revolve
>
> And tread this way the ways of men
>
> And know the ways of God,
>
> And thus I stand.

My blessings are with you.

Andrew Carter - 17/12/2014

NOTES

TRANSCRIPTS FROM THE

MASTER K H

BOOK TWO

NOTES

NOTES

Let us consider the Divine Will impulse, this you can relate to a plane that corresponds to a constellation, and through the inter-connectivity of that constellation with the solar system, the rhythm of life impulses upon the plane of Atma. The Divine Will has its focal point for the involutionary manifestation of form within the Monad. The One Life focussed within, and embodied as a representative of the cosmic life stream and the syntheses of being, the Monad represents the highest point upon the path of evolution, for a continuity of consciousness from a monadic level brings about an alignment with all that you may perceive as truth, and, of course, truth is love, the love impulse from a cosmic level of truth is an integrated aspect of the Divine Will impulse.

Here we seek to understand the word '*impulse*'. This produces a rhythm, the impulse is not the rhythm, it is the underlying factor for its continuation of life force energy interwoven with the love energy. Wisdom is the result, through the conjunctions of this Divine Will impulse upon the brain consciousness, because there needs a certain amount of will to be impressed by wisdom. Love and intelligence are not enough. Intelligence transposes wisdom into an intelligent format, love will be the agent for its manifestation, and here you need to understand that manifestation of love requires an objective point of focus within the three worlds, and you may understand this as service.

What does this word '*service*' bring into our consciousness? How do you perceive it? Service to what? To another person, to a group, to humanity? This may seem to many all too much, as your understanding of the word 'service' is limited to your personality expression, it denotes servitude. This, my brothers, is far from the truth. So, take for one moment, a realisation that you have been incarnated for a purpose, a destiny, and that reveals your service. Now, it is not service in the sense that you carry a burden of responsibility, and you have to carry out all this within your life, just, for example, like a job. It is a job, it is a place of work, but not in the sense of how you understand it upon a physical level.

I wish to explain the difference here. Your work upon the physical plane provides you with the financial resources for living, or, we refer to it as the economy. In many cases, this is the primary reason for your work situation, although there is an aspect of resonance here with your emotional and mental bodies. The emotional body is the factor that will reveal to you whether your job, your circumstances, are in resonance with the Spiritual Man, and forget not that the Spiritual Man is the higher aspect of yourself, it represents and is your purpose and destiny. Now, if you have no glimmer at all of the Spiritual Man who, in those moments of emotional and mental silence gives you realisations and impressions, you would know no insight, then you will be very confused as to the concepts proposed.

There are many names given to the Spiritual Man. This aspect of yourself, whatever it is called, is your link to the worlds that vibrate at a higher frequency than those you are familiar with. If you are impersonal about all this, you will receive a small portion of understanding. Is your purpose what you are living today?

Now, outer happenings and events are but a moving picture of life through eternity, these are the result of forms and movement and as you are probably quite aware, are very limiting in a physical sense. Purpose does not rely upon economy, and by that word, one aspect of economy is finance, another is time, perception of time is a very interesting thing. One thing that limits the perception and the purpose is the fact that you use up time, you have this precious aspect of divinity, for this example I will use the day - twenty four hours - from the time you rise to the time you retire. How do you consciously view the day? Mostly by what you can cram into it. Those who follow without question the social structure, are doomed to repetition, the repeating of patterns from the time you arise until when you retire. View your day and you will know what I am talking about. Now, if there is no understanding of anything else, well, you will want to fill your day.

Now, consider there *is* something else, and consider that what you are familiar with is, and I quote, "your physical body", and in this context also your etheric body, your emotional body and feelings, your mental body and thoughts, that there is a correspondence to those three on planes higher than those three. So, for example, you can become the recipient of consciousness from those planes into your thoughts and feelings. Now the problem occurs when you are engaged in outer world activity, the mind and emotions become fully submerged with whatever you are doing, therefore, you separate the Spiritual Man from the Earthly Man. Recognition of the Spiritual Man is not enough if you then forget about him when you are engaged in outer activity, and to an extent, because of this, your day can become a survival course, relaxing, if that is possible, when you have no other commitments. In this scenario your earthly self will also see the Spiritual Man as a commitment.

Now, purpose cannot be perceived from outer activity and the need for economy, and if your purpose is starting to manifest, it cannot be linked to economy as economy is related to need. All things are perceived from the earthly self that manifestation requires economy and remember, I have placed the very important aspect I am referring to as finance. So, consider for a moment whether your purpose requires economy to manifest, or whether your purpose pursued will manifest the economy. I have to warn you that literally taken will not relay the truth of the statement, because the Earthly Man will not perceive the truth and react upon the statement from its level of consciousness.

To embody this concept we have to incorporate in the consciousness time, and see time as an opportunity to reach out to those higher planes of vibration and consciousness, because there will lie your purpose, which is not an individual affair, it may be perceived as such, but not from those levels.

Now, if You can create time, and in many cases this will be very difficult, to reach out to those higher planes, then time will be viewed, as I have mentioned, as an opportunity. This opportunity represents the concept of the Eternal Now. The more you slow down those three lower aspects, the closer you come to the Eternal Now, and that represents the point that elevates the consciousness in a vertical movement into the higher corresponding planes. The Spiritual Man knows your purpose and the Spiritual Man has many friends that form a group. From the perspective of the Earthly Man, a group is something that has the same identification and interest in a particular subject and they may well meet, or in these days of instant communication, it may be via the internet and its many forms.

Let us consider the group I am talking about, it transcends time, location, interests, and will also transcend the physical plane itself. Think about the simplification of this proposition. You have made contact with the Spiritual Man, you may well be in communication, although your Earthly Man may not realise it. You will realise it more as your purpose unfolds, meaning the purpose that has its origins with the Spiritual Man who holds this purpose, waiting for the Earthly Man to make contact. Now, your purpose will also accelerate your consciousness, because your purpose is held by the Spiritual Man. Then, as I proposed, the Spiritual Man has many friends that form a group, and here we can now use the words *group consciousness*.

So, just for one moment, consider first a group upon the physical plane; now if that group is separatist to other groups, then that separatist ideology will impregnate and affect the thinking of anyone who joins that particular group, therefore, they will become like everyone else in the group, quite mindless of their activities. This is a group of earthly men unaware of the Spiritual Man. Now, if the group is a group of spiritual men, then that is different; they mostly will not know each other, and could be anywhere within the world, but this is the thing, their consciousness will be of the Spiritual Man, and because of this, they will share their consciousnesses.

Ponder this firstly, it means your consciousness will not only be impressed by the Spiritual Man, but also all the others within the group. Can you imagine the expansion of the consciousness of the Earthly Man as a result? How does this affect economy? It means that if you pursue your purpose, because it is there to be pursued, and you consciously undertake to do so without bringing in the limitations of the Earthly Man, then economy will take care of itself. But one has to use economy to manifest purpose, and that does require time and stability of finance, and this is the key, it is the plan itself, so if your purpose is aligned, or is attempting to manifest a portion of that plan, then the plan itself will provide the economy. If love is displayed through your purpose that is of the plan, then your purpose will, through Law, attract to you the means by which you will be able to manifest this purpose. I present another clue to this, *"do not think in isolation."* Think as a combined group consciousness, realising that the group itself will respond according to the Law of Love with the purpose and the plan. The methods of the Earthly Man for manifestation will not work in this instance, he can only manifest a form within a form that is already in manifestation; as time goes, it will be short lived, and if it concerns purpose and plan, it will not manifest at all. Therefore, the activity of purpose goes on within the plane of the Spiritual Man. Now, when the Earthly Man realises this, he has to adapt to the concepts of the Spiritual Man, a difficult task as the Earthly Man has to accept that he cannot manifest in the ways he has always known.

Meditation can manifest your purpose, but do not expect it tomorrow, or maybe next year, or maybe never. It will manifest your purpose rather rapidly though, if you connect purpose to your meditation with the motivating power of the Divine Plan. "How can I do this?" you may ask. The answer to this lies in relegating all preconceptions of purpose and plan away from your thinking and feeling, then you will be in a position to receive instruction, but be aware what others may say, not directly because directly is addressing your personality, your Earthly Man. Most of what you hear is of the Earthly Man, but it doesn't mean it is to be ignored, because that particular Earthly Man may be on the level of the Spiritual Man, be a friend with your Spiritual Man. You may not have much in common, but underneath all that, there is a common purpose, the upliftment of human consciousness into a synthesis of consciousness that is group consciousness that understands love, and displays love, has purpose and is aligning with the plan through selflessness and becoming a part of the One Life.

We now have to consider what is the motivating power for manifestation. So, there requires a preparation firstly to relinquish the motivating power of the Earthly Man.

Meditation

Prepare to enter meditation.

Realise you are doing this as a group. (This may be so physically, but if you are alone physically, just call to mind this fact at the onset.)

You quieten your lower bodies by an identification with the space, as the place of harmony where all exists in perfect cooperation.

The inner vibrations of the space have ceased to be dominant, thus affecting your aura and centres, for what remains vibrates on the level of the Spiritual Man. It is not the Spiritual Man, but the plane and vibration where the Spiritual Man functions, thereby bringing your Spiritual Man into a resonance with your Earthly Man, who benefits by this relationship.

You will now be slowing down and through your resonance with the Spiritual Man, perception of time will change. Understand time is also slowing down; this, you appreciate, is physical time.

Then a wonderful thing occurs, if only briefly, you find yourself on the periphery of the Eternal Now, where there is no time.

Try not to be disturbed by this, retain your identification with the Spiritual Man and slowly, through this action and approach to the Eternal Now, you become the Spiritual Man, he has descended into your consciousness.

You may feel you are losing your identity with the Earthly Man. Allow this to happen; the Spiritual Man has embodied itself into your consciousness, therefore, your Earthly Man may disappear briefly, be aware he may return abruptly, as he is not used to this place.

Before he does this, the Spiritual Man invites you to travel upon a line of light from your head centre into a place which is the home of the Spiritual Man, a sphere of soul consciousness; many others reside within this sphere.

At the centre of the sphere is a smaller sphere, in comparison with the greater sphere, which is of blue light.

Try now to perceive your position within this greater sphere. How far away is your Spiritual Man from the smaller sphere of blue light?

Now, from this position, your Spiritual Man will move closer, but first understand this blue sphere represents the Divine Man, and there lies purpose, and also the plan for your purpose, because this smaller blue sphere is linked to an even greater sphere that relays divine consciousness and pure plan, and the motivating power then comes into activity through your resonance with the Divine Man, to allow your Spiritual Man to move closer.

Realise you are on the periphery of the Eternal Now, the Eternal Now is the result, and taken from a conscious perspective, is a part of the small blue sphere, or is your method, in this instance, of moving closer. The Eternal Now is love, it is a cosmic love so allow your heart centre to resonate with the Eternal Now, this is through your will, its use is through belief, that is the only way; believe it is done. Believe you are now part of the Eternal Now through the heart, and you will perceive your Spiritual Man moving closer to the small circle of blue. He will only go so far.

Now, from his new position, he will be receiving more energy exchange from the blue sphere, and as you are embodying the Spiritual Man, you also, as you are not apart from him, will be impressed with these energies and they will process firstly love and its energy consciousness.

Pause to allow this to happen, make this a creative imaginative process, but also realise a connection into your head centre, then the Spiritual Man, then the blue sphere containing the Divine Man, the energy consciousness of love comes down this line of connection, allow no thought to enter, just be with this, side-step all your conceptions on love.

Pause. Through this interaction and play of energies, visualise how the Spiritual Man, moving even closer to the Divine Man, stabilises his position.

From his position, the blue sphere intensifies with energy.

Now imagine you are the Spiritual Man upon his own plane. Your consciousness elevates to that position, and, as we are working with Triads, you, the Spiritual Man, using your imagination, create a line of light from the blue sphere, the Divine Man, to an even greater sphere of light above it.

So, the connection now becomes the Spiritual Man on its own plane, the blue sphere (the Divine Man), to an even greater sphere above, and from this greater sphere now emanates the energy of will and purpose that is the motivating power of the plan.

This enters into the Spiritual Man, you will have no thoughts on this as you are the Spiritual Man, just this stream of energy.

Pause to side-step all your conceptions of this. Your Spiritual Man may move even closer to the blue sphere.

Precipitate now the energy consciousness that has been received by the Spiritual Man, so you imagine that line of energy consciousness from the Spiritual Man into your head centre.

This light also moves outward into your aura.

The final point of this is to send this energy consciousness out via the Ajna centre into the etheric body of humanity.

Relaxing now the attention and focus.

Now you are awake within the room, you are aware once more of the space, and to remind you - there lies the Eternal Now.

I suggest some time within the space and Eternal Now, and as you are aware, there is no time. This will assimilate the energies of your meditation.

Three minutes have now passed. Become fully aware within the physical plane, and I suggest you move around. Before you do, it would be useful to sound the OM into the space thereby releasing the energies into a full manifestation. Sound it naturally, let its pitch automatically occur.

Now, within that meditation, I mentioned to you to side-step your conception, firstly of love, and then to side-step your conception of will, purpose and plan, and this is a good way to expand the consciousness towards those concepts presented, because they may, to a great degree, seem meaningless to the Earthly Man, or will have no relationship to him. Forget not what the Earthly Man represents, it is your mental, emotional and physical activity within the sub-planes of the physical plane, therefore, all understanding will be from this level. To understand this, try now at this moment to formulate what love is, what will is, and purpose, and what do you define as the plan? Now, there are two aspects of you, the one I have just mentioned, try to formulate what I have presented from the level of the Earthly Man, which is your conception of life as you have experienced it from yourself within these experiences.

It is not wise to spend too long on this, as you are probably not getting very far as you will be trying to understand them from the self. This is why you have to side-step yourself.

Now, if you try to formulate these concepts into an understanding straight after the meditation presented, you will be thinking from the other aspect, the Spiritual Man, which takes into consideration the many, so think now from the Spiritual Man as it relates to humanity. You also will be thinking not from the aspect of time and what is going on now within humanity, as this will give you a distorted reality, as the concepts will be then based on what is perceived as reality due to present day events, which will restrict your consciousness within them. These need to be side-stepped

So, how does the Spiritual Man understand the concept of love? How does he view it? I have mentioned 'the many', now the Spiritual Man has incarnated a portion of himself many times, and you, at this time, are its present incarnation. The experiences of these incarnations have served to evolve the Spiritual Man on his own plane closer to the Divine Man. This is the case when its incarnations have been successful from his perspective. The Spiritual Man cannot move closer to the Divine Man without the Earthly Man recognising the concept of the Spiritual Man and moving closer to him, and this does not mean moving out of the physical plane to greet him, it means creating that channel in consciousness whereby his consciousness can 'descend', although this is not the correct word, into the consciousness of the Earthly Man. But realise this: the Spiritual Man is already part of the Earthly Man, but that portion of himself lies dormant. I say this to give you an understanding, not that this is the fact for you, so every incarnation is the result of the Spiritual Man sounding his note into the lower frequencies, and that note attracts substance. That substance is what consists your bodies, therefore, your bodies possess the sound of the Spiritual Man. They also possess the different facets of the Spiritual Man from previous visits to the earth plane.

Now, to awaken the Spiritual Man is to awaken him within yourself, and one of the things you will come to understand is love which is not a separate affair. The more the Spiritual Man enters your worlds, the more you will become the conscious soul incarnate, thus you will become a magnetic force in the world of forms. Picture yourself as a magnetic force in the world of form. If you have a glimmer of your purpose, then you will be relaying this purpose out upon the etheric network and, through attraction, your story will unfold. This is the story that the Spiritual Man has written as he sounded the note for your appearance. Realise this appearance is not a random event, it is part of a sequenced order for the enfoldment of the Spiritual Man for manifestation of his consciousness within the Earthly Man for the redemption of matter, for the upliftment of consciousness, and remember, brothers, this is not an individual affair, do not self-contain yourself within the Spiritual Man. He knows this is the danger that is presented, as that can feel good, a sense of peace, a sense of security and harmony and, therefore, the Earthly Man wishing to retain this state will isolate himself from any challenges as confrontations in the outside world, in short, the environment.

This is not the way of the Spiritual Man, because the Spiritual Man now is also the Spiritual Warrior. Understand now, this is purpose in action; also understand the Spiritual Man is intelligence. Many disappointments can occur if you are expressing your purpose and love, and engaging with groups of Earthly Men whose consciousness is of the Earthly Man, they will not understand you. Realise you can be in a room full of these people and still contribute to the upliftment of consciousness by just being there, you do not have to say anything, your Spiritual Man will be stimulating the other Spiritual Men present into a conscious activity with that portion that resides within the Earthly Man, because you are a living channel for the Spiritual Man. Although, I must say, some people will find the light uncomfortable, and some people will find the light, if it is stimulating an interaction between the Spiritual Man and the Earthly Man, very relaxing, to the point of sending them to sleep.

Now, to be a warrior is to engage in the battle. To explain this more fully, a change of vibration is necessary, so the Master M can give insight. Thank you for your attention.

When we talk about the warrior and the battle, does this not give you an image of a physical battle? That may be so, but the warrior I am speaking of is the motivating power of the will to go forward, regardless of the obstacles and the challenges. We need many warriors to implement the plan, and it is the plan that matters. Can you devote your time to the plan? Can you sit down and meditate every morning and devote that time to the plan? Can you see this as more important than your job of work? More important than the food you eat? More important than the sleep you enter into every day? It is this sleep I wish also to talk to you about.

During your day, and realise that is part of a cycle, it is not separate from the next day or the one before, your thoughts, feelings and actions will have created a moving forward of energy into the next day. I use days as an example, but if you use your intelligence wisely, you will realise there are greater cycles; expand your thinking into these cycles. Your motivating power of purpose goes beyond the cycle of a lifetime, propelling you into future activity. This moving forward I speak of is the evolution of the soul. What has your day accomplished regarding the evolution of the soul? Is it propelling you forward, as I have mentioned, or has your day fixed you to the previous day? In this case, you will be relying purely on physical energy for the next day, in fact, you may not have had the motivating power for years. The result of this is fixation to ideologies, to identifications, to people, to a way of thinking, (we shall examine your way of thinking in a moment), physical identifications inevitably fall away at some point. Throughout your day, all is recorded on a sub-conscious level and also, and this you must realise on a planetary level, all that occurs is recording because it is part of the planetary life, and that is One Life. When you disconnect with physical plane consciousness through sleep, it is then possible, through this, that the sub-conscious will be allowed to surface, because your surface mind is not active in physical life, it is not now the controlling factor as it is during the day.

If I dare say that if your Earthly Man, and I am using the same terminology in this instance as this is what is being projected, is the controlling factor during the day, then it will simulate your sub-conscious into activity during the night. All aspects of similar vibration that reside within your sub-conscious will tend to surface if your day has not been harmonious, you may not be aware of all this activity on waking, but it will only serve to keep you within the confines of the Earthly Man, and the result will be your dreams experienced. If you think this out, you will understand what I mean.

Now, if you are aware of the Spiritual Man, you can put this to good use on retiring and consciously make an effort to place your consciousness within the sphere of the Spiritual Man before you fall asleep. This does not require some complicated ritual, although you must become aware that the energies of this coming age may stimulate that aspect in you, then through your action and identification, you will be achieving a continuity of consciousness with the Spiritual Man, in fact more so, as your waking consciousness will be rendered quiescent. Then, on waking, you immediately become the Warrior and enter into meditation; you will then be initiating an aspect of synthesis that is the motivating power, the Warrior I am referring to works very dynamically on subjective levels.

Can you, my brothers, become the Spiritual Warrior, as the first battle is the battle of the self? As I am involved with the first aspect, the aspect of will, it is apparent to me that your personal will is an individual affair, one of self-initiation and purpose that is in line with certain requirements for your individual self. I am not talking about the incidentals of life, you place too much importance on those, specifically for your spiritual growth. "If I deny myself a new shirt because it is a materialistic need, then I am being spiritual." I have to say on that sort of attitude, that denial is also of the individual self, you are better off buying the shirt and maybe on the way out of the shop a person might be sitting on the pavement asking you for money. You may feel very uncomfortable with that, but it is your opportunity to give help, and think on this, if you had not bought the shirt, you would not be in the position to help them.

Your personal will has to give way to the will of the One Life, to understand this is to enter into the mysteries, realise there is a greater will than your own. Look around, all the Kingdoms of nature and the human Kingdom are held together by the will, so therefore, everything is a part of the will, it is just that each part is different to another, and yet it is all part of one thing. Will is the energy force and substance that creates, substantiates, and produces movement, life, and appearance. It also produces transformations, once you realise you are only individual regarding appearance, then you will function within the greater life; this is the battle you face.

Now, once you enter is some conscious way with the concept of the One Life, then your goals will change from an individual perspective to the group perspective, in short, you will want to help change the consciousness of your brothers, who seemingly are unconscious, to achieve fundamental principles of, and I quote, "Goodwill". A change of vibration to a fourth ray transmission. This goodwill is a radiatory energetic effect of the One Life within one of its centres that represent, and is, humanity. This centre bringing down into your understanding on an individual level, is the throat centre, so it is quite understandable that goodwill will bring about harmony, which will produce the perfect note. It matters not whether you are perfected or not, because if your note is the clearest it can be for your particular key, then it will resonate with the One Life. To change the vibration of your note within a certain key requires a more expansive consciousness, the only way is through consciousness, then through consciousness, the desire to be this, that, or the other disappears, because you realise that will only produce in harmony and your sound will be flat.

Your knowledge and mental striving produces a complication of vibratory tones, because it is from a lower key, therefore, these tones I mention will be lower tones, and your sound will reflect these tones, you will have subscribed yourself within yourself. The sound of the Spiritual Man is upon a higher key and its tones are varied so to reach this higher key is to make no sound at all. The many sounds of humanity do not help this, but if you stop trying to sort yourself out, and just be silent, then you will hear the notes of the Spiritual Man, and these notes will translate to you as inspiration, wisdom, and intuition. Because each note carries an abundance of sound they will reveal truth, they will carry the tone of love, they will be projected with purpose and motivation, and though this silence, will come many realisations. You may not hear the notes from the Spiritual Man as in a tune, as you would understand it.

The more you can stop playing your individual notes as in relationship to your individualisation, meaning the separated self, then you will enter into a different rhythm. This rhythm will bring you into resonance with the Spiritual Man, you already are not separate from the Spiritual Man, but you do not understand or resonate with him. We find integration in a harmonious progression of silence, when you have become attuned to the key of the Spiritual Man, then your original key will be in harmony, it will then sound out into humanity as a part of a group sound, also through your individual interactions, and there will be many that will be attracted to your sound, they will seek to be what you have become.

If the lower key starts to attract you to its sound, and the higher key seems too much of a difficulty to sustain, then you are probably expecting a lot of yourself and are going too high on the scale, and this you cannot do, because what you will hear is but the higher note of your original key, and this will be astral sound. These sounds will seek to control, mislead, and disrupt the sound coming from the Spiritual Man, your station will then be distorted sound, in a sense you cannot listen to the sound of the others unless they are attuned to the Spiritual Man. You will know and recognise this by the quality of their sound and their intention behind its projection. Yes, this is related to speech, which is the obvious identification, but their sound also goes with them, the aura carries sound and so do the centres of consciousness, each centre is resonating to a note and carries its own energy. Discord occurs when one or more of these centres is not in harmonious resonance. "With what?" you ask. Well, this is, of course, the Spiritual Man, but the higher centres or the head centres are the governing factor for the lower centres; are they awake to the Spiritual Man? And to appreciate this, you drop your focus into the heart centre.

Meditation

I am now leading you into a meditation.

You need to quieten all the other centres and create a silence, but you are aware of the sound of the Spiritual Man, you identify with this above the head.

In this silence, the sound of the Spiritual Man becomes stronger, it is starting to affect your other centres.

Now create a direct line of contact with your heart centre, and slowly there comes a magnetic resonance.

You are aware of it lifting the vibration of your heart centre to the key of the Spiritual Man.

What may occur is a great sense of joy and freedom.

You will find also your aura will be uplifting its vibration so you are now establishing a resonance of soul with the Spiritual Man, your heart centre and your auric field.

Allow this to stabilise into the key of the Spiritual Man.

Now bring a note from the Spiritual Man into the solar plexus, do this from the heart centre.

Allow the solar plexus to stabilise into its new vibration. You also need to move all lower vibrations out of the solar plexus into the etheric, then out through the aura.

Your solar plexus will now be resonating to the key of the Spiritual Man.

Re-establishing your resonance, Spiritual Man, heart centre, aura, take the vibration into the sacral centre from the heart centre, moving the unwanted vibrations out into the etheric, then the auric field.

Allow this to stabilise via your focus on the Spiritual Man, you will find that your vibration is increasing so it is time to take the sound from the heart centre into the base centre.

Remove any unwanted vibrations and sounds into the etheric, then the aura, and as you do this, the vibration continues down into you earth centre, both centres are then uplifted into the key of the Spiritual Man.

Your focus now is on the throat centre, removed unwanted vibrations into the etheric, then out through the aura.

Now sound your note. This you will do through the medium of OM. Do this with purpose and conviction.

Focus now on the Ajna centre, view this as six inches outside of your physical. Your Ajna centre can be visualised as resonating with the Spiritual Man.

Now sound the note as the OM, and through the Ajna into humanity.

Imagine this as perfected harmonious sound precipitation into the consciousness of humanity.

You are held now in a balance of vibration, take a line of light from the Ajna into the cave in the centre of the head, and up into the head centre.

Sound your note as the OM, which projects a line of light to the consciousness of the Spiritual Man

The Spiritual Man has his place in the great centre of consciousness. There is a focal point within this centre that emits a key and note that is higher than the Spiritual Man, and this radiates throughout this centre of consciousness. The Spiritual Man is aware of this and is evolving towards this key.

So, as you are vibrating to the key of the Spiritual Man, attune, if you can to the higher key of the focal point of this centre of consciousness.

You could go further from this focal point to a higher focal point within a greater centre of consciousness. Dare to be inclusive in your attempt to perceive these sounds and vibrations.

Then it occurs to you, everything is in motion, nothing is separate, the greater sounds spiral down into the lower sounds and then back again into the greater sounds.

There are many higher sounds that are beyond our registration, so visualise this spiral of sound from the greater sounds into the lower, then back to the greater, and as you do, allow the greater sounds to penetrate into the lower kingdoms, firstly humanity, then the animal kingdom, the flowers and plants, then the mineral kingdom, and back to the greater sound, but see this greater sound moving outward through these kingdoms. This you will do rapidly, as the greater sound should not be held in any place of consciousness for long.

You will now have achieved a high vibration and motion to bring this to stillness within the Eternal Now, and to stabilise your energies, sound the OM into the space; this will align you to the space, then relax your attention.

Thank you for your participation.

The Master KH:

The concept I wish now to convey to you is the relationship that exists as the result of purpose that manifests as regeneration; also, as a secondary subject - reincarnation.

The purpose is buried within the essence of your being, certain aspects of consciousness are there, and can be dormant from the aspect of externalisation, so purpose lies within your subconscious. It lies within consciousness itself, and the third aspect that will unfold this purpose is the surface mind, so clearly you can see there are three aspects here relating to purpose, and specifically your purpose, for your manifestation into form and appearance. I might add that consciousness itself is subject to the evolution of the Spiritual Man within the causal sheath and its place within the ashramic group consciousness.

Now, will that relates to purpose is a specific stream of energy, will holds the creativity of the logos in manifestation, but on an individual level it is will that holds the form in physical manifestation. So now assume the will energy carries purpose. We have discussed that this purpose is related to the plan, so your resonance with the Spiritual Man will create a condition whereby the purpose will unfold in consciousness and impregnate the surface mind, registration of this is through the consciousness aspect as you relate yourself to the One Life. If you have accepted the principle of the One Life, and the One Life has responded to your ability to conceive this as a fact of life, then the surface mind will register the consciousness of the One Life, and that exists within everything you have just meditated upon, the major centres of the One Life.

I bring your attention to the three kingdoms below the Human Kingdom, if 'below' is the right word, this is only regarding the fact of humanity's individual expression. These lower kingdoms are not separate from you, they also possess purpose within each form. I illustrate the purpose contained within a plant, the purpose contained within a crystal, and this purpose is revealed in their appearance, but hidden within their microscopic worlds, I give as example the geometries of a crystal. Now, think on this, because you have accepted and thought about the concept of the One Life, you have become receptive to purpose, not just your purpose, but the purpose of the lower kingdoms, you will then be informed of their purpose and become aware of their etheric energies, and these energies carry the plan.

Yes, the plan can be seen in a plant, can be felt and impressed by a crystal, and can be touched by an animal. If you have not accepted the One Life this will not be possible, because the will related to the purpose carries the sound of love, another thing for you to think on, nothing is indivisible within the subjective realms, appearance leads you to believe otherwise. Now, the principles of the lower kingdoms are a subjective part of the human kingdom, a little thought will reveal this.

I wish to add another word to your concept and that is *growth*, leading to purpose, growth, regeneration. I have placed the word *growth* between *purpose* and *regeneration*, expanding the concept and allowing you to understand the original concept. The growth of a crystal is almost unperceivable from the time frame of a human consciousness, it may take millions of years. This is the densest of matter within the One Life as far as appearance, but not within its microcosmic worlds, as an investigation into them will reveal that there is memory contained within the formation of their geometries through their growth over a vast period of time. The motion of their growth comes from the creative process of sound; from out of the earth comes the manifestation of this sound in the geometric form of a crystal, so you could say everything that has appearance is through sounds, so they contain sound, so a crystal's geometries possess sound, and sound produces vibration. Resonance occurs through harmonious sound; as a crystal is a stable form, then its sound will be a constant rhythm. When you hold a crystal, this rhythm, through the synthesis of human and crystal, increases its rate of sound and blends with your sound, it is a possibility then that if your sound is inharmonious, then the potential of the crystal is to balance this sounds to its optimum vibration.

Now, crystals and minerals are an Informing Life, they contain the plan, they contain the past, the present, and the future, because what is in appearance now is from past plan, so it is not inconceivable that they also contain future plan. The plan radiates from a level of consciousness above the human; the human may not be in tune with the plan, and may not ever understand that there is a plan, but the crystals and minerals absorb this plan into their structures. Quartz carries incredible memory and the capacity for memory, and will emit energy, in the right hands it will respond to the intent of the user, so I am presenting a proposition that a quartz crystal, through its radiation, combined with the intent of its user, gives forth healing energies.

So, healing is connected to sound and vibration, and the key to its solution is light and the etheric body. In this context, I present to you the word '*luminosity*' - this infers an intensification of light, a state that is continuous light velocity. If you think about what I have presented, you will probably refer to the light emanating from a lighted object that you can physically see with the eyes, and that light will light a room, a street, the sky. It all goes beyond that. There is light that is imperceptible to you, but nevertheless is luminous. What about the aura? Everything has an aura light upon another level, the etheric level of existence. What is contained within this aura is the blueprint for the existence of its material form. Now, the light you may perceive from a plant is the energy emanating from the plant, but underlying this is its etheric structure; it is an Informing Life, it has colour and may have scent, but what else can it tell us? That the plant is luminous to the crystals and minerals, it has escaped from its kingdom through the luminescence of the sun, that great radiatory source of life energy, and again, perception of this is probably that you appreciate its light and warmth.

Now, I would like to take you beyond your present conceptions; if you can accept the fact of the aura, let us consider the human aura. There are many sub-divisions within its field, each sub-division is a vibration which is the result of sound. I am separating vibration from sound to give you an understanding, their clarity and pitch depend upon the Informing Life, and there is a possibility of three informing lives. All these sub-divisions carry information and knowledge, and their sound also depends upon their geometries, the higher sub-divisions are also an Informing Life for that which lies below the human, and, I must say, this is not in status, as the word above and below can denote some sort of superior position. Throw that concept away, all is part of the One Life, and the One Life would not conceive it that way, as all progresses in unison and the below also informs the above, and the above is the below to yet another Informing Life, but all part of One Life, whether planetary, solar or cosmic.

Integration of a stable geometric form within the aura brings it into a synthesis, if the higher sub-divisions are informing the lower sub-divisions, then you will perceive that the aura creates a luminosity, a brilliance not perceptible to the human eyes, but felt through the auric eye. There are many factors here for discussion; I briefly wish to mention the brain consciousness within this concept as the Informing Life, within the sub-divisions lies the aspects of human nature: to think, to feel, to act - each one informs the other, the physical informs of the condition of the other two. You probably have realised the information coming from your thoughts and feelings inform your physical body, but also your physical body can inform you of incoming energies from another source, also you can take this back out to the feelings and thoughts. Your brain consciousness informs those three under discussion. If the brain consciousness is all there is, the Informing Life will be dominantly within the lower sub-divisions, all what will happen then is that the information and knowledge contained within the aura will be of a quality reflective of that level of consciousness. You will understand then that the Informing Life will only communicate through their aura on a horizontal plane within those three levels, and the information projected will be of a quality reflective of those levels, according to the information consciousness. There will be but a dim light, there might not be the physical appearance, mannerisms and behaviours will also be an indication of the information contained within the aura. Please think of this information as changeable, but not adaptable, as within its narrow band relating to the sub-divisions, it can only inter-exchange on those levels.

It is worth going into a state of pondering to try to understand what I have said, relating it to the environment. Have you come to any conclusions from your effort to ponder on this, meaning have you perceived the different states of man? If not, take yourself to where there are people, view them. They are physical, as you will see, but around them is their aura and this is what is carrying the information from their Informing Life. See them with your physical eyes, and then your auric eye, which lies just above and between your physical eyes, and also be aware your higher sub-divisions, if they are active, will also bring you into a realisation, as those relate to the Spiritual Man and carry information from him, this you can use with this exercise.

Then become aware. What information do these people carry in their aura? This is done as an observation, you may also register the need to be detached. Now, the information may be chaotic, all manner of tones, colour and mixed geometrics. This is reflective of the Informing Life in the lower worlds, and there may be quite a lot of it, because the information of the lower worlds is denser and also reflects on the fact. When one is engaged in these lower worlds with mind, emotion, and speech, which you are creating all of the time when you stop one train of thought and lead into another, what happens to the first train of thought? It is continuing within the aura within the subconscious which the aura is also a reflection of, it is echoing itself. It is the same for feeling; if your feelings are undesirable, then they will continue within the aura, even though you have, to a degree, stopped feeling them. They, again, are submerged within the subconscious, which is, as mentioned, a part of the aura, in fact, it is the lower sub-divisions that are not registered by the surface mind.

All this is present within the aura. Your aura goes before you, and auras communicate with each other on their own energetic level, much of this you are not aware of, but, nevertheless, it goes on.

Regarding the earlier proposition that thoughts and feelings continue within the aura, have you ever suddenly started to think something you were thinking about, maybe ten hours ago, or suddenly started to have feelings that, and this is the difficult one, you felt maybe two weeks ago, or even five years ago? Similarity of experience brings about similarity of thought and feeling, because you already possess it in your aura, and also your centres of consciousness, all is in correspondence. If the indwelling consciousness identifies within the lower worlds, then you can understand how you can repeat a pattern, but also understand your aura will be communicating your patterns to others through what it contains. This Informing Life is circumscribed within humanity, its affects on other kingdoms will be undesirable, in fact, it is an affect in itself. As far as consciousness is concerned, there are sub-divisions within the aura that are capable of receiving consciousness from a highly evolved Informing Life. Now, do not immediately think of this as separation from yourself, therefore, leading you to believe it is something else, or even worse, someone else. Part of your aura is of a vibration that has its place within a higher sphere of consciousness, accept that and we can start to accelerate the process of integration. You are not aware of these sub-divisions even though you may be affected by them, but you do not register this fact. You might to a degree register some of those energies and see my last statement as an insult, but ponder the fact that there is vastly more you can be capable of registering.

It might be wise at this point to present a meditation for your understanding. This, in a way, will also be a healing meditation.

Meditation

Identify now with the space, and then the Spiritual Man above the head.

The Spiritual Man, for your identification, is a centre of light and consciousness.

The space to you may, from a physical perception, appear empty. It is not, it contains many sub-divisions of vibration just the same as your aura, except your aura is circumscribed by an Informing Life, which is your present state of consciousness. The space is not circumscribed, it is endless, and it is timeless.

You focus now intently upon the light of the Spiritual Man above the head and request that the Spiritual Man project his light into the space that surrounds your aura.

You must realise the Spiritual Man at this point will be projecting three different energies of light. If there is a perception of colour, go with this.

Now these three energies are of different frequencies, all are one as the identification for this is the word *divine*, so realise they consist of divine mind, love and will.

Imagine these three entering the space of the room; you will probably start to respond to this and feel a sense of vibration.

The outer sub-divisions of your auric field will start to recognise these vibrations.

At this point, enter into communication with Divine Will; this communication will proceed within the highest sub-division of your aura. This is not limited to the periphery as each sub-division also has a sub-division, so within all seven sub-divisions there is a space provided for Will to enter, and as you enter into communication, and remember this will be varied, not just the word, you start to perceive above the Spiritual Man a cloud of energy, this is the Divine Man trying to make himself known.

Some of the energy of that could is dropping down into your head centre, then into your brain consciousness.

Now shift your attention to Divine Love, it is within the space.

Start to communicate; you will find the vibration will change to a slower rate as you will perceive it, but may be more penetrating on some of the sub-divisions.

You may feel this energy on the body; it may be hitting the information that resides there. Relax with this, you may be necessary for you to breathe in the energy of Divine Love into your being.

Continue with the communication using the Law of Substitution, if required.

When your vibration has stabilised, the cloud above the head starts to form into a shape, this is the Divine Man giving you an image of itself in the form and shape that will represent Divine Love to you.

Once formed, identify with it as a symbol of the Divine Man and love.

Each one of you will experience something different. I will pause for a while so you may integrate this.

PAUSE

From love the space now calls you to identify within it the energy of Divine Mind, your sub-divisions of the aura respond to the light of the Divine Mind.

As you communicate with its essence, see no separation from your mind to the Divine Mind.

You experience its light on many levels of your aura and then what happens is a clarity of brain consciousness occurs, and you realise and feel your auric field has been cleared of all the information that the Earthly Man has accumulated and held onto.

The Spiritual Man is still above the head, its light now is very bright.

The Divine Man is not now perceptible, because you can now, if you wish, throw a thread of light from the Spiritual Man upwards into the One Life; it will disappear out of your imagination into unfathomable realms.

The Spiritual Man now starts to project into your aura new information. You do not need to put this into words, although the power of word may enter.

Geometries, the language of the One Life may enter.

Colour may enter as this will be changing the life substance of your aura.

Number could be important.

Keep your identifications on the Spiritual Man, he will know when enough has been done.

Relax your attention and enter back into the present, when you are ready.

A recording of experiences will be useful for you, particularly any of the above mentioned, as they can be retrieved by the brain consciousness when needed. They will have a specific relationship to the aura, and can be used to stabilise and inform the aura when you require to do so, as each are identified with by your consciousness and carry a specific vibration that will align certain sub-divisions into a geometric symmetry.

Geometric symmetry is the structure of the One Life. and from this the many forms make their appearance, so you understand from this that the structure is upon, as far as you are concerned, a subjective level, although this subjective level is true reality and the objective, or appearance, represents the reflection in a denser form for which you use the word *matter*. This is the substance of the lower worlds. You are the interface between those lower worlds, and I use this term broadly, and the worlds of spirit. So, your aura is the interface between the two, and the way it links the two is through geometric symmetry. It is difficult to understand this as your concept of the aura is from the 'I' identity, always relating it to yourself, your progress, your interactions and how it affects you. Now, to go beyond this comprehension it necessitates your acceptance of the One Life and your place and function within it. If you are functioning in geometric symmetry, then you are a One Life within the Greater One Life. There is no difference between the two except the ring pass, not of consciousness, but within this geometric symmetry all of its parts are in communion and communication.

Can you imagine what this means? Take yourself as a One Life, that means you will be in a full conscious awareness of all aspects of yourself, because your geometric symmetry will allow you to do so. You will realise you are more than the brain consciousness, you will recognise the centres as a higher consciousness, and your aura as a transcended pathway into even higher states of consciousness. You will gain the knowledge and the wisdom from the Spiritual Man, in many ways you will become the Spiritual Man incarnate, then the Divine Man, or the Third Man, (which is more of a cosmic nature than a planetary nature) will start to relay purpose. The purpose, you will know, is not individual to you, but you will know this is something you have to externalise, all incidentals then become unimportant, playing those out will not be part of your life, you will have greater things that concern you.

So, ask yourself: Are there any auras that are relaying the information from the Earthly Man? There may be many, but ask yourself: Have they penetrated my aura? Have they affected and disrupted the information I am carrying due to the unfoldment of my consciousness? What wisdom do I need to deal with this? Logical interpretation of how to deal with these questions will not work, because there will be no answer, so you will continue to be affected by the Earthly Man and all he represents. You may try the attitude of acceptance, but at the end of the day, you will find the battle between your Spiritual Man and your Earthly Man is enough to handle. So think on this: these auras will be backing up your Earthly Man even though you have, to a certain extent, relinquished some of his tendencies and your focus is the Spiritual Man, but you are living in the world of the Earthly Man and pressure will come to bear upon your aura.

The family aura is a powerful medium for the Earthly Man, and will seek to eliminate your Spiritual Man, so the auras of the Earthly Man will be stimulating your Earthly Man, which will suppress the Spiritual Man. Now, all this is on the physical plane. On the spiritual plane, the Spiritual Man has many more friends than the Earthly Man, which can also inform your aura, it's just that you cannot see them, so they are subjective, they all work together. Now, if your light is luminous, your Spiritual Man will be active. Now imagine that the Spiritual Man of those who are consciously, and in consciousness are identified with the Earthly Man, their Spiritual Man will be inactive as far as the connection between the two. If the Earthly Man is penetrating your aura and consciousness to the degree that it is impinging upon your ability to be of service, then seek up to the Spiritual Man for help.

Now, you will not know how this help will come, but I can tell you this: your Spiritual Man will stimulate the Spiritual Man of the Earthly Man that are causing a problem. They will not know this, but will suddenly find, for example, a change in attitude will occur, or a situation may arise whereby their emphasis upon you will diminish. Because the Spiritual Man is an Informing Life to the Earthly Man, for the Earthly Man to take notice will require a situation that will cause the Earthly Man to think about itself. Some will, some won't, but the circumstances maybe will demand this to happen. You, in the meantime, trust, and that trust is in the Spiritual Man; allow him to sort it out without allowing your Earthly Man to take over. You may not understand all this until it happens, then you may remember these words and seek a greater contact with the Spiritual Man, and maybe that is what you are required to do, because if you overcome these Earthly Men, then you will encompass the One Life. Your service to the One Life will expand and is this not what your heart desires?

In a group recently, the words were impressed *"Love is Peace"*, as this, you may say, has to do with your heart's desire, to embody this love so you can love others, and then be at peace. A wonderful thing to desire, and you will probably wish that others can experience this love and peace, and harmony will exist, and in a way many strive to give others this love and peace, and wish for the Earthly Man of others to be at peace. This is a devotion to others, and is viewed in a physical manner according to appearance, according to situation, and yet this is not reality.

The appearance can be deceitful, it can be a self-fulfilling prophecy. You have to develop what I call *soul sense*. This is the developed perception from the Spiritual Man, this is the sense of reality, the seeing through the outer garment into the subjective worlds, the identifying of the information contained within the aura. Through the alignment of the brain consciousness with the consciousness of the Spiritual Man, this is what you will develop, and it needs to be developed and understood, otherwise the Spiritual Man will only remain as something you become aware of in meditation. This soul sense relays information from the Spiritual Man to the Earthly Man, and the Earthly Man back to the Spiritual Man; it is a two-way flow, when there is a flow, and that flow then attracts the attention of the Divine Man. Soul sense is your way of being at peace within the Spiritual Man, by the acquisition of wisdom and the embodiment of love. The Spiritual Man gives the Earthly Man love, so the Earthly Man will acquire the peace of understanding. This is important for your growth towards the Divine Man.

The development of soul sense will enable you to move forward with your realisations and increased awareness, because these do not necessarily bring peace, as they open the eye out into the world. The eye I refer to is the Third Eye, this is the eye of vision of the Spiritual Man, and what does he see? He sees reality as against non-reality, and through this seeing he relays into the brain consciousness all those things that are not of the Spiritual Man. Are you starting to realise what can happen? You are becoming aware of the Spiritual Man, your mind is expanding, you are more creative, you receive ideas, and yet within your environment you are perceiving more and more of the Earthly Man than ever before, this is through your awareness developed by your contact with the Spiritual Man, which then creates within your imagination. At first it will be concerning yourself, and then others, and you must not confuse the two - this is where the soul sense needs to be developed. The Spiritual Man cannot do this, but your Earthly Man can if he has somewhat realised himself as a part of the One Life, he can separate the aspects of the individual identity of himself and others. His soul sense then develops and his energy changes, his aura will then contain different information.

I give an example here whereby if there is no soul sense, there is no discrimination. This lack of this discrimination will be reflective in the information contained in your aura. To further the concept, your aura is magnetic and radiating. If that specific vibration of discrimination is not present, then through the aura's magnetic field, you will attract those who seek, and I can only say from your understanding, "to take advantage of you". If you have started to develop the soul sense, then discrimination will be present in the information contained within the aura. This will then have a radiating affect upon the auras of those who are seeking to take advantage of you by repelling the information contained within the aura that is seeking to, in one instance, control you, and in another to change your information into theirs, and then they will become a controlling factor in your life.

An attribute of the soul sense is also observation; there are many ways to observe. The soul sense observes via the Spiritual Man and his eye that looks out upon the world, therefore my brothers, he doesn't criticise or judge, he just observes. Why should he do any other? He has no agenda, and that is the difference, but through observation he knows how to act and this is why the soul sense is necessary, to relay this into your surface mind and, of course, through this you will sense and feel liberation and freedom. Your soul sense comes into being from the point of stillness deep within the heart, aligned with the Spiritual Man who then looks out through the eye of vision and the brain consciousness, or you could say your mind is then receptive to the energies and inspiration from the Spiritual Man via the head centre. Both the eye and the head centre are then registered into your consciousness.

We are approaching a new age, and part of the problem now faced is the devotion and idealism of the old age, which has become entrenched within humanity. It, therefore, is very powerful still upon the mental and emotional planes; it could be said it is still somewhat the line of least resistance so, therefore, you develop the soul sense without any previous understanding. Some of your understanding may well be of the soul sense, but it is useful to put aside all previous understanding to allow you to develop the soul sense, and then your impressions will be very different from the previous as part of consciousness you have embodied. If you cannot change your opinion, or I should say, have a fixed opinion, then you are still under the influence of the previous age. The soul sense relays the consciousness of the Spiritual Man, it will help you not to become fixed within any ideology. Love is not a fixed ideology; it encompasses everything, it enable you to move from a fixed point into a new area within the One Life. The soul sense gives you no fixed point, it allows you to move within all the fixed points of consciousness, expanding your awareness through the mind into the wisdom, creating concepts through identification, then moving on, always retaining the truth in relationship to the One Life.

Can you develop this soul sense from your present life circumstances? Is your life circumstance circumscribing you within the Earthly Man, or, as mentioned before, the Earthly Man of others? I invite you now to try to install this soul sense within the activity of your brain consciousness. You will have already done this to a certain degree, because of your previous meditations, and your assessment of the insight I have presented. I will try to make this simple, but highly energetic.

Meditation

Attune now to the point at the centre of the circle. You might know this point as the Point of Stillness deep within the heart; if you have followed that work, you know this point to be representative of the Eternal Now as far as vibration is concerned, you also know it is the point where spirit and matter converge.

So, start to go inside via the space, but retaining the space you need to develop a multi train of thought; this is abstract thinking and it also concerns light, and surrounding your centre point, your point of stillness, are three layers so as you go inside, you touch first the layer concerning light. This is for this meditation and progressive exercise, the light of mind.

Through your imagination, you reach the layer of light and as you do, you experience its vibration and imagine a band of light. This your third eye is perceiving, and at the same moment, this light reaches upwards into the centre of consciousness which you have come to know as the Spiritual Man, and then it descends down from the Spiritual Man into the cave in the centre of the head, lighting up the brain consciousness.

This is the third aspect concerning the soul sense, and this light discriminates the thought patterns of the Earthly Man, whether yours or others.

PAUSE

Move your consciousness back to the space and the centre point.

As you pull your mind inwards, your imagination conceives the second layer surrounding your centre point and this is love.

You pass through the layer of light into the layer of love. You feel its vibration and then perceive, with your third eye, a band of love.

A line of this love moves upwards to the centre of consciousness of the Spiritual Man, then rapidly moves downwards into the cave in the centre of the head activity, the brain consciousness, with love and unity. This aspect links you into the whole, it is the second aspect and underlies the creative processes of the One Life, thus you are developing the second aspect of the soul sense into channels and pathways of the brain consciousness.

PAUSE

Focus back to the space and the point of stillness, your centre point.

Between each integration you will have paused to assimilate, allow each vibration to do its work and not enter into any thought processes, they could inhibit the integration of the soul sense.

Bring yourself inward, you pass through the layer of light, then the layer of love into an intense vibration of will carrying purpose.

You see a band of this energy in your imagination, and you rapidly move a line of this energy upwards into the spiritual, and then back down into the cave in the centre of the head, and into the brain consciousness, activating the dormant activity of the brain consciousness with will, the carrier of purpose.

This is motivating power of the Spiritual Man and the Divine Man, this is the first aspect for the soul sense, it is important for the other two.

All these three energies are now present in the cave.

PAUSE for a while.

Now, from the cave you imagine them ascending back up to the Spiritual Man, and then back down to the cave, creating a flow between the two, and then imagine the soul sense as an energy centre of consciousness within the cave in the centre of the head.

These energies now need to precipitate outward from the Spiritual Man and the cave in the centre of the head to the Ajna centre, via the third eye, and as you have already been assimilating them there, release the flow outward via this centre into the consciousness of humanity via the etheric network.

PAUSE

Focus back to the alignment of the point of stillness, the Spiritual Man and the cave, and enter into a void, a place of non-activity, of anything.

PAUSE

Enter now back from the void and open up to physical plane reality.

You must now nurture this soul sense and realise there is a light within the head that has been birthed by the Spiritual Man in cooperation with the Earthly Man, via the initial point of stillness within the heart, therefore, this light is a means of communication between the Spiritual Man and the Earthly Man. If you keep this connection by realising every day this light exists, then you will be building upon its light. You do not have to worry or strive to understand the soul sense, because by not mentally, or should I say intellectually, identifying with it, then the soul sense will naturally develop. The more you step outside from yourself, the more this soul sense will relay its purpose and intentions. Many realisations will occur, let them naturally precipitate into your mind, but always retain your point at the centre of the circle, and your identification with the Spiritual Man.

I now give over this instruction to the Master M, who wishes to relay to you some insight.

Thank you. I seek and endeavour, at this time, to initiate a renewed purpose, a renewed motivation, as far as you are concerned. There is much that depletes your energy; there is much that adds to your confusion, yet if you may realise it, we are on the threshold. This represents to you a transference of consciousness, not it its totality from a concentrated focus upon the aspect of love to the intermediary level of wisdom into the centre of consciousness that represents will and purpose, in a sense, and you have been instructed upon the soul sense.

I now present to you the monadic sense. This is quite different for you to understand, and I cannot initiate this for you, but only try to give you a measure of understanding.

Firstly, all your understanding needs to change, there are many states of consciousness governed by certain aspects of the divine. Upon the plane of Atma there exists the will and purpose, and below, you will understand, exists love and wisdom. As I mentioned, wisdom is the pathway to Atma, and this you experience as love and will within your lower states of experience. But the influencing energies that flow into and through the state of Atma are those of Cosmic Love, something very different from your present experience, and it is this that I refer to as the monadic sense. This is the sense of oneness, this is the sense of purpose that is manifested because of this oneness, and this oneness referred to is the oneness of yourself within the harmony of the One Life, so this oneness is not, from your understanding, individual to you. This is absurd as oneness cannot be contained within an individual aura. If so, your purpose is then centred within yourself and your life experience.

Yes, I am talking about life, and the life thread is within and connected to your heart. Can you imagine not being individual, and if you did, you would worry about what you would lose of yourself not being individual. I tell you this: what you would lose, you don't really need. That word *'need,'* is very appropriate for this concept. What is your need? All that I am saying you will instantly relate to your individual experience and see it that way, and that is another word for presentation - *'way'*.

In what way is your need individual? Your concept of individuality will say many things concerning the self that lives and moves and has its being upon the physical plane, and the need on that plane is great in many ways. If your life upon this plane is governed by your need within it, then there will be no fulfilment; that would be impossible. Now, I must say there are basic needs and everyone one the planet should have those needs met, but then there are many other needs. At this point, you would start to intellectually try to work them out and, of course, the intellect will think horizontally and then, according to devotion on the extent of it, and also I might add, the sense of a challenge, the challenge of the self, your eternal battle because you are individual, then you will try to correct some of the needs you will deem unnecessary, and not worthy of yourself as being spiritual. Being spiritual is embodying the monadic purpose related to the plan, through the developed monadic sense, then the Divine Man manifests and descends into his earthly garments and walks among men.

So, it is best to develop these senses of soul and Monad, and not develop any more confusion with the individual Earthly Man.

Master KH

So, you have pondered the concept of not being individual, and you are not sure what to do now. Ponder the concept that you have lost all those needs that are individual, and you are part of the One Life. Realise everyone you meet is also part of the One Life; they may still be individual, but also realise their problems of being individual have also been your problems. They might, in appearance, look totally separate from you, but they are not, as you are now not individual, you have no responsibility for them, you just understand this concept, and when you walk out into the world and see the trees and plant, birds and animals, you realise they are also a part of the One Life and because of this appreciation, you will be moving closer to the heart of the One Life.

You can now imagine you are not individual, because you certainly are not individual upon other planes, so why should you think so on the physical plane? You sometimes attempt and want, (and this is a need of many) to be part of those planes that are not individual, and seem so far removed from the physical plane that you would wish to be there, and not up-on the physical plane, because that plane of living is all too much for you.

I mentioned a word a few pages back, and that was '*being*', and now I have to say to you, to enter fully into those higher planes of existence, you have to integrate your being upon the physical plane, you have to overcome it; you cannot overcome it by attempting to move away from it. Those who have mastered the physical plane have had their being upon it, and some still do; it is not a problem for them as it is for you, you fight continually for one thing or the other, or you just hide away in a cupboard, and this is not the way. I mentioned the importance of that word earlier and we can say there is a way, many now are starting to realise this. The way is not easy, as it confronts you all the time

Now, have you pondered upon being part of the One Life? Has your outlook changed, but is maybe still confused? The way will give the answers. What is the way? It is very easy to say what is not the way, and this can be your problem. You identify too much with what is not the way, so the way is not fully seen. The path is a darkened way and you cannot see where to go; you will not see if you focus upon what is not the way as you will be identifying with it, because you will judge it and want to do something about it, and then you will realise you can't, so then you will be shouting about how bad things are. You will never find the way if you do this. One observes and through this, if your purpose has any clarity, then you can use your observation to further the plan by changing the polarity of what you perceive as being not the way. What is not the way is very attractive in that it attracts your attention, therefore, you will be caught up within it; what you see in humanity echoes itself from the mass consciousness into the individual consciousness. If you put aside your judgement you can see this, and you will see it better if you lift your consciousness to the Spiritual Man, and ride above the masses with the help of the Divine Man.

Once you find the way your need will change, because the way will lift your consciousness and identification away from the fractures that exist at this time, because as the need changes, then within your consciousness these fractures will lose their power and leave the mind; they will become fleeting thoughts, thus they will create space within the mind, not because they have left, it is possible for a short period of time to experience a void, but then the opposite polarity will enter. This is because of the time continuum. Now, thoughts that leave, which will then seem quite incidental, have been repelling thoughts producing a cloud across the mind for anything other than their energy and substance. Once gone, magnetic thought enters, which is the opposite of the repelling thought, but what does this magnetic thought concern?

Magnetic thought is the thought expression of the One Life, a synthesis of thought, future thought, so in this instance, understand that magnetic thought is future thought upon a time continuum. It is on a continuum because it is being projected in cycles according to, and I will use the word, 'need' of the One Life for the evolution of its planetary life. In regard to all this, we place the aspect of consciousness, so future thought contains consciousness, as parts of consciousness yet to manifest, and this is the difference between what you could logically interpret and what you could intuitively interpret. In one example of repelling thought, now you can relate this to past, evident in the present, but it is not present, it is past, thus you are attempting to move forward if you are starting to have a conscious awareness, but your repelling thought is dragging you backwards from the present that has the potential of future thought. So, instead of moving forward, you come to a halt. How many of you feel this as being stuck, as everything being mundane, with occasional excitement of breaking the mundane, but mostly you break through the mundane into another area of the mundane, therefore, the excitement is short lived?

Magnetic thought is very interesting for you to consider. The lower planes of manifestation concern time; beyond that plane lives the Spiritual Man upon a timeless plane, who has his place in a centre of consciousness where it can be seen lies future thought, or slightly better put, the consciousness that is being projected for the next step in the evolution of humanity. Forget not this also concerns the lower kingdoms and this consciousness concerns the plan. So, understand then that the Spiritual Man impresses you with future thought and future potential; the problem here lies that if you still identify as an individual, by that I mean a separate consciousness, then you will relate to time and One Life time as an individual, you all understand how limited this is. If you disassociate from that aspect of time which is material in nature and casts a shadow of dissolution, you then can start to perceive what is meant by a continuity of consciousness. So future thought is a future consciousness brought into the present via the timeless reality of the Spiritual Man and the immortal essence of the Divine Man within the sphere of the One Life, but it doesn't stop there. Expansion is something that is going on, on all levels, and there are many levels of cosmic life that you have no experience of. The Divine Man is an informing life to the Spiritual Man, but there is also an informing life to the Divine Man, and if you have managed to understand what you are to the One Life, you will be thinking within the solar spheres, as well and the planetary spheres.

There is a need for you to assimilate what has been said, so I would like to invite you to meditate.

Meditation

I would like you now to become silent, but not silent from an individual way, silent within the all-encompassing space you are within and are part of. You are part of this space via the etheric network that interconnects all living things within the space.

Pause

Now, contemplate the One Life by expanding your mind into the One Life, not through thinking, but through feeling.

Pause

Now contemplate your place within the One Life. What is the One Life informing you?

Any reaction to this of an uncomfortable nature will be informing you of any repelling thought processes. They will relate to your need of a physical nature.

Realise this is your need, at the present moment, that is carried forward from the past.

If there is required a transmutation of thought related to need, then imagine a light in the centre of the head, this light possesses the energy of magnetic thought and will attract the appropriate energies from the One Life to relieve any discomfort.

Your consciousness moves outward from the centre of the head, yet retaining this centre, and through this moving outward, energy moves inward towards the centre of the head, and down into the centres that are in a place of discomfort, it also moves within your aura because most discomfort you feel will be of an emotional nature.

Allow the One Life to pour its energy through your physical body.

These energies have not come from a specific centre, but from the whole.

When the discomfort has gone, or you may not have felt discomfort, now is the time to contemplate magnetic thought. Remember this will relate to the future, but with this aspect, forget any preconceptions of past, present, and future, for example, a past which has been experienced, present is being experienced, and future will be experienced.

Contemplate this for a moment: that in any given moment, you are either past or future.

Pause

Now bring this period of contemplation to a close. Integrate by exercising a period of no thought, just a state of being. Attempt to feel this with all your senses and body, not just the mind.

Now, throw a line of your consciousness aspect from the centre of the head, through the head centre and up into the One Life. This line will anchor into a higher place of consciousness.

You may be approaching this place of consciousness, or you may not have come anywhere near to it, but at this point, hold yourself in alignment and start to visualise your line of light, see it as three strands of energy intertwined.

It is time to activate magnetic thought. Imagine down this line, the energy consciousness of this higher place descending down the line into your own brain consciousness.

At this moment now, visualise this energy consciousness also ascending, and then each time it descends it bring with its descent yet another aspect of consciousness from this higher place of consciousness, where you have anchored magnetic thought.

Then on the ascent of this energy, realise you are creating "the way", and your consciousness is travelling upon this way.

What are your needs now, at this moment?

You will find that your individuality has changed, and you will wish to project this stream of energy consciousness to others, and this you can do at this time.

So, stay with the flow of energy consciousness. You now need not to try to keep it going, as the consciousness itself has taken over.

Before you enter into projection, visualise the etheric network.

Pause

Now you need to open the gate of the Ajna centre, your third eye is already active through your progress through this meditation.

Imagine your Ajna centre six inches outside your physical brow. The first action of precipitation will be to flood the etheric network with light. This is the lighted way.

Visualise the higher place of consciousness building in light intensity.

Now slowly open the gate to the Ajna centre, and then you are fully looking out onto the etheric network.

It is now open. The light from the highest place of consciousness descends rapidly down into the head, out through the third eye to the open door of the Ajna centre, and out into the etheric network, flooding the network with light.

You now, as a group consciousness, will keep this flow going.

Pause

Now, while keeping this flow going, you will change its identification, and this is to the heart centres of humanity, because that is where the need lies.

You now perceive many, many lights upon this etheric network, the flow of energy is still going, but with a dual action of thought.

You invoke the love aspect from the higher place of consciousness to descent into the heart centre of humanity.

Do this with purpose, and realise that as you are a group consciousness, you are working with a group; you may be alone, but you are also a group, and you may well be doing this as part of a physical group.

Visualise the energy of love pouring out to humanity and visualise humanity receiving it, and all repelling thought disappearing.

Pause

It is time to close the gate by fully focussing into the head centre and the higher place of consciousness - the thread between the two is still there.

You become centred, experiencing a state of being, relaxing, then back into physical plane reality.

Record any results from the meditation.

From this a realisation may have occurred, that magnetic thought receives impressions from a higher plane of consciousness, so it is not positive to this impression, it is negative, meaning receptive. I am talking about polarity here, not the psychological aspects regarding these poles; again, this requires you to shift your thinking away from existing parameters.

Through this impression, two avenues open up: one I have mentioned is future thought, and the other is radiating thought, but let us not confuse the two through logic. These two aspects I have identified with are the result of magnetic thought that is impressed by a higher plane of consciousness. Future thought is the result of magnetic thought that relays purpose; radiating thought is the manifestation of this purpose exoteric within the lower planes of human endeavour.

So, I ask you, is all that I have mentioned of a vertical or a horizontal nature to you? Magnetic thought is neither, it is the point at the centre of the circle; future thought is vertical in nature and there is much that can be said about this. Radiating thought is horizontal in nature within the lower words, projecting the aspects of the higher plane of consciousness that is synthesised within magnetic thought. Your understanding, therefore, needs to be of a vertical nature, and if you take what has been said about the point at the centre of the circle, then you will see that there is a lower part of the circle if you take a horizontal line, and a higher part. So, radiating thought affects both halves of this circle, the lowest part representative of the lower kingdom, and the higher of the kingdom above the human. Believe that as a human you can be radiatory to both, although you perceive both halves as being not part of your human existence horizontally, because all this is above, and all that is below, as you would perceive it, is part of the One Life, so through radiatory thought, you extend your consciousness into both and then both aspects impress your magnetic thought with the consciousness that is of those kingdoms that reside within the lower half of the circle, and the higher half of the circle. So, in this context regarding the One Life and the two halves of the circle, you can relate to planetary thought.

You can see I am relating many aspects of mind for your consideration and stimulating you to think about them. Planetary thought concerns the whole, what you see and experience in physical expressions, and also what cannot be seen, in this respect feelings and thoughts. Obviously we have dealt with those two regarding the third eye and aura, but moving beyond that to the unseen worlds of the higher planetary, the lower planetary life being but a reflection. Now, if you relate to the concept of worlds within worlds, you may gain an understanding, the world that you are so familiar and live within is just circumscribed by the higher planetary life, this will enable you to think vertical, horizontal and circular. You do not have to understand this concept as the concept itself will give you insight, you just have to make space for it.

Now, if you think circular, you will see the physical plane, counting inwards, is the fifth circle in. That is where it starts concerning the lower aspects of this circle, that of intellect, so the emotions are the sixth circle in, and the physical body is the seventh. I have mentioned sub-divisions - each circle has seven of these sub-divisions, the seventh circle, through its sub-divisions, also incorporates worlds within worlds and what is unseen. You only need a microscope to prove that, down to the very atoms that are also a world within themselves.

To understand this, each sub-division of the seventh circle is then sub-divided seven more times, so in totality the seventh circle comprises of forty-nine other circles going inwards, and there exists in these circles many lives that affect substance. For example, your physical body is made up of these lives, but these lives are unconscious of that fact, and experience life according to intelligence, and react accordingly, but in totality, there is a life that informs this multitude of lives that make up substance, in the case of the physical body, it is manifested form. Now, ponder upon what informs this life that informs the multitude of lives, and in the case of the physical body, it is the brain consciousness.

For an identification of these lives I have quoted, let me say they are devas. The devic life runs parallel to the human and they are the builder of substance, and on the lower levels of the planetary life, they react without question to the informing life that governs them. This is true also for the next inter-pregnated level, the emotional, which also is made up of seven sub-divisions, and each sub-division also as seven sub-divisions, again making forty-nine circles for our identification of understanding and there, what is found, is a multitude of lives, but these lives are different to the physical body, and they also have an informing life over them, and this informing life is informed by your brain consciousness.

Can you see a picture building up here? Can you see the connections to the consciousness resident is then your brain consciousness, and how it would inform the informing life that instructs the multitude of lives that make up, as in the first case, your physical body?

The mental plane also has seven sub-divisions, but the mental plane is very different; this is where the transference is made into the higher planetary life, the unseen or, shall I say, the unsensed. You will link what I have just said to the previous instruction concerning the soul sense, the monadic sense. These seven sub-divisions also have within each one, seven more sub-divisions, making forty-nine, but the difference here is that the lower four circles are of the lower planetary life, which constitutes twenty-eight circles, but it is in the seven circles making up the fourth sub-division that the transference is made into the next seven sub-divisions that make one sub-division, and what do we find here but the soul sense and magnetic thought. So, these sub-divisions mentioned, making fourteen circles, require your attention.

Now, repelling thought lives below these in what I will call 'the soup', where nothing can be seen with clarity, all is part of one state you could say, a soup is the whole. It is, but the consciousness of this soup cannot separate its ingredients, it is not aware of what constitutes its state, and within its state some of the ingredients are more active than others. It has not the capacity or measure to control what precipitates out of the soup. Do you understand what I am saying? This represents what is going on in the lower circles relating to the concept that is being projected. The seven levels of the fourth sub-division of the mental plane is where it all happens regarding the transference I have mentioned, the sub-division above this on the third level has filtered through into the fourth sub-division. Its seven levels then become highly volatile, creating a duality, the brain consciousness registers this duality, firstly as being impressed by higher concepts, and secondly dropping into the depths of what I have named 'the soup'. You can view this as a transference into the third sub-division, and at the same time a transformation is occurring within the soup that is revealing the very depths of its nature. The informing lower lives are having to adjust to the aspects of consciousness that have impressed the brain consciousness that is transferring itself into these lives. This you can perceive as a period of adjustment when some of the old thought and feeling patterns are relinquished, and the new are taking their place.

It is very difficult for you to understand that there is an informing life above your brain consciousness; it is outside of yourself, but it can overshadow you, and it does overshadow many people, but whilst they are fully identified with their brain consciousness, then this informing life cannot enter. But this informing life has a relationship to the other informing lives I have mentioned, and the multitude of lives that reside in substance, so it is well worth while forming a relationship with this higher informing life within your brain consciousness, hence the reference to magnetic thought and soul sense. As you are a whole within the One Life, then you will appreciate the fact that the higher planetary life that you are made up of, that constitutes the multitude of lives we have spoken of.

One has to ponder at this point what your brain consciousness, as the informing life, is impressing upon the multitude of lives that make up your existence. The nature of mind will affect those lives, as they can only respond to the consciousness that informs them, so if the informing life to your brain consciousness is the One Life, then the One Life will harmonise the multitude of lives. I have mentioned the sub-divisions and the divisions within each sub-division; we are going to work with this concept in a very different way, linking it to the multitude of lives.

I perceive at this point that it would be useful to focus upon the emotional body, and for the meditation I am about to present, I suggest you view your emotional body as having seven selves, seven informing lives, and these seven informing lives inform your multitude of lives that make up the physical body, and also the multitude of lives that make up your mental body, and they in their turn represent each one of them, a multitude of lives. Can you understand this concept of worlds within worlds regarding the concept of a multitude of lives?

Meditation

Prepare now to enter into a state of oneness.

Pause

To do this, you bring your attention to your auric field, it is electromagnetic; this, you realise, is a vibratory field of sound, a mixture of energy and force. Its vibration increases.

You take one breath, one breath of life, and as you exhale, your aura opens up into the One Life, expanding your consciousness into the

One Life, and the vibration of your crown chakra increases in its velocity.

The One Life now has a direct means of communication to your brain consciousness via your heart centre.

The vibration within the crown descends into the cave in the centre of the head.

You contact now the deva of your emotional body to inform him you will be working with the seven selves that make up your emotional body.

Your first body appears before you, which represents the lowest sub-division.

How do you perceive your emotional self?

What does this self require from the One Life?

How do you need to adjust your thinking regarding him, and what energy does he require from this integration?

Retain your connection to the head centre and the cave. Once you have been informed as to the need, project the appropriate energy from the One Life via the third eye as a stream of light upon this self.

This energy stream then transforms this self and integrates into the One Life and the brain consciousness.

As this self integrates, the second self appears. Remember, you are working up through the sub-divisions. This, I realise, is a hard task, but if you can take the attitude of the observer, you will be safe from emotional reaction.

How do you perceive yourself? Everybody's experience will be different.

It will become quite apparent very quickly what this self will require.

Extract from the One Life the appropriate energy and project it, via the third eye, upon this self.

This self quickly integrates into the One Life and brain consciousness, and then the third emotional self appears before you.

This emotional self could appear rigid. This could be the case, as it may appear totally opposite to any proposition.

This self may need the energy of love, or it may require intelligence, or will.

Release this self into the One Life, then back into your brain consciousness, then back into your body through the light you will project upon it.

There is a freedom connected with this integration, and as it integrates, the fourth self appears.

How do you perceive this fourth self? It is an emotional self made up of a multitude of lives, but there is an element of the mental self within it, so this emotional self is also a materialistic self.

You need to stay removed from this self as the observer. You will need to be the informing life for this self and pour the light of the Triad of Divine mind, love and will upon it to render it in line with the Divine Plan.

You may be tiring at this point so it is worthwhile projecting up to the Spiritual Man for added energy, which you now project upon this self.

The integration of this self starts to happen, and as it fades into the One Life and the brain consciousness, the fifth self appears.

This self presents a void for you, and perception of this self may appear rebellious. It is open to your individual interpretation; this emotional self is waiting to be stimulated.

It is your creative emotional self.

Your heart centre resonates with this self.

When you have achieved a harmonic resonance with it, then pour the light from the One Life upon it, and experience its integration.

At this point you become aware of the Spiritual Man above the head and the sixth self makes its appearance.

This self is the lower aspect of the Spiritual Man. You just need to reaffirm its connection.

If there is any problem here, it will be from your sub-conscious, so any light projected upon this sixth self needs to be projected upon it into the sub-conscious downwards, and as you have integrated your other selves, the process is rapid, connecting your sixth self into a synthesis with the Spiritual Man, allowing then the seventh self to appear.

Your emotional seventh self has a different identification, it is probably because the activity within the lower emotional selves has not been allowed to function, therefore, it has lain dormant, and of course has no influence upon the brain consciousness.

You imagine this seventh self. In your inner vision realise this is something new to you.

This seventh self is already surrounded by light, it is the light of the Divine Man.

You stand face to face with this self. It is the exact image of you, but it possesses none of your problems, none of your expectations, none of your needs, none of your desires, because it is beyond all of these.

This self is the immortal essence of the Spiritual Man, impressed by the Divine Man.

More so, this seventh self is a reflection of the Divine Man.

You realise once more your alignment with the One Life and before you integrate this seventh self, you enter into a process of communication, because this seventh self can alleviate your problems, your expectations, your needs, and your desires.

You feel a release on those levels and your seventh self is gradually synthesised into your brain consciousness.

Relax your focus and attention.

When you are ready, a record of this meditation would be useful for you. I will leave your to do this.

As you assimilate the result of this meditation, I would like to say to you that your identification requires you to focus upon the higher selves; if you identify too much with what was impressed by the lower selves, then you will stimulate those lower selves into activity, and it is this activity that will imprison you within them. Your consciousness needs to evolve, unless of course you need these lower selves for whatever reason, because they serve you in some way. This last statement is worth considering so I will repeat it, "they will serve you in some way", and as, to a certain extent, the sixth and seventh sense have been dormant, then your consciousness has not evolved into them, so to an extent, you will not fully understand that statement.

Now, each lower self you would have perceived in a certain way, and because you will have perceived its problems, so you will probably have related these problems to your brain consciousness and the past, so you would also have deemed these lower selves as a problem within themselves. It is a mistake to assume this because their integration is not from the fact they are a negative influence to you, it is the fact they are a positive influence upon you when they are transmuted and allowed to be themselves, functioning within the sub-division of life. So, the higher sub-divisions are the influencing factor upon the lower sub-divisions, then they will function according to the higher, but within their own worlds, and, I might add, with greater creativity. They have to function within their own worlds as this is your means of communication into those worlds, so you take this concept of communication from an inner relativity into an outer relationship. You cannot transfer yourself into the higher sub-division without retaining the lower sub-divisions, because what use would you be? If this is what you seek to achieve, then you will only reach so far, and certainly it will not place your consciousness into the higher sub-divisions, you will end up in a void. The void would not be a transitory state, but an illusionary place that will attract your attention and bring you within its imagination, so the higher sub-divisions speak and act through the lower; you do not speak from the higher, you speak through the lower impressed by the higher. If you think you are speaking from the higher, then you are certainly disillusioned as you are not living in those planes, as you are still physical, and if you are trying to attain the higher planes by disowning the physical, then you will not reach them. There is a way to reach them, and this is through sacrifice, and to understand this is to break through your existing interpretations of this word; there is no pain involved, only the pain that you could experience of loss.

What would this incur? Certainly there are aspects of yourself that you would not be willing to sacrifice. This word is related to a plane that is of the first aspect, and this is will and purpose. This probably does not resonate, but can you resonate to the word *dedication*, and also *'commitment'*? Through this there is a sacrifice, it is the sacrifice of your time. This is a most difficult thing to understand, although it is most simple to the intellectual mind, to dedicate oneself to the Spiritual Man requires time on all levels. When you reach the Divine Man, there is no question regarding this.

Now, the condition and state of human consciousness does not help you regarding time, all the diversions are all around you, taking up time, but also consider there is physical time, emotional time and mental time, relating to spiritual time.

So, the first consideration is spiritual time, although, as I have stated, upon those spiritual planes there is no time as you understand it. They are also regarded as formless; to understand this quickly is to realise our mental thought (air) is regarded in this aspect as being form, along with everything else that lies below it, in the descent into matter. The laws that govern these spiritual planes are quite different from those that govern the form nature, and bear in mind, the form nature is but a reflection of a formless spiritual nature.

So now consider: how does spiritual time relate to your time? In the first instance, your time is subject to the process of rebirth and incarnation; there is birth, growth, maturity, decline, and then disintegration, to be born again at some later date. You could say everything is subject to time and growth, but also it is subject to regeneration and persistence. Within these cycles there also occurs a growth in consciousness, and this occurs when you make the space for spiritual time, but you have to realise what the difference is. When spiritual time is embodied by your physical time, then a wider consciousness occurs and there occurs an ascent in circumstances. Now, this ascent is something that, as I have mentioned, sacrifices certain aspects, you cannot ascend the spiritual ladder unless you have lightened your load, and this is through mental time, and your identification with mental time.

How much thinking do you do? How much of your thinking concerns yourself? How much thinking concerns the mundane? Is your thinking purely from the surface mind? Are you not registering what is above, with symbology, the sky, and clouds? And are you not registering what lies below: the crystals and minerals, flowers, plants and animals? Do you also not register, and this is important, those who are a lot younger than you, the children of the world, or those who are very much older than you? The child you have been before in this life. Have you forgotten how to play? Those who are much older you have experienced in a different lifetime, but that memory has gone and it is wise not to retrieve any of those previous lifetimes, you will not acquire a true representation as the memory lies in the past, it does not lie in your consciousness. It may lie to your sub-consciousness, but then so does all the information from the media, all that you have learnt at school, and all the history of past ages, so if you try to retrieve a past lifetime, you may well retrieve a mixture of what I have mentioned, coloured with what your brain consciousness requires you to retrieve, whether that is good or bad, because you will be seeking answers, or it is a glamour for you to rise above your mundane life by retrieving a life of importance. I am not criticising you with my statements in any way, I am trying to stimulate your spiritual time in a useful way.

So, back to mental time. What are you thinking about most of the time? Is it your daily life from dawn until dusk, and the chores that are involved? Spiritual time can exist for you in the tasks that you carry out during the day, so the function of mental time exists in two ways regarding spiritual time. The first is quite easy to understand, the study of spiritual concepts from a source that you are comfortable with; the second is thinking about spiritual concepts and relating those to life. This requires an interface between thinking about the concepts you have read about, and those you haven't - these are the ones that concern the over-shadowing wisdom.

Can you give yourself mental time to think about something, but you are not aware of what that something is? In this instance, you are giving over fully to spiritual time. It is worth taking that last sentence into meditation to fully understand it, because this represents the transition from the Earthly Man to the Spiritual Man, overshadowed by the Divine Man. Can you now see that you are the three and yet you are the one? So, emotional time has its place also concerning spiritual time; emotional time doesn't identify with your emotions regarding any problems you have at present, or of past, although the two are the same in reality. Emotional time is a sensory condition, an ability to feel, not from an emotional state as you understand that, and there is so much discussion upon this subject of emotions that to spiritual time is erroneous, it is outdated, it centres upon the self and its problems, so therefore, it exacerbates the problems, meaning the brain consciousness re-energises the problems of an emotional nature. You may then say, "I thought I had let go of that emotional problem."

Enough said about the emotional nature. Emotional time and the ability to sense is also part of spiritual time via mental time, and is relayed through impression. Emotional time represents aspiration, the excitement concerning the creative processes, it is not to be overlooked and relegated into submission via the mental control. The mind then would struggle in three directions, the emotional time is something that requires integration and coordination, rather than suppression, otherwise the mind has to deal with the emotions itself, and also the Spiritual Man. Emotional time senses the Spiritual Man so it also related to spiritual time. Can you imagine mental time based upon the three aspects of mind as previously mentioned? You may well relate to this, as that is what could be happening, so release your feelings to also experience spiritual time, but not from its emotional nature. I will explain this further.

The emotional nature referred to is of the Earthly Man, which you all understand. Opposite this are your feelings towards the Spiritual Man, which were, until now, of a devotional nature to some ideal.

Now it is towards what your feeling can interpret from the Spiritual Man the concept of feeling, meaning what you can sense, which is totally different because your senses are aligned to the Spiritual Man, especially if you allow for physical time. There are two aspects to this that need to be considered, the first is the ability to create the space to allow the physical to sit down, to give it spiritual time, as the essential point at the centre of the circle will then tune in, so to speak, to what is seeking impression and which you will be able to sense. The second aspect is to bring yourself in line with the concepts that reside within spiritual time.

What concept do you wish to understand? You may say, "I don't know, spirit will inform me at the right time. It is meant to be when it will be." And so many go on with what they understand, that they will be informed when spirit deems they are to be informed, and all they have to do is wait. They may wait, and wait, and wait, and then they may say, "I am not getting much at the moment, I have no direction. Spirit are not telling me anything." We'll, where shall I start with this? First of all, right timing is everything, as this is part of the manifesting process, the creative process; the release of an idea requires the nurturing of an idea, it needs to be created in substance, it needs to be given life. The life aspect is the power behind the plan, the plan is engineered within spiritual time, and it is governed by right timing; the consciousness concerning the plan comes from outside of spiritual time.

Let us identify now with solar time, with an identification with cosmic emotional time and cosmic mental time, which seeks to create a condition of receptivity to that which lies below it, so solar time impresses spiritual time with the consciousness of the plan, on that portion of the plan that requires the attention for recreating an evolutionary condition within the lower planes to lift those planes in vibration, and into alignment with the purpose of solar time. On those levels this is right timing for their evolutionary growth; it may not appear so on the lower planes, because the lower planes are influenced by the law of Fixation, or you could say they have created the Law of Fixation, as it relates to the Law of Karma. This Law of Fixation you can identify with mental time, whereby mental time becomes concrete, inflexible even; the highest of intellectual thought which is a portion of mental time can be of a concrete nature, meaning, for your understanding, there is no movement in its ideology, it believes what it believes, and knows it is right, without any possibility of thinking beyond it boundaries.

Going back to the quote concerning right time and the belief that all you have to do is wait, that belief says it is always right, that those who wait have a divine right, that they are living in spiritual time. Far from it; they aren't giving time to anything. This is the impress and ideology that needs to be removed, there is no divine right; only when you can touch solar time will you have acquired an aspect of divinity, this is not the time to wait, the plan is seeking manifestation, the first aspect of the Divine Man requires your attention, this is right timing. If you ignore the first aspect of the Divine Man and focus on the second aspect of the Divine Man that isn't the second aspect at all, but an emotional reflection which has no relativity to emotional time, then you will remember all sorts of problems. The third aspect of the Divine Man now will also not be known; a relativity here is mental time, intelligent activity related to the divine plan, as sensed in emotional time.

It is quite absurd to think you will be told anything, this is not the Law, you have free will, this is the Law of Choice and cannot be interfered with. You make the choice to work with time within all those levels I have explained, or you choose not to and wait for the right time. So, solar time is impressing spiritual time; solar time is the impressing agent and spiritual time is the receiving agent, and spiritual time does not question this, it reacts to what it receives and passes it on down to mental time, and here the problem lies. The concepts, and the consciousness related to the concepts, are for you to understand as transformation, not that you will be transformed by them, not unless you recognise transformation as a requirement for you to undergo. In this recognition, it will be seen that spiritual time then becomes the impressing agent, and mental time is the receiving agent, and in the previous relationship of solar time and spiritual time, we then can conceive that mental time does not question, it reacts to what it receives and passes it down into emotional time.

So, can you see more fully where the problem lies between spiritual time and mental time, and how it would restrict the sensory perception of emotional time and the requirements of physical time? Become aware of your concrete thought that clearly identifies you as a self-identity, break through that barrier, see and understand things as energy and how this energy can transform the physical substance of circumstance. You have aspirations. Do you feed the substance of those aspirations with energy, the energy of spiritual time, or do you just not relate the affects of this that can occur within physical substance? If you have an aspiration, vision, or goal, do you add these times zones to the promoting of your vision or goal, or do you see obstacles in your way? This is your fear, that the obstacles cannot be transformed, and the power of your thought concerning your vision will not remove them, hence you have an apprehension concerning this. If the vision is in line with the plan, have no fear about the obstacles, as they too will be transformed. You have to trust in your vision and give your vision time to manifest.

So, it is a good time to meditate upon these concepts that have been presented, and also during this meditation, come to a conclusion upon your mental selves, as you have previously done regarding the seven emotional selves, as this teaching upon time will be the step that leads you through the door into a more profound relationship with spiritual time, and the result will be the descent of the Spiritual Man into the lower aspects of time, more so mental time as that is the bridge you have to cross to dissolve all concrete thought, and as emotional time allows the element of water to flow, and within spiritual time there is also a higher element of water, which we call love, the two combined in unison will melt and wash away concrete thought; it is just if you can prepare yourself for this to happen, because the familiar you are comfortable with, the familiar creates an instant reaction to what it is confronted with and behaves accordingly. This is called the line of least resistance; you have flowed with your thought and emotion along this particular channel many times, it is familiar, but it does not serve you. Never become fixed and have a rigid opinion; concrete thought can lead to concrete emotions and a concrete body. You can, if you wish to see this, observe other people regarding the condition of their thoughts in relationship with their emotions and physical body. It is shocking to see this happening.

So, if you can now find some physical time and prepare to enter into a transformational meditation.

Meditation

Can you now slow down your physical clock. Do this with your eyes open, preparing the space through the eye triangle, and you will feel your aura vibrating with the higher planes of the space.

You become aware also of your head centre and you place a focus there. You will feel a further vibration within your aura.

You need not make any connection to the Spiritual Man or the Divine Man, just be aware that they are there by identifying with them in your conscious state. - say "I am aware of the Spiritual Man. I am aware of the Divine Man".

All this with your eyes open. You have given yourself over to physical time, now give over to spiritual time by closing your eyes.

You are aware of two spheres of light above.

The first above your head is clear and full of energy.

Above that sphere is the second sphere, blue in colour.

There is a third sphere above these two, it is not so tangible as the other two, but it now moves down into the blue sphere and passes through into the second, and passes through into the head centre, then into the cave within the head.

You are aware now that solar time has blended with spiritual time. You may find your aura will increase once more is its vibration.

You can open your eyes at this point if the vibration is too strong.

In fact, before we carry on, it would be advisable for you to do that. This will release some of the vibration into the manifest world. Yes, it will emanate out from you in concentric circles, but do not direct it, just let it happen.

Now bring your attention to mental time, still with the eyes open.

Now close your eyes and visualise your first mental self. This mental self will appear to you in many abstract ways. It represents your first understanding, also life through thought. How does this self view and understand life?

There needs to be an energy exchange between this first mental self and the highest emotional self, so initiate emotional time. This is through your sensory perception, just identify with this.

Call upon your higher emotional self to integrate your first mental self into the One Life through spiritual and solar time.

Forget not the spheres, they can be used in the process.

Be creative and imagine your mental self, transforming if necessary into its divine blueprint.

As the integration is complete, your second mental self appears. How do you view him? Your sixth emotional self will know what to do.

See this emotional self approaching your mental self. He is surrounded by light and places his hand upon the shoulder of your mental self. All is transformed within the light of the sixth emotional self.

Certain aspects of thought from this mental self you may perceive leaving him, do not dwell on these, just feel the freedom it creates within you, and that within, do not forget, is the sum total of all your selves related to time, so as you release this mental self into the One Life, your inner self realises the liberation within all your other selves.

Again, do not focus upon the individual parts, just stay within spiritual time.

Pause

Then, from out of this spiritual time, your third mental self appears in your vision. This mental self is the logical self, the analytical self.

How do you view this self? I suggest to you it may be critical and judgemental, but this mental self has not acquired love. It stands for pride and will say to you "I do not need this love you are suggesting". But the fifth emotional self is what it needs to integrate it into the One Life.

Retrieve your fifth emotional self who encompasses love and allow him to approach your third mental self. There may be a rejection to start with as this mental self, as I have said, has pride, a powerful energy of protection for this self.

Now imagine your emotional self pouring love upon your mental self, and remember all this is occurring within the spiritual time over-shadowed by solar time.

I will leave you to integrate this mental self.

Pause

You have worked very well at this process so far, so I feel we need to continue.

Take your focus briefly into the spheres - I will remind you, the one above the head is clear and full of energy, above that is a sphere of blue light, the third sphere you have brought into the cave is the centre of the head. Because of the nature of this sphere, it will be influencing your brain consciousness to adjust to this process.

Now visualise your fourth mental self, he will appear gradually into your vision.

This self is very powerful, it contains all past selves and represents to you the dweller on the threshold.

Your fourth emotional self is not capable of integrating this mental self into the One Life because it is part of it, so you will need the help of your spiritual self and your divine self represented by the sphere, but also your fifth mental self is beyond the threshold, so now imagine your fifth mental self approaching your fourth mental self with all the energy, light and power of the spheres.

Many things at this point may well occur, but realise the fourth mental self will finally give way and be integrated into the One Life.

There has been a transition now, and all you see is your fifth mental self.

It's just now a matter of visualisation, the work has been done, but first, pour the energy from your fifth mental self into your third emotional self. You will know what that energy needs to be.

When that is complete, your sixth mental self appears. This is your higher mind.

How do you view this self? This self is your inspiration, his thinking is far beyond a normal range of thinking, his frequency is higher than that.

Tune into his frequency, be receptive, feel yourself resonating with him.

Now you are entering truly into spiritual time, and all those other times mentioned become receptive.

Just give over to this frequency, which radiates light. See this light emanating from your sixth mental self.

It enters your aura; there is one thing you need to do, and that is to flood your second emotional self with this light. Maybe you need to visualise your second emotional self, but maybe not. This light is an integrating light.

Now what happens is that behind your sixth self, there is an even greater light, the light of the seventh mental self, who adds his light.

As it floods your second emotional self, it also floods your first emotional self.

Pause

You will know when an integration into the One Life has occurred, and then there before you will stand your Buddhic self, the soul within the ashram.

Now is the time, although you have done a lot, to sense the consciousness of the ashram via your buddhic self.

If you have no image of this, create one. Remember the ashram is group consciousness within the central consciousness of the ashram, and therein lies the purpose of the plan.

Realise you have a role to play in that purpose and that plan.

It is now time to relax the attention and come back into physical time reality.

Your impressions would be welcome, and recording them would be useful. How did that go for you? Have you some idea of the consciousness of the ashram? Have you realised that a shift is required when identifying with all these aspects of time and their concepts? The shift is from what I have spoken of, from an identification with yourself, as in 'my mental time', as an example, to 'the group's mental time', and spiritual time is the giving over to ashramic group time.

You have now achieved many integrations, the purpose of which was a unity with the One Life, and the One Life has many parts, all parts are like a hologram. Think of the One Life as a hologram; no matter how small something becomes when fragmented, the One Life can still be seen within it subjectively as the idea and design from the creative process of the One Life, and objectively its image pictorially will be seen on all of its parts, whether those parts are joined together as, for example, an object, or not, such is the beauty of the One Life and the love of the One Life within its parts.

Contemplate and think about this concept you are portraying in appearance as a manifestation of the One Life, but all you can see is yourself functioning within the One Life. If you have grasped the concept or functioning purely within your life circumstances and environment, the One Life is but a dim vision. There are many who are unaware of the One Life, and many whose vision is clouded, so to increase your awareness and realisation of the One Life is to spend your spiritual time in service to the One Life, in short, you are spending your spiritual time acquiring and becoming receptive to the ideas and the over-shadowing wisdom that is, you could say, the knowledge of the One Life that is held in substance, so that its parts may abstract the wisdom, and do not forget the dual aspect of wisdom is love, and the monadic aspect of wisdom is also will, or, for the relaying of this wisdom, purpose, so its parts can profit from this exchange within the One Life, and energetically relay the consciousness that is held, and by that I mean, is waiting to be manifested. This is all worth thinking about, but not intellectually as there would be no understanding, so your thinking needs to be from within the One Life, which is an abstraction from the normal range of thinking, which you can say is a certain frequency. Lift the frequency by rendering the normal range of thinking into no-thinking, then, after a short time within the void between the two, a higher frequency of thought will enter and touch the brain awareness with the consciousness, and the process of thinking that is relative to the new frequency.

Many aspects of the One Life go unnoticed, because we do not sense them; their frequency is above our sensory perception. Now, to understand this is to realise that you separate all aspects of yourself, rather than view them as a whole, working together. For example, you perceive your senses are a different aspect of yourself, from your thought and your thinking. They are not at all, they are integral to your brain consciousness, and they relate to your level of consciousness and the ability to discriminate. They are also not separate from your aura, or your other centres, or chakras upon the body. Once your senses become a unity, a One Life within the One Life, then your perception will change. The Spiritual Man will instruct of this unity of the One Life to such a degree that whole life perception will change. Whatever form or appearance you have taken within the One Life is subjective in nature within the One Life, and your manifest appearance is of great value towards the evolution of the One Life.

What then is your purpose? Can you conceive you have something to offer? If you utilise the aspects of time I have projected to you, you will find out. Do not accept what already is, that is the manifest product of a previous inspiration from within the One Life, and the higher consciousness of that One Life that is but a distortion of its original blueprint, and the design that had been created for its manifestation. But behind the manifestation can be conceived the original idea, so in the present you are living the ideas and ideals of a past idea that has been distorted away from its original concept, and concept relates to conception, the birth of an idea. So, think about this, that your spaces of time that you create will have nothing to do with what is, and the reality of what is other than this, can be used in synthesis with the new ideas that are there upon the subjective planes, so realise what is upon the manifest planes, which is a distortion, the One Life through its own life-cycle, which is vastly different from our life cycle in manifest form, although from another perspective, our true life cycle is just as great as the life cycle of the One Life, if you can perceive the meaning behind this statement.

The One Life is evolving, and as we are part of the One Life, so our purpose also is to evolve. Within the D.N.A. lies the purpose that will motivate that evolution, so the purpose, the creative potential for your manifestation, lies as a blueprint in those microcosmic levels within the physical form; it is there because you have incarnated. It mostly lies dormant until such a time as you become a bit more consciously aware of something other than your normal existence. The ability to function within the world of past condensed inspiration that has become a sequence of living events, a conformity of rules and regulations concerning physicality, You conform so easily to this past initiative that is a distortion, and you do not realise it; you are also not helped by those around you who, for this lifetime, are fixed and concrete within its ideals and cannot break free. Indeed, they do not even see the need to break free, such is the state of affairs that exist from one age to the next. The One Life, as I have mentioned, is evolving, therefore, different energies are being projected into the consciousness of humanity, and are seeking to lift the consciousness of humanity into the energy consciousness of those energies that are passing into and through the One Life.

Here you can understand the fact of solar time as the source of the energies coming into the One Life. Always there are transformational energies being projected, and impressing upon all the kingdoms of the planetary life, none more so than those impressing the consciousness of humanity at this time. This is the purpose now being relayed into humanity, via the One Life, and this purpose has a plan, so it is seeking to stimulate that plan which already has the D.N.A., or blueprint, for your activation into the purpose and the plan, it's just that you haven't arrived at the place where you will know, without a doubt, where your purpose lies within the concepts that humanity has, at this moment, endowed within itself, which is reflected in its behaviour, attitude, and the way its consciousness is governed by past ideals. You have to realise most of what you see and experience are past ideals; here and there the new ideas are starting to manifest. If you think about it, you can see this duality going on. Two opposing forces playing out at this time between the past age and the new age that is rapidly trying to impress the consciousness of humanity.

It is time to reflect upon this and see where you stand between the two. Are you part of the past? Or are you part of the future? If you are part of the future, then you may feel apart from the manifested past that, at this moment, is still the dominating force in life and circumstance. You, therefore, will question yourself, and to such a degree that you will conform to the past, as I have mentioned, so you will go through life restless and wondering why. So many people are depressed within your culture, and yet nobody has questioned from the consciousness of the One Life, why! It is, to a certain extent, within many that they are perceiving, to a degree, within their physical bodies on this level, that they will be conceiving that the answer lies on that level, or if not, and they have become aware to their emotions, they may perceive many things on that level. You have integrated the sub-divisions of the emotional plane of consciousness you have been in, and maybe have transformed that consciousness, that emotional state of being, to its highest place of reality within the One Life and, therefore, you will be wise to your emotions. It may well be worth it to consider that proposition. Have you changed how your feel? And have you integrated this change within emotional time that then blends with physical time? And has your physical body received this change? Your centres of consciousness will indicate to you whether this has occurred.

If you are struggling with this new state of feeling within the physical body, then your physical body is fighting the change, your essence of appearance for the physical body is not adapting. Your brain consciousness is confused between the old and the new. Why is this occurring? Because your new feelings and emotions are from a higher source and the energy of them has not been embodied by the brain consciousness. How you think about this is very important because the old enemy of man may wish to retain its control; it has embedded itself into the very cells of your body. It is a past conscious pattern of energy exchange that is from the past, which was quite fitting to the past, because that was, at the time, the energy consciousness of the One Life wishing to change humanity's consciousness from an even more ancient consciousness from a time before that. Humanity has to catch up with the consciousness of the One Life, so you will be struggling with physical integration, and, more than likely, your thinking will be confused. What is the One Life trying to say? How can transformation from the past age to the new age occur? This wisdom of the new age is what is over-shadowing, it contains the plan, it contains what I will call *the new language*, not as in the changing of words, but the use of words; how they will form mantric verse, and their quality of sounds creatively expressed through the wisdom in a language that the past language will understand and think about. But there are others who will not understand and be over-shadowed by a cloud of unknowing.

So, to be wise to the emotions is to be in touch with the wisdom, not from books, although there are certain books that do relay this wisdom, and they will all say that what has been written is for the future. The Tibetan states this, and the transmissions from the Master R also reiterate this, but then think on this, that if you have become a representative of the future, and you have grasped some of the concepts of the future, and have embodied them, and are displaying them, then you are living the future in the present. So, even if an instruction is clearly written for the future, you will understand it very quickly, and the new language will start to impress you. This language, you could say, is the intuitive language. The intuition is a wonderful way of receiving the wisdom, but the new language is not just the intuition, because your language will be just the same, with maybe different words arranged in a different sequence that will be abstract and in most cases, not understood. How many times do you ask, "What does that mean?". You have received an impression which you regard as intuitive, but you haven't got a clue what it means. There is no consistency here with the brain consciousness, it is still holding onto the past by telling you it does not understand what it has just been told, so the left and right aspects of the brain are not in a harmonious resonance.

You may say that the intuitive part of the brain is merely dormant, and it is, but your intellectual brain has to be prepared to integrate the intuitive part of the brain. If you conceive that you think from the past, then if you inform that intellectual part of the brain to that affect, you will be informing your consciousness that it is required to expand its realities and integrate these realities, and if you do not understand what the intuition is telling you, then think about it within spiritual time and then another insight will occur. What will you do with that? Add it to the previous impression and relegate it to your sub-conscious because you cannot consciously understand it, and you need to understand, beyond anything, you need to understand all of your life, and this is also the past pattern you have been indoctrinated within. This is the control that holds you and why it is said your soul is imprisoned within the three lower worlds, but it is very hard to see that when you are controlled by your own thought patterns and feelings, as such, your physical condition. Can you see the limitation of all this?

The problem here lies with rules. You must consider that rules are not laws; rules are made as a means of control, to control certain elements that would cause chaos if these rules were not in place. So more and more you seek to control the negative behaviour of yourselves, I say this because you are all part of one humanity. I am not saying that you are displaying, or you think and feel according to this negative behaviour, I am saying, at one time, you were displaying this behaviour in the past, and not necessarily the immediate past, as in who you are now. This is what humanity faces and those who have transcended the separation and have spiritual values, have to conform to those rules that have been made to control the negative aspect of humanity. So, those who implement these rules have a resonance with them. Here I am talking about the negative aspect of rules, not those people who are trying to help with those rules that already harmonise humanity and retain the sense of freedom.

Common sense should be a rule, and if you displayed common sense, then a lot of rules would disappear. Those rules are of an active intelligent nature that is manipulated from a materialistic viewpoint, this is the substance of the past. It is present upon the earth as it is the foundation of the earth; there is a problem when also the energy of concrete science is added to the equation. Can you see the control, therefore, of those two energies upon humanity, especially if humanity is calling forth the need for them? Rules are based mostly upon physical time and those who enjoy all aspects of physical time, and that is not using physical time to enter into spiritual time. Recognition of this will precipitate in your consciousness the urge to rebel, wise discrimination will guide you away from many situations; abstract realities are more of a reality than physical reality.

You may be realising that physical reality, as far as humanity is concerned, and by this I do not mean all of humanity, is not really a reality as a reality has movement, fluidity, progression, and is for the most part a future representation. I am writing this insight for those who have an understanding and can use this understanding to help others. For the most part, reality, to many people, is clouded by the limitations of mind; they see what they want to see and they see no further. If people recognise that what they see, think, and feel is not true reality, then they can start to enter into a different state of being. I seek to break down the concretised state of life that you have entered, the fixed attitudes of mind, and the somewhat chaotic state of emotion, and that is not necessarily displayed, because when the emotions have become numb, there is a fixation of mental activity that is connected to the numbness, and this is not a very good place to be.

How can I relay to you the fact of soul? How can I relay to you the fact of Monad? And how can I relay to you the fact of the centres of consciousness related to soul and Monad, and the lives that live and move, and have their being within these centres of consciousness? The journey towards the soul requires the treading of the path, a spark of light within the mind, and this is the problem. Can you imagine a new beginning? Can you accept, at this moment, that you have reached the number nine, the conclusion of a cycle, and are about to enter into the number one? You may say "I have not concluded a cycle, I am meditating, I have a goal in sight so, therefore, I haven't reached identification with the number nine, it is not possible to enter the number one". You may also say "I am already on the path of the soul, and I am aware of the Monad". Well, at least theoretically, and maybe your awareness of the soul is, to an extent, theoretical. It doesn't matter whether you are an aspirant, probationer, a disciple, and it doesn't matter also that you haven't, in your mind, reached the number nine.

You are thinking too linear, you don't necessarily have to have completed a cycle to start a new one. Initiation is not that you complete a particular initiation and then start another one, this is the thinking that needs to be transcended, this is the thinking you have grown up with, but, you do understand, you can have more than one job on the go at the same time. So, if you are aspiring towards a particular initiation, or shall I say, expansion of consciousness, as the word 'initiation' conjures up all sorts of thought concerning it, and that would limit your expression regarding it and, of course, the danger is that it would swell your ego and increase its power. Ponder upon the fact that you will be expanding into a certain area of consciousness, but at the same time, expanding into another area of consciousness. Each area of consciousness contains certain qualities and certain vibrations, it will not be self-contained as it will be receiving from another area of consciousness and also transmitting its qualities and vibrations into an area of consciousness that, for your understanding, lies below it.

Expansion of consciousness is not like reading books, because with books of any import, they have a start and a finish, an alpha and an omega, but understand this, each book will link to another book that will carry your consciousness to enquire. Never take things or others on face value. The enquiring mind is the discriminating mind, but it is also the mind that seeks answers to the many questions of creation, of life within creation, of what is the purpose of your creation, and what will be your creation, what can you achieve?

Perhaps you need to enter into spiritual time to use what I have said as a seed thought.

Meditation

I suggest you enter stillness.

Look into the space as a timeless entity, this will allow your three lower selves to become receptive by giving way to the space, by this I mean your physical body will not disturb you.

Adopt this principle for your emotional self as a complete unit.

Then your mental self as a complete unit.

This now allows your causal self to over-shadow the others.

A complete resonance occurs.

If you will kindly also focus upon your head centre, do not think about this, understand that this will happen. You do not have to strive for it to happen, as your thinking needs to stop.

So, allow yourself to sink into this state of stillness.

Pause

Now bring to mind the words '*Expansion of consciousness*'. There is no process required for you to enter into this.

Part of you will because of this form we are using, entering into another area of consciousness, you may not be aware of it, but you will be aware of the awesome silence, and this is an indication for you that this is happening.

Pause

These words will mean that you will have certain realisations and understandings that previously you were not aware of.

Something may filter into you at this stage, but do not worry if it doesn't, because retaining this stillness is bringing about a certain vibration that will be changing the vibration of your higher centres. You may be aware of this as you may feel the energy, or you may not, but nevertheless, it will be happening, if you are still experiencing the stillness.

Pause

Now, reduce the words *'Expansion of consciousness'* down to just the word *'consciousness'*.

Retaining the stillness, you perceive the shifting of your identification from yourself with the original thought concerning expansion of consciousness, to the polarisation to consciousness itself.

Ponder upon the levels of consciousness, the aspects of consciousness, remember there is no intelligent thought involved here. Just allow consciousness itself to impress you.

Pause

In this moment of impression, realise that consciousness is not just above, but below. You know the meaning of this, so incorporate both of these in your impression of consciousness.

Realise now as an analogy, consciousness is the intellect of the One Life. What is the One Life relaying to you?

You enter into the attitude of the enquiring mind so that you can focus upon what was presented earlier.

"What is the purpose of my creation?"

This is deeply esoteric and is connected to your impression of consciousness. It takes you also away from any self-identification.

I will repeat that so you can assimilate the vibration of its intent.

"What is the purpose of my creation?"

Pause

You now need to super-impose any realisation of this upon the next seed thought, which is "What will be my creation?" This is what you have to give to others.

You now need to enter more into the thinking process and what is known as *thought form building*, especially if you are starting to grasp what your creation could be, but hold no fixed personal identification with it.

Be creative with this process, take notice of everything that enters the mind, no matter how abstract. You are training yourself to attune to the higher realms of consciousness, and the knowledge and the language they use.

If nothing comes from this, do not worry, it will be affecting your sub-conscious, and the many sub-divisions, and the multi-consciousness that live there, stimulating the dormant aspects of these to precipitate at another time.

Pause

To help this process, imagine waves of consciousness entering your auric field from a higher source. Visualise this higher source as you are shown - you will all be shown it slightly differently.

Realise all these aspects of the higher source are part of the One Life and will blend into a synthesis, and remember those waves of consciousness are light, and as they reach the earth, you visualise them impregnating the lower kingdoms as they move from lower, to animal, to plant, and then mineral.

Remember also each wave carries a certain vibration and quality of energy consciousness. Colour may also be involved here.

You may find once these waves have reached the lowest kingdom, the mineral, they proceed back upwards to the higher source.

A good way to visualise this is to see concentric circles coming down from the higher source, through the aura and lower kingdoms, then back up, so you have a two way flow that is in constant movement. You have the ability to speed up or slow down this movement of consciousness.

Pause

The time is correct to slow this movement down until finally there is no movement.

Stay within the timeless space and stillness for a short while.

Now relax your attention and then record anything that was inspirational and insightful.

As part of this meditation, you focussed upon the lower kingdoms. Realise that these lower kingdoms also have within them sub-divisions and certain varieties of species representing all aspects you will find within yourselves; the further into material manifestation you go the fewer sub-divisions will be displayed, until finally the mineral kingdom has the least sub-divisions of them all. At this point it is wise not to assume that the mineral kingdom is the lowest aspect of consciousness because of this; it may be, if you relate it to self-consciousness, but the mineral kingdom relays a greater consciousness that contains within its consciousness all the sub-divisions of all the planes, those that you are familiar with, and those you have little understanding of.

The greater consciousness is seen in a crystal and a mineral, an aspect of this greater consciousness is revealed through their geometries, so to expand your consciousness is to realise that behind every mineral, crystal, and element is the idea for their manifestation, they are just an objective manifestation of an idea, and that idea has a purpose. Also realise energy is also involved here, so if you hold a crystal or mineral, there will be an exchange of energy, because their objective manifestation relates also to your objective manifestation and will have a resonance with it, so you will be impressed through an aspect of the Divine Plan held within a crystal or mineral, because otherwise it would not exist.

There is a line of connectivity through all the planes that exist within the One Life, so there will be certain crystals and minerals that will be upon your line of communication and consciousness, which will expand your consciousness, and also deal with those sub-divisions that are not communicating in a harmonious way. They are the stable structures created by the divine idea, so to perceive this idea is to look into their structure, to break through the physical object into their microcosmic worlds. The only way to do this is from your third eye. So, when you hold a crystal or mineral, your physical eyes see its outer manifest form, and your sense of touch relays this fact - it feels solid.

Now, if you look into the space to bring your third eye into activity, which remember is etheric in nature, and then bring it to bear upon the crystal, you will see into its inner worlds, and its inner worlds will take you into the higher worlds via its geometries. I realise this is very abstract for your understanding, but I am trying to inform you that consciousness is not just about going higher. I use the word *higher* for your understanding, because if you go lower, so to speak, you will find a correspondence of consciousness, and this concept of higher and lower you need to understand if you wish to embody the Spiritual Man and be impressed by the Divine Man. I say this because to embody the Divine Man is something very different to any of your experiences. You cannot enter into the higher planes of consciousness without entering into the purpose and understanding of the kingdoms below the human kingdom.

When looking into a crystal or mineral, always place your identification within the Spiritual Man, so it is the space, the third eye, identified within the Spiritual Man above the head, then focussed into the microcosmic inner worlds of the crystal on an etheric level to perceive the idea of its manifestation regarding the Divine Plan, and its relationship to the Divine Plan that is held within your own microcosmic worlds, it is within your D.N.A. When you connect in this way with crystal and minerals, you realise your basic foundation and structure within your original blueprint and design; an adjustment takes place within all your bodies and sub-divisions. This exercise is worth trying, as it will connect you to the earth itself as a whole, because the crystal or mineral you are holding is a very big part of all the other crystals and minerals that compose the earth itself, which came into physical manifestation as the result of an idea that created the sound necessary for it formation, so you could say that crystals and minerals are condensed sound, and contain the essence and origin of that sound, so they carry the intention of that sound and the thought behind.

The thought behind the sound has a plan and a purpose, and, as I have already stated, the crystals and minerals contain this plan and purpose, each variety contains a part of the plan, but the thought also contains the future as it had an intention that will culminate many millions of years in the future. As a human you are part of the plan, you display the plan just by being human so you also possess the future of the plan. If you can become as one with the will and purpose of the plan, then your future is revealed and you will proceed with great rapidity upon the path to enlightenment, and because you sense the future, then you will become the future and you will enter into a continuity of consciousness, you will see yourself as part of the One Life, and that is Immortal Life.

So, there are those who possess a continuity of consciousness, and there are very many who only possess a consciousness that has a ring pass not of the personality that is the extent of their consciousness, and that is a limitation to one life time, in this respect it is the life time of a personality, therefore, the personality consciousness perceives it that way, and when the personality fades away, so does the consciousness. The light that shines through all of this is the Spiritual Man. When the personality consciousness fades, it does so through the stages of its incarnation, so physical consciousness becomes astral consciousness, then mental consciousness, back to the Spiritual Man. So the concept I am wishing to impress upon you is that if your spiritual, astral, emotional and mental consciousness is in tune with the spiritual, and is attuned by the Spiritual Man, then those states possess the energy consciousness of the Spiritual Man, it is then, as I have stated, you enter into a continuity of consciousness. This you do by having no personality thought, because, as I mentioned, thought is creative, and what created the crystals and minerals? It was an idea, then a thought, then the sound. How can you not think about yourself? You can think about yourself within a continuity of consciousness regarding idea, thought and sound in relationship to the Spiritual Man, and your creative expression within the three worlds of personality regarding the idea, the plan, and a goal, but most people think of themselves within themselves and all that they can achieve for themselves; this is desire that is comfort, that is control. A continuity of consciousness does not do that, it realises it has no need for those things, but do not take the opposite to what I have said if you are taking it from the personality, because then the personality will only do all those things I have mentioned according to its understanding, which will then lead you into the suppression of the personality.

All these things I have mentioned can be from the Spiritual Man, but the identification is different, and because of that it allows you to be yourself for more creative, expressive, and expansive within the personality worlds.

I wish to present to you the word *'purification'*, the symbology for this is water. Immediately your mind will identify with the physical body, and mostly it will be because of a religious nature, because that is where your knowledge concerning purification has come from. Even those who have not identified with religion will still make that connection, and why is this? It is because for the last period, and this spans many centuries, the emphasis has been upon religion. Referring back to the continuity of consciousness, therefore, your consciousness in this life has been impressed with the experiences and consciousness of previous lives. Now, you may start to understand how and why your consciousness, at this time, identifies as it does with the word *purification*.

Another word I wish to present is *'illumination'*. As you shift your consciousness from the word *purification* to the word *illumination*, you will also perceive and understand this word from your previous identification, which will see this word as being something beyond yourself. So purification you identify with yourself as a physical act, and illumination you see as a spiritual acquisition, and something that only a few have achieved. If I said to you the two are part of the same thing, you would ask, "Why? I don't understand that."

First I wish to inform you that words are very limiting and restrict your freedom. Again, here is another word that you probably bring a physical identification to - *limiting*. "How can a word restrict my freedom? It doesn't stop me doing things." Well, if you do things according to your understanding of words, you are limited within your freedom, limited to your understanding of words and what they mean, but words have many meanings, depending on the consciousness that uses them and displays activity upon them.

There is another word that you probably relate to physical motion - *'activity'*. You must realise I am playing with your understanding. I am not trying to confuse you, although, if you stick rigidly to one specific interpretation of a word, then your brain consciousness has been conditioned within the boundaries of that word, in short, you will probably be confused. Now, if you can adopt the attitude of motivated discovery and drop your prejudices, then you may get something from this. If you wish to stay rigidly within your present concept of word, so be it.

Let me test this out and go back to the two original words - purification and illumination - and my proposition concerning them. Now, if this proposition relates to your understanding, then you will be acting upon that understanding and using all sorts of methods to purify the body, and all sorts of methods to gain illumination, you might achieve some sort of success, but you will be limited, and part of you will know that, and you could be miserable within your efforts of purification and your search for illumination. One will be playing off the other, and in your quest your mental body will be stimulated, causing you to think too much, you will be preoccupied with all the facets of these two words and inevitably you will fail, and may even give up the quest. Take heart. I am going to reverse these words for your understanding, so now think about illumination as being physical and purification as being spiritual. How do you feel about that? You may say it doesn't fit. It won't unless you gain some sort of understanding you can work with, and then apply to other words, in short, turning your understanding on its head.

One thing also is required, the will to evolve as it is the will that initiates the search for understanding, and purification that creates the condition for the will to illuminate the physical worlds.

The Master M wishes to inject some illumination:

"If you expand beyond this word purification, and see that this word presents no boundaries for you, you will realise it has a relationship to fire. The fire of spirit is the purifying agent for the consummation of spirit and matter, it is the will that brings forth the fire, it ignites the soul into activity, it burns away all opposition to its purpose. The purified soul of man creates the flame, the flame of life, the problem comes when the flame of purification descends from spirit into the plane of mind. Have you an illuminated mind? Your mind is not your brain consciousness, your brain consciousness reacts according to your experiences. Your mind propagates your will to discover, it receives the flame and starts to think, it thinks other than the limitations of word so your mind then feels; it feels the light, it attracts the light, it absorbs into its body the over-shadowing wisdom. The purified soul transmits the fire into the heart, and then the heart illuminates the body, and the flame it creates moves back upwards. This is the activity of the Spiritual Man who also moves the flame back to the Divine Man, so can you see that the word activity is not just physical? It concerns movement, movement of consciousness, of energy, of thought, of wisdom. Enter into this activity.

Let us explore the concept of word form. Commonly, if you want to understand a word, you will resort to a dictionary or, to use your language, you will "google it", and there presented will be its meaning. There may be extra presentations of its meaning, giving you an idea about it, which will then assimilate its meaning into your brain consciousness. Now what you have done is to give this word form, in actual fact, it already has form because of its explanation, its form then becomes embodied, so to speak. So in this respect, if you believe that all that has been written about this word is all it has to offer, then you will have given the word concrete form and this concrete form will become part of your brain consciousness, to be replayed when the surface mind encounters the situations for the use of the particular word in question, whatever that may be. So your expression of this word will be reflective of your understanding of it. Now, this word in question is connected to many other words so if you concretise a word, you limit your expression of the word within the boundaries of the word itself. If you think beyond the word, then you become connected to other words beyond the normal range of perception of word.

You can have a very extensive vocabulary, but if you have no sense of the words, which means you do not feel the energy and consciousness of the words, then you are still limited within the concrete form of each word expressed. This is concrete intellect that expresses words because it has memorised then, this is being clever, but not clever enough to realise what lies beyond. They are purely expressive of feeling and thought, and are, by their formulation of sound, naturally limited within their states. But other words require the attention; you cannot say one word is on the same level as another word, and words produce sound so your words are going up and down on a musical scale, and this is rightly so, but are they in harmony with one another?

Now, realise also that there is sound that is imperceptible to your senses. This sound you could also relate to a musical scale. This intangible sound is beyond your physical senses, and your brain consciousness. Now, when you go beyond a specific word and also connectivity of word, then you will perceive this higher intangible musical scale, until you go beyond word itself, and this is silence. Then you will perceive the divine truth, your senses that are beyond the physical senses will relay to you what lies beyond word into creative word, therefore, word takes on a different meaning and becomes mantric in nature. Yes, you can have a very expansive vocabulary, but do the words mean anything to you? A word, or a concept expressed in words, is a doorway into further higher concepts and the over-shadowing wisdom, so if you live life as a discovery and enter into exploration, you can understand this on a physical level, but adopt the same principle to the power of thought, try to discover beyond your thought, do not limit your consciousness to the familiar, attempt to journey to new areas of space and understand the Spiritual Man is waiting to go on that journey with you. Stimulate your enquiring mind, always seek beyond, and look to new horizons.

You could relate this to the climbing of a mountain - if this is how you perceive your journey, then instantly your identification with a mountain will bring out of your sub-conscious the fact that this could be a test of endurance and requires determination. It also suggests that you could fail in your attempt to reach the summit of your mountain. This mountain is not someone else's, it has not been placed there by the Spiritual Man, or indeed the Divine Man, as the challenge you face, it has nothing to do with anyone else but yourself. If you have a big mountain to climb, then you have a lot to learn, and if you proceed to learn and acquire knowledge, then your ascent is more gradual. The mountain represents yourself, your limitations, your barriers, your restrictions, and it represents your journey to freedom. You can be guided up the mountain and shown the way, but if you choose another way that looks more inviting, you may fall, and if you think you can climb this mountain without a guide, then the mountain will not reveal its summit. The guide will never tell you, he will advise you and for a lot of the journey, you could say the guide is the Spiritual Man, he will meet you at a point where you have left a portion of the mountain behind, and this portion represents your limitations concerning glamour and illusion. He will then journey with you until, at another point, the Divine Man will appear and lead you on until you can reach the summit.

Let us enter into meditation to find out what this mountain represents to you.

Meditation

Ponder upon what has been relayed to you regarding word, and that word and concept are doorways into expansive knowledge - this you are seeking. Adopt an attitude of discovery

Now, realise humanity has a mountain to climb. Visualise humanity's mountain.

Realise if you climb your individual mountain, a portion of humanity's mountain will disappear.

There is a word that can help achieve this. You have come across this word many times and are probably very familiar with it. So, you need to initiate a renewed motivation towards this word, this is your will to discover, then it will open a door for you.

If you are aware of your group, or are sitting in a group, then the door will open for the group.

You are aware of the light of the Spiritual Man above the head, you may experience a small dot of white light briefly in your inner vision.

Now bring to mind the word *'truth'*.

You see a mountain in front of you, this is your mountain, although at some point, as you travel this mountain, it will become the group's mountain.

Certain aspects of the mountain will be revealed to you as you start to climb upwards, but first, as you view the mountain, and do this in detail, observe all its aspects, then project the word *truth* into its image.

Waves of energy pervade the mountain and transform it into a different image - or not, as the case may be.

It reveals where there are, and I will use a past reference, obstacles. In fact, they will become more abstract to you.

Start to ascend, this first part is the physical journey. It will present no problems for you as your sense of discovery retains the will.

Pause

You are now on another portion of your ascent. This could be difficult as it concerns your emotions. Whatever your mountain reveals to you is representative of your emotions in the form of imagery.

This, you realise, needs to be transformed, or it may not present a problem for you.

Use word and sound to continue your journey upwards until what lies before you is a visual representation of your thought-life in the scenery and difficulty that the mountain represents to you.

Further up the mountain you see a light, this is the light of the Spiritual Man, and you become attracted to this light.

However you visualise this part of your journey, you know the Spiritual Man offers you freedom from your thought-life, and that aspect of you that is still at the centre is attracted towards the Spiritual Man, and you ascend further up the mountain.

To achieve this you need to relinquish your thought-life, especially as it concerns yourself, and ask yourself why you would not want to do that. If you manage to do this, you will then perceive that the imagery of your mountain is not so much of a challenge.

The light of the Spiritual Man will be easily attainable and you will move closer to it.

It is important that you move into this light and be absorbed into the light, so you move closer.

There is no reason why you should not move into the light. If it is a problem, then what the mountain will show you is your own limitations and restrictions, which you are cherishing, as you will be gaining something from them.

If you communicate with the light of the Spiritual Man then he will project this light upon those limitations and restrictions, but you must be prepared to address yourself in this respect.

If you cannot do this, it is wise to descend the mountain. Otherwise, proceed into the light of the Spiritual Man.

Enter into the light, and within the light you see approaching you an image of yourself.

It is bathed in light, it is your perfected Spiritual Man, but it is you. You may wish to enter into communication, or just be with the light.

Allow any distorted images of yourself to fade away at this point of convergence with the Spiritual Man.

The Spiritual Man now steps forward and merges himself with you. The two have now become one, and you experience an activation of your head centre.

A line of light is projected upwards from your head centre, this is towards the Divine Man, who resides higher up the mountain, although at this point the mountain, as you see and experience it within your consciousness, has disappeared.

There is no mountain. It was representative of your past experiences, your past and present thoughts and emotions.

The Divine Man resides within a centre of consciousness and light that is beyond thought and emotion. It is just pure being which emanates pure love and pure purpose.

So now enter into a resonance with the Divine Man from the place where you now find yourself embodied by the Spiritual Man.

You will register this resonance as a vibration and that is all that is necessary. There is no need to strive towards anything else.

You are just required to be in resonance.

Pause

Abstract yourself now back into the physical world.

Presentation Two 19/4/15

NOTES

TRANSCRIPTS FROM THE

MASTER K H

BOOK THREE

NOTES

NOTES

In this presentation I will be relaying many concepts that will warrant your investigation via word form. I have touched on word towards the end of the last presentation whereby you perceive and understand a word according to your knowledge of it, so you could say you have given a word form, form meaning a physical representation of that word according to, in its first instance, its creation within a language, and its documented meaning according to the language.

We have already discussed the words *purification* and *illumination*, and reversed their identification to give you a flavour of how to expand your thinking processes to go beyond yourself. Now the question arises, "Why would you want to do that?" Well, ask yourself - have you no problems? Are you happy in your present understanding? Immediately when questioned with this your mind flicks itself into a reaction according to your present understanding, and to you that would mean if you are not happy there, you have to do something about it. You might have to start reading books to gain knowledge, you might have to go on a course, and that would cost you money. Is money more important than your consciousness? More important than your spiritual growth? So, understand this, at some point you will have to undertake the task of your spiritual growth, it is best to do it now.

A course may be useful, also a book may be useful, but they will only stimulate your growth. Now, one of the biggest problems is inertia, the putting off of what you could do today until tomorrow. You fully understand that statement, but what really happens if you are within inertia is that you put it off in this life, and the tomorrow is the next life, and what could happen in the next life? The power of your inertia has strengthened and once more, you put off until tomorrow what you could do today. You can see I have expanded your time concept of this statement, and, of course, time on your physical level waits for no man. Self-consciousness is a wonderful thing; it stimulates your thinking to realise that you are in inertia. The Spiritual Man reveals your self-consciousness to you. Many people do not even realise their consciousness, they just register their environment, and consequently their thinking and feeling is of the environment; there is no separation between them and their environment, so they create that environment within their own lives and, of course, a lot of this will be emotional in nature.

Why am I mentioning this, because it concerns other people? Because you need to understand the world you live in without any misconception concerning yourself, and without any misconception of the path towards the Spiritual Man, and then the Divine Man, although he only appears when there is no way back into your state of environment. So, are you the environment, or are you a self-conscious being living in the environment? Are you living the human experience with your consciousness in the environment within the Spiritual Man? If you have embodied the Spiritual Man, then your consciousness is not the environment, you will see your environment as truth in form.

How can truth be within form, when form is not a reality in itself? It is a distant reality of the great design, but first we have to think about the concept of truth, so we also have truth in spirit, and, of course, there is one ultimate truth that lies far beyond comprehension. Truth lies within form, it's just that you have to delve under the surface to understand what the form represents, and to do this you have to go beyond form, into form to find its structure, its make-up. How a form is responsive is a different matter. To achieve self-consciousness is to relate yourself to others, can you see yourself in others? Do you understand the truth of others and the truth of yourself, because self-consciousness is achieved through truth? So, why would you not pursue truth?

I realise I am asking a lot of questions, but I seek to break through and create a spark in your mind, I seek to activate more fully the Spiritual Man. You may say, "I am already self-conscious, I know myself, my positive and my negative traits, and I am seeking to correct my negative states. I help others, but I am also working on myself, and I am self-conscious of this." Now, no matter how self-conscious you think you are, there is always another step, another level of self-consciousness, and I might add that if you are aware of your positive and negative traits, and are working on the negative, then you are not self-conscious, you are self-conscious to a certain extent by this recognition, but the recognition itself lacks truth. So, to understand this you have to assume there is no positive and negative, there is just the truth of yourself in self-consciousness, identified as a whole within the oneness of the One Life, so do not separate yourself into positive and negative because then you will be in conflict. It is obvious if you really think about it. Those who are conscious within the environment do not have this problem, they understand, to a degree, the positive and negative states mentioned, but of themselves they have nothing to give to themselves, recognition is limited to others, not themselves, and yet you have to recognise the truth in form of others.

So, the difference in recognition comes to those who are pursuing the path to, and I will say, enlightenment, but then, as I have said, you separate yourself into positive and negative, and the battle commences, and you run here, there, and everywhere to transform your so-called negative states, for which you have a language, for which is now becoming the past. Why split yourself in two? Because you must understand that the will is part of what is called the life stream, which also gives purpose, so why exercise this potent, divine energy upon yourself? Now, the positive and negative is a balance, so you are, through your pursuit of self-consciousness, trying, through your positive will, to destroy your negative and, in this instance, traits. I will say this, if you succeed in doing this, your positive will also be destroyed by your will to transform yourself into an enlightened being.

So, I have presented two particular conditions people find themselves in. What does the person who is conscious within environment

ANDREW CARTER

do about this? Realise the truth of form, which, you could say, is also truth of environment, and exercise certain measures to abstract themselves from it. I do not just mean physical abstraction here, because that is the last act, if that is necessary at all! It means to abstract the mind and emotions from the environment and that is via releasing your consciousness from it. But how can you do that when your consciousness is the environment? Develop another aspect of your consciousness that is lying dormant, so for those who are reading this, it will probably not apply to you, because if your consciousness was within the environment, then you would not even pick up this presentation, whether in book form, or orally spoken.

For those of you who are receiving this presentation, then you will be able to inform others, although this may not be easy, as the first thing this particular group of people need to do is to achieve and dedicate a small portion of time to enter into the state of silence, in short they need to enter into the first stage of meditation. Just simply become quiet and place an identification at the top of the head, realising this is of a higher intelligence and that is all. It is no good mentioning the Spiritual Man and certainly not the Divine Man, as that would be that. You might want to do this and relay many other things, but realise this, that you will not be relaying the need of the person or group, you will be exercising your sense of superiority, and an over-developed intellect, and the need for recognition. This aspect I am relaying relates to the second group that is trying to destroy these negative traits. They are trying to feed themselves with confidence and recognition, trying to energise these positive aspects, and this is part of their problem. This is one way that will destroy their positive aspects, although I have stated these forms will not exist, so putting it another way, they will be separating themselves from themselves within the whole, and their particular place within the One Life.

So, the second group need to realise pretty quickly that a satisfaction of your own knowledge relayed to others is separatist, as you are going beyond yourself. This is the so called positive path that shares knowledge to give a sense of satisfaction, and to big themselves up. Here we see the emergence of the ego with knowledge. Some-times there is a need to stretch people beyond their limitations through a concept that is beyond their understanding, but then this concept is brought down through the levels. Another state to consider is the emergence of the ego through love. What does this represent to you? Maybe it is positive love as against negative love, both these represent to your consciousness an identification with your consciousness concerning their meaning. Realise that positive love displayed is just the same as negative love, it is just on the same continuum. If you are still thinking and feeling positive and negative, then it is just a different aspect of the same thing.

So, the emergence of ego through love can take on many forms, but it still relates to form, and the more you attempt to display love, the more you will be (a) doing it because it is the right thing to do, and (b) doing it because it will give you a satisfaction and a response. This may seem harsh, but this major concept I am projecting will lift you into a higher state of registration, so let the move to the third aspect of emergence of the ego through will, this is interesting. Now, these three states do not unfold one after the other, they are all going on at the same time, and because of this you will observe, in this second group, a backwards and forwards movement between these three states, you will not perceive a balance. The third state is the one that will concretise your thoughts and feelings, and fully identify you with the positive and negative, and you will exercise your will in a full belief of what you deem as positive. Those who do not agree, you will exercise your negative will upon them. You need to remember I am not referring to the physical action of will, but your thought and feeling towards any given subject and, of course, a subject leads to the subjective.

So, have you now gained some sort of understanding regarding the concept of positive and negative, to lead you from this second group into the third group that is fully self-conscious and is adjusting to the overall consciousness? What is required is adjusting to the state of neutral. To be neutral means you are neither positive, nor negative, therefore, you are not fighting with yourself, you are in the place of neutrality, which means your consciousness has lifted out of, and above, the identifications of the positive and negative.

Can you do this - give yourself no thought? Do not accept yourself, do not understand yourself, just be yourself, because if you just be yourself, then the neutral will bring about any adjustments you need to make as a natural process, and this is what people cannot conceive, that there is a natural process that relates to the neutral. Do the crystals and minerals, flowers and plants, and animals identify with the positive and negative? No, they just evolve through the seasons, there is a natural process concerning their growth. Now the concept I am relaying cannot be contained within those lower kingdoms as they are not regarding the human being evolving consciousness in the same way, but they do give an example of what I am trying to project. So the second group needs to obtain, from out of the positive and negative, the state of neutral, and if this occurs then the positive becomes radiatory and the negative becomes magnetic, and this is the achievement of self-consciousness, because self-consciousness is not ego consciousness, it then thinks and feels beyond itself into the overall consciousness. The more you attain the aspects of self-consciousness, each aspect then is magnetic to the overall consciousness, and in so doing, is radiating into the human consciousness.

So, the neutral gives you radiation and magnetism. If you place what you conceive to be your negative traits into the state of neutral, then you will become magnetic to the neutral, and if you place your positive traits within the state of neutral, they will become radiatory, then the emergence of the three states of ego - intellect, love, and will - become transformed into the higher aspects of divine mind, love, and will, a transference will occur. The stress of the positive and negative will disappear, because your identification will be the neutral. This neutral represents everything and nothing; everything the overall consciousness, and nothing self-consciousness, because when self-consciousness occurs, there is nothing that you cannot bring an understanding to, because everything contained within the overall consciousness can be magnetically attracted into the self-consciousness.

I wonder if this is breaking through into your thought life and your sensitivity. Your sensitivity is all important, because to enter into the state of neutrality requires a sensitivity, it's the transference of your sensitivity from the positive and negative states in the neutral. Neutral sensitivity does not identify with positive and negative sensitivity, and when you negate these it naturally unfolds. You see, no effort is required; once you apply effort, and by that I mean you are giving a lot of your energy towards it, then you will enter into the positive and negative states. Where do you want your energy to go? And this is not just physical energy, it is emotional and mental energy. How much of this do you give to the positive and negative states? And, of course, these states concern decisions; what decisions do you enter into concerning these states? The neutral is the place where decisions are not necessarily made, they just occur and through this recognition of occurrence, you automatically go the right way, because decisions are all to do with the right or wrong way.

Let us take one decision of a very every-day nature. You go to a café to meet some friends, or you are on a course. Now, you may perceive what I am now presenting as being very mundane as against the teachings upon the higher spiritual world, but they require your attention to release you from these limitations. Now, if you are in group two, you will be confronted with a choice and a decision; your decision may be based upon your friend's decision, or it may be based upon you being good. What drink will you order? Will it be a coffee or an herbal tea? I use this as an example; and maybe you will chose something sweet to go with it. There could be quite a discussion concerning this regarding the aspect of being good, and what *is* good for you? What is good for you is not to enter into this exchange of energy, as you will be identifying with the positive and negative - the herbal tea is good for you, and the coffee will stimulate you. Maybe you need some stimulation, certainly towards the Spiritual Man whose essence is imprisoned within your positive and negative.

But what about the something sweet? The icing on the cake? So much energy is given towards this decision and the reasons why you should have it, and the reasons why you shouldn't have it, that you plummet deeper into the positive and negative. This is a very simple example, but also there could then occur an entire discussion upon this identification. You could say this is an aspect of self-consciousness. "The coffee is not good for me, and the herbal tea is good for me." This is not self-consciousness, it is consciousness that lies within the environment, because you would go with whatever feels right at the time, without the need for decision, without the analysing of what the choice represents, therefore, there is no energy given by the consciousness to the positive and negative. The consciousness will then not be in conflict. Of course, the portion of the consciousness that creates the conflict is the intellectual mental body that is over-shadowed by the environment, so decisions occur when there is a choice to be made. Life is full of choices, they are everywhere, there are more choices than ever before, a bewildering world of choice, some would say more freedom of choice, but there is no freedom if there are decisions.

So, once the word '*decision*' is activated, you enter into a state signified by the positive and negative, and the conflict occurs. Now, the freedom mentioned comes when you enter into choice itself, and not decision. Choice is related to the neutral, the neutral doesn't analyse the choice, it just makes it. It doesn't work out what is good for you, or not good for you, it knows the answer, so it does have freedom of choice. This comes from within the neutral that contains potentiality, it is a sphere of consciousness that has birthed by rising above the positive and negative, it bridges between the worlds of time and the timeless worlds, in contains both, and what starts to enter this sphere is the energy and consciousness from those planes above the strictly human. So, this neutral holding place of potentiality, because of the energies that it contains, and it can bridge dimensions, starts to shift the identification of the brain consciousness away from the positive and negative. It recognises them by the sheer fact they are displayed all around, but does not think that way itself, There is a withdrawal of identification from their existence, safe-guarding is necessary so that the neutral sphere can develop. This sphere is your means of communication to the Spiritual Man, because the Spiritual Man is timeless and the Earthly Man lives in time, and the more it builds, the more there is an automatic communication between the two, and the Earthly Man transforms and releases much of what concerns it, so the vague outline of the sphere develops when the consciousness starts to withdraw from the environment, and develops self-consciousness, and as that happens, the overall over-shadowing consciousness starts to enter via the development of the sphere. All these three aspect then are all happening at the same time, one way towards the Spiritual Man, another from the Spiritual Man to the Earthly Man, and what happens then is that another sphere is created between the Earthly Man and the Devic Man of the three lower kingdoms. Energy consciousness exists through all the potentiality you have by moving your thoughts away from the positive and negative, because the overall consciousness, you must realise, just doesn't lie within; what lies above you, so to speak, it lies below you as well.

Now is the time for you to enter into meditation.

Meditation

Bring yourself to a point of receptivity, rendering yourself at one.

Just experience the silence as a state of tranquil activity.

You ponder on the state of neutral. You identify this as a sphere of transmission from the worlds of time to those that are timeless.

You hold this sphere in your consciousness and imagine the zone within the sphere where this happens, reality, in one sense of the earth plane, into the reality of the spiritual plane.

Use your imagination to transmit between the two, between the timeless and those which you are familiar with and live within, which are of time.

Try to experience the difference without, in any way, trying to formulate any experiences.

You could imagine within your sphere a horizontal line so the top half of the sphere is the timeless zone, and the bottom half represents time. This line is what you will be removing during this meditation and subsequent meditations, as this line is the barrier between the two.

See energy moving between the two halves of the sphere. This starts to weaken the line, but it cannot disappear. If it does, you are going too fast.

Now, take your focus away from the energy interaction. This does not mean it will stop, energy continues beyond any withdrawal of focus, because you have set it in motion.

Take as analogy the wheel, which slowly comes to a stop unless you put a brake on it. So, if you take your focus away, but don't put a brake on, then it will still flow, and at some point there will be a perpetual motion. This is what you are seeking to achieve.

With that in mind, you place a fixed point of identification within the top half of the sphere and then shine a light upon your consciousness that lies within the environment.

You are seeking to abstract that portion of your consciousness back into your self-consciousness, which is identified with the sphere.

This may be confusing for you, but realise your consciousness can be part of the environment, if you choose it to be so, when it is necessary. So, I am referring to that portion of your consciousness that is of the environment and causes you to be the environment. This is the part of you that is imprisoned within the environment, so expand your vision into the environment.

The environment may also be represented by a sphere; how you imagine this will be variable, but between you and the sphere of environment will be lines of energy. Don't confuse this with lines of light.

Those lines of energy are symbolic of your self-consciousness that is environmental; part of these lines of energy require you to abstract them from the environment, and a part of these lines are the energy consciousness of the environment.

You renew your connection with the upper circle of the sphere of neutral and then proceed with the work.

There is a possibility that there are seven lines. Take the first line now to abstract your consciousness from this line.

You need to perceive what aspect of yourself is imprisoned. A word will now be impressed to you which represents part of your consciousness that needs to be abstracted.

Once you have found the word that represents a part of your consciousness through this realisation, through word, it will then abstract your self-consciousness from the sphere of environment.

This will be automatic and what will be left upon this line will be the consciousness of the environment in connection with the word.

Send light from the upper circle of the neutral upon this line of energy, and it will then dissolve, and all associations with the environment will lose their power over you.

There may be minor realisations of what they could be. Do not identify too much with this, just realise a part of the Spiritual Man is being released from his imprisonment.

Now attempt the second line and proceed in the same fashion.

Find the word, then abstract your self-consciousness, then shed light upon the remaining energy.

I will allow a short period of time for you to do this.

Pause

Now approach the third line. Maybe you will have noticed that the sphere of environment consciousness has weakened.

This third line, potentially, is more powerful than the other two, as it is fixed within the positive and the negative, right and wrong. It may not necessarily be, so don't approach this line through my suggestion, expecting it to be so, but also be aware of the necessity not to bring your existing thought life into any sort of activity, as it could stimulate your line, rather than release you from it.

You are now fully aware of this line so project along this line golden energy, this you will draw from the heart of the sun.

Imagine this how you will, then activate the word form in relationship to this line of energy, abstracting your consciousness away from the sphere of environment.

Your Spiritual Man now sheds his light upon the line and it dissolves.

Enough work has now been done.

Surround yourself in golden light. This, for your attention, is the light of transmutation.

Then completely release your focus.

There will be certain important aspects of this meditation that will be required to be recorded. Please discuss in due time any of your results. Repeat this meditation, which, in a way, is a healing meditation, as many times as is necessary to abstract your consciousness from the environment; be aware this will highlight aspects of your own behaviour that is of the environment, but slowly, through many realisations, you will see these affects after the first attempt. You may not register them all, but realise as you abstract, a portion of your consciousness is then absorbed into the Spiritual Man. By that I do not mean you will lose a part of your consciousness to the Spiritual Man, but you will gain a certain amount of consciousness from the Spiritual Man, this will be via the breaking down of the line of separation that exists within the sphere of neutral. Instead of, symbolically, a horizontal line within the sphere, there will be a vertical line, but realise this will take time.

Now, there is a certain energy that will help with this process, and it is one of three particular energies that are associated with the life of the solar system; it represents spirit, soul, and matter, or I should say, it governs these three aspect that exist within the solar system. In its totality relating it to the solar system as a whole, meaning a complete state of consciousness, an entity in itself, it is the heart centre. But to our planetary life, it stimulates the spirit or the head centre; the soul, the heart centre; and matter, the base centre. I am referring to the sun. Now, the sun itself has a purpose; it has a Monad, and in that respect, represents one of the seven solar systems, each central sphere of life represents fire - I will come back to this discussion later on.

Now, the energy that the matter aspect generates for its purpose of manifestation in relationship to the sun, is fire by friction, which, in the first analysis, relates to time, and for our discussion, is the energy consciousness of the environment, and if you look at the environment, if you have managed to abstract yourself from it, you will see it at work. Friction causes heat, it causes conflict, it is related to karma, it is the energy that stimulates the need for transformation, it does, to an extent, relate to the Law of Economy. This friction can slow things down, it can put a brake on you if you engage with this energy through the energy consciousness of the environment. Now it is a different matter if you utilise this energy for the purpose of the plan, in conjunction with its companion energy, solar fire, therefore, the two working together, I use the words for your understanding, *constructive*, and *destructive*.

Constructive energy is the life stream that stimulates the builders in line with the great architect and the plan. Solar fire is etheric in nature so once the consciousness is abstracted from the environment, then this energy starts to work within the higher sub-divisions of the etheric, emotional, and mental divisions. There is a reference to this energy as it relates to the heart centre, the sun itself is a heart centre, and so do you possess a heart centre? Is your heart centre a fire, or does it burn with a dim glow, while fire by friction governs your life, therefore, your lower centre will be highly active, but not in consciousness? The Spiritual Man moulds the energy of solar fire, so once a line or lines have been connected, then solar fire will ignite your head centre via the heart centre, and you will realise many things in your thoughts that go beyond the consciousness of the environment. You will become self-consciousness within the planetary consciousness, you will go beyond yourself. Can you believe this potentiality exists?

I have said this before, but you need to be reminded as it may not have been registered, solar fire delivers your consciousness into the overall consciousness, which is also knows as group consciousness, but the statement *group consciousness* can have lower identification if you are not careful in your thinking, so what you probably understand as group consciousness is probably mass consciousness, and, for your understanding, this exists in the animal kingdom, but all too often it also exists in the human kingdom. So, even if you understand group consciousness and have displayed it in your life, there is still some sort of separation here, so I use the term *overall consciousness*, because that doesn't leave anything out, because all aspects of consciousness are useful to you, even those aspects that really cannot be classified as consciousness, they probably relate to instinct, although you must understand that instinct is a primitive term for survival. Instinct I am referring to relates to the consciousness of the environment because, if there is a lack of self-consciousness and automatic behaviour, then it is indeed instinct, just like the animal kingdom as an analogy. It's just that within a human, it is a higher distinction.

Rules produce this aspect of instinct, perhaps I need to alter the word to relate it to the concept I am projecting, so I will use the words *auto response*. Even if there is a great deal of self-consciousness, this auto response will exist; it certainly exists in environment consciousness and, of course, auto response can be passive or aggressive. There are certain laws that humanity has tried to create to make the world a better place, but mostly they work with fire by friction; now, if solar fire enters into humanity, then humanity will have to get rid of many rules, because the overall consciousness of humanity will not require them, why should it?

So, here we see an overall consciousness that is abundant and contains the over-shadowing wisdom, and the overall consciousness of humanity, a mixture of many states, but as none of humanity abstracts itself from itself, then solar fire will act upon fire by friction and the aspects of the environment that are imprisoning your consciousness will slowly disappear, as there will be no interest in them. So it is wise to ponder seriously upon where your interests lie. Is it with solar fire, or fire by friction? How much friction is there in your life, and that includes your inner life? Bear in mind, if you are transiting from fire by friction to solar fire, there could be friction, or, I will use a better word, *tension,* so you have to be selective with yourself and this is, of course, self-consciousness.

How much light is there in your life? Is your mind a fire with the Spiritual Man, a solar fire, although I have related this to the heart, is also of the mind, you could say solar thinking, although the higher correspondence to this statement is vast in its connotations. A short meditation at this point would be useful to attain the energies and energy consciousness of solar fire, so prepare to identify with this.

Meditation

I have related solar fire to the sun, and also the Spiritual Man. Link these two together into the head centre, which accelerates the energy of your etheric body.

Let us now make a further connection. You realise the Spiritual Man has a line of energy to the Divine Man, experience this ascension, and the solar fire of the sun related to the solar system.

You are now going far beyond the planetary scheme.

Link the Divine Man to the solar system, you do this by visualising the solar system and the constellations beyond, but having done this you identify the Divine Man with the spiritual consciousness of the sun, and coming from this consciousness via the constellations, are the energies of divine service of the divine idea and intent.

These energies, seven in number, enter the earth's atmosphere. Some are more potent and intense than some of the others.

One is receding, it is idealism and devotion, one is gaining in intensity the energy of divine manifestation, and one is just starting to manifest harmony through creativity and sound.

I will mention two more: the first compassionate wisdom divine love. This energy stream has been the impetus for the manifestation of the solar system; and the second the Divine Will and purpose for its creation.

There are two others, and they are highly active: science and intellect. We will not focus upon them.

So, hold in your mind the Divine Man and the spiritual consciousness of the sun as I introduce you to electric fire. This was meant to come later is the presentation, but you have called forth this instruction.

Electric fire is a combination of these energies that carry the prototype for the Divine Plan, and the consciousness of the Divine Plan as formulated by the greater consciousness that lies beyond the solar consciousness.

See these energies blend into one energy stream. Visualise this energy stream travelling along the etheric network of the planet into the consciousness of humanity.

Then drop the energy stream down into the lower sub-divisions of the etheric network, into the three lower kingdoms.

See this stream having a transmuting affect.

Once it reaches its lowest level, it travels back up through the etheric sub-divisions and takes with it all that is not in line with the plan, back to the spiritual consciousness of the sun.

Pause

Bring your consciousness to your head centre and identify with the magnetism of the earth.

Relax the attention.

Record impressions, please. How did you experience electric fire? Did you create a free channel for its entrance? Electric fire stimulates solar fire, you become aware of it when you have touched the Divine Man in consciousness. Do not try to understand this statement from the intelligent, as you will give yourself an understanding based upon your intellect, and place the Divine Man apart from yourself. He is not. It is just that you are not as aware of him as the Spiritual Man, and you are not as aware of the Spiritual Man as you are the Earthly Man, and that is not surprising; that is the world in which you live and move and have your being. But there are clues to your identification with the Divine Man, and if you have travelled the pathway of consciousness enough, you will be instilled with purpose and you will have a plan to the extent you will be following your purpose.

If you have understood the concept of the consciousness within the environment, then you will understand this: there is no choice in the matter if you have touched the Divine Man, he will be influencing your brain consciousness, your everyday consciousness, so that this everyday consciousness relates the essentials of your purpose; you will be living your purpose, whatever that may be, and it will certainly be of benefit to others, even if you consider it is of no consequence. It is of great consequence because the few become the many, and you have to realise your so-called small part is but a portion of the greater part, on the etheric level of consciousness your small part will be connecting with all the other parts that are in resonance with your purpose, and the information in your aura will be relaying this purpose. Can you imagine when your aura touches another aura, and you do not have to be standing next to that other? The information of your purpose will affect the information within their aura, all these unseen things happen on the level of the etheric.

You may say, "It would be great to see this happening". That would not be wise if you are not initiate in consciousness. If you have too much of an everyday consciousness that separates one day from another, one week from another, and so on, you would not understand what you saw, and it could affect you badly.

Now, imagine also if your purpose was alight with solar fire, then your aura will be attractive to others, and they will behave in an agreeable manner, but also solar fire can be combustible, so never throw intent upon others, and affect their Karma. Too much of that goes on. But you can heal with solar fire, especially on the level of the etheric, to then merge with fire by friction onto the physical to change the consciousness of the physical that is in distress; its substance is struggling to maintain its health, the devic lives are behaving according to the brain consciousness and, of course, in healing if the brain consciousness is rendered neutral, then the affects can be almost magical. The healing energies reinforce the devic lives to their purpose, and their purpose on this level is to maintain physical appearance, through regeneration. You do not need the brain consciousness for healing - you require intuitive consciousness.

Now, the devas that exist within your appearance will respond differently when solar fire enters the system, by this I am referring to the human system. The devas concerning solar fire are of a higher order than those within the human system, they are informing lives and they are conscious of themselves, unlike the devas of substance, or the devas related to fire by friction, as this keeps things separate as a natural law of substance, solar fire will integrate the substance of the lower worlds, creating order through the energy consciousness of divine magic. Once this integration occurs to a great degree, and a higher order of devas governs through the second aspect of love, then the energy consciousness of electric fire can safely enter, but it does so very slowly and is controlled by the Spiritual Man with an understanding by the Earthly Man, although the Earthly Man will be struggling to relinquish old ways of thought, feeling and action; his life will be turned upside down. But although this may be happening, he will know beyond doubt of the existence of the Spiritual Man and, therefore, will arrive at a state of tension; this particular position is when the consciousness is training itself to receive more insight, more realisation, another expansion.

Stay relaxed and focussed at this point, just wait. Your existing consciousness will be seeking to know, and this is the problem, so the Spiritual Man will only allow a certain amount of electric fire to filter through into your system, if you can trust in the Spiritual Man, and do not have this need to know. When you come to know, it will be when the Spiritual Man and your purpose are aligned into your brain consciousness, so this need to know will transfer into a knowing, and when you need to know from the aspect of the Spiritual Man, then it will be given.

So, you need, if I may use the words again, to *step out of time*, and the more you do this, then electric fire will descend and the Divine Man will make his approach to you. And what will you do with this? If you have stepped out of time, it will not govern you, then you can say you have relinquished environmental consciousness, and each day will not be separate from the next. You may say, "It isn't, I go to work just like the previous day, I have my meals just like the previous day, I watch the television and go on the computer, just like the previous day, so how can it be separate if I am doing the same things?" That is just the point I am trying to make; these actions are perpetuated by environment consciousness. "But I have to go to work," you might say. That is true, but what will you do other than work? And also, you can work and have other channels of thought, the Spiritual Man gives you this ability to think in two directions, especially if you are doing something in the lower worlds that, for you, is automatic and requires very little of your time.

Now, the Divine Man allows you to think in many directions, I will refer to this as spiral consciousness, and at any given moment you can bring a point of identification to what you are functioning within. How great or less is your spiral? The spiral of the Earthly Man is subscribed in horizontal planes, the Earthly Man is lateral in his thinking, so the lesser spiral as regards thinking has a very limited range of thought; in fact, if your continuity of consciousness from one day to the next is not separate, as I have mentioned, then does it concern a period of time watching a television? It requires no thinking to do this and you may well say you are relaxing in front of the television. That could be true, and if you are, you are then receptive. This teaching may, at this point, seem too basic to you, but you have to understand certain things concerning energy before you can move your consciousness into higher planes.

So, what you are watching on the television is impressing your consciousness, because you are receptive; everything you encounter affects the consciousness in some way. Many things drop below the consciousness, other things continue to impregnate the surface mind, because the surface mind is the environment mind. Watch and listen to the television too much and your thinking will be the television, and if you look, the television is a rectangle with four corners, and everything is contained within those four corners. So, spiral thought on these levels will be a mess and self-contained within itself. The higher and lower spiral needs to be in resonance. Can you not see the futility of life without the higher spiral? So these aspects of everyday consciousness are not a continuity of consciousness that does separate one day from the next, because you have not stepped out of time, you are perpetuating time, individual time.

There are many individuals who use time in the ways I have mentioned; they are stuck in the environment, but one thing I have to say is that if you are selective, you will escape the separation of time. Learn to think, I am continually saying this, but I seek to motivate you to think beyond yourself. How much do you talk about yourself, and your desires, your problems and your wants and needs? Do you want to become the centre of your own universe, or do you wish to be part of a greater universe? This the Divine Man can give you, but you have to try to contact him, and that is through thinking, not about yourself. Now, if you contact the Divine Man before your day starts and make further contacts during the day, not by thinking about the Divine Man, but just thinking, attending to your silence, then a continuity can occur from one day to the next. But, the Earthly Man is very good at staying where he is; this thinking, I am proposing, is very uncomfortable for him, because he has to make an effort, he has to conform to a different rhythm, a different state to what he is familiar with. He will not enter into a "perpetual evolution of time".

Not all time is the same; you regard time as the same time as it always has been, it is just time, but the substance that makes up any particular time period is different from another time period, so there are longer and shorter time periods. The time you live in now is different from the time 100 years ago, the substance is different. You may ask, "How can it be different, time is just time?" Well, the Divine Man answers this question, as I invite you to cast your mind back to the meditation and the seven streams of energy consciousness. Their rhythm and energy consciousness pulsates and, for your understanding, each energy ebbs and flows in greater or lesser degrees, so the mixture of energy within the whole of their combined substance changes. You could relate this to a musical instrument, if such a thing exists as a seven string guitar; each string represents a stream of energy, but the guitar has six streams and so one of these streams of energy is kept at bay and only a percentage of its energy potential has a manifesting quality that enters our time space continuum. This particular stream is of great power, it does to an extent, underline the other streams just as the second stream does, but not to the extent of the second stream.

So, there are six streams; one of those streams is, for our analogy, starting to be played. This is the fourth stream, so their combined energies produce a stimulation of consciousness in ever changing patterns of energy, therefore, what you regard as just time is not how you perceive, because *time* is the word given to a period as related to night and day, and their accumulation via number, which you then relate to years. So, are you living in time? Can you move with the perpetual evolution of time, or are you stuck in time? That is quite a dull place to be, this is the ordinary life, the human existence within the lower worlds of consciousness; what exists beyond this state could be called extraordinary, you will not be circumscribed by time.

I think you have a need to visualise these seven energies in motion through time.

Meditation

So, become quiet at this point as I am required to abstract your consciousness out of time.

An identification with the Spiritual Man is necessary at this point.

You visualise a circle with a horizontal line; in the bottom half lies your consciousness in time, which it probably is at the moment.

You focus on the Spiritual Man in the top half of the circle and the horizontal line turns and becomes a vertical line.

Take your consciousness to the top of the vertical line and there you find the Divine Man.

Your brain consciousness, at this point, is changing its rhythm and vibration into a different higher state of vibration.

You stay focussed on the Divine Man, and the vertical line becomes a point in the centre of your circle.

As it becomes a point, you enter into a state of no thinking and stand on the threshold of the perpetual evolution of time, an eternal continuity of consciousness.

Stay with no thought.

The point at the centre is the gateway. There occurs an energy exchange between this point and your third eye, via your vortex of energy, about six inches outside of your brow, the Ajna centre.

You are required to stay magnetic for three minutes.

Now, the point opens up, the gateway extends your consciousness out into the solar system.

There in the distance is the sun, you identify the sun as physical and experience its photons of light. Use this energy to regenerate your physical - these photons stimulate the cells of your body.

Take three breaths, with this in mind, your power of visualisation will determine the effectiveness of this.

Look now beyond the sun; this is taking you fully into the perpetual evolution of time.

You are now in a timeless state, but even within this timelessness, there is movement. This movement is the movement of consciousness, so beyond the sun you perceive another centre of consciousness outside of the solar system.

You travel along a line of light to what I will identify for you as the sun, Sirius.

Your crown centre expands on contact and instead of photons of light entering, it is information of light. Do not think about what it could be, otherwise you will click back into time as you know it.

You will have various experiences at this point.

You are required to spend three minutes in connectivity by allowing your centre system to collect the information.

Focus back on the Ajna centre now, and the earth beneath, allowing a portion of this information to enter the earth geometries.

Bring yourself back into time.

Assimilate and record any experiences.

Now take your mind back to the point at the centre of the circle.

Slip into the timeless state by visualising this point and circle, go beyond the point into the solar system and visualise the sun, and coming through and from the sun are these seven streams.

You see their colours and their rhythms; they spiral, interchange, pulsate with different intensities.

You imagine this flow as almost musical, in fact it is regarding sound. Experience this show of light, and you also see these energies dancing around the earth.

You see them entering the etheric network; as they flow through it they carry consciousness, so you will perceive areas on this network where they are unable to flow.

Which of the seven streams of consciousness are unable to flow? What is the consciousness or opposition to consciousness that is blocking them?

Use your creative imagination, what do you need to learn from this?

Fix your mind upon a stream of consciousness, what is its energy consciousness?

Register what it is trying to inform humanity, what can you gain to give to humanity to uplift their consciousness?

So now fluctuate between the perpetual evolution of time, and time as you know it, to register the insights.

Expand your mind towards these insights. Do not allow existing memory to formulate your insights.

Become one with the consciousness of whatever stream is impressing you with insight. Is it will, love, intelligence, harmony, science, devotion, or magic?

This is inadequate terminology, so go beyond this simplicity of identification. Do this by the transference between time and no-time.

As you start to identify insights, you can open your eyes into time to record them, but keep your consciousness on the threshold. You can transit both states with eyes open. This is the intuition working for you.

Now experiment with this. Stay for a while in the perpetual evolution of time to expand your insights beyond your initial registration.

Let the words come into your mind. These are not intellectual words because you are not thinking at all. They are your words, but not your ideas. Give over to this.

During this process, add the ingredients of your purpose.

I will now leave you to fully enter into this process.

Finish when you have completed this stage of development.

Have you gained something from this process? If you have tried to intellectually create this process, then you will still have been within time and your intellect, which has its agenda based on memory. This process does not concern the memory; it concerns the timeless memory that is the wisdom and this wisdom is many things, a multi consciousness, so do not try to understand this wisdom from your present perspective.

So, you give over your mind to this wisdom, you realise the Spiritual Man is your higher mind that is not separate. Have you achieved to bring the spiritual into your lifetime? Have you realised you can flip between the two, time and no-time? But this no-time is not static, it is every changing, just like what exists in time as you know it, but what exists there is not subject, it is subjective. Now, if you can utilise this approach to all aspect of life, not just what you regard as spiritual, then you will be getting somewhere, and the more you achieve this, the less you will be subject to time. But then there will be that aspect of you that will keep reminding you that you are physical, and time may once more move into your consciousness, with all the mental thoughts that exist there. So, there is a need, when this happens, to transmute them. I will call this *'thoughts in time'*, and that is what filters into your brain consciousness from the mental plane, and is displayed by others, and all aspects of your material world. It is quite understandable that you will be in duality.

The Master DK wishes to impart some insight concerning this.

Thank you. The first thing I wish to convey to you is the fact of impression and this I will take up with you in two ways. The first, impression that is received via your senses that is coming from the three lower worlds; and the second, the impressions that can come to you from the higher planes.

The first, you will understand, is registered in many ways, sight is a good example of impression. The physical eyes have a limited range of vision, but there is a connectivity immediately to the brain consciousness, therefore, you see and perceive what you see; thoughts are then formulated according to what you see in many ways. What are those thoughts made up of? This depends upon the quality of your inner vision.

We also have to take into account your sense of hearing, the two go together. How much do the sounds of the lower worlds penetrate into your inner sound of silence? Your previous instruction on time is quite appropriate here, as is your ability to move from one to the other, and also transfix yourself in both at the same time. This is a possibility, and, on a very simple scale, denotes initiation, your ability on these levels not to be influenced by them. Many thought forms exist on the mental plane that are undesirable to you, many astral energies and images are ever more undesirable.

Do not become sucked into the undesirable. You can love the undesirable. Do you understand that, my brothers? It is an enigma for you to love the undesirable. You can, because you recognise what it is, and what it represents, and what is its influence. This is truly the sacrifice of self, the will to become whole within the whole, as the whole contains the undesirable. Notice the word *desire* fits in with this word. No, you do not desire many things that your vision and hearing inform you of, but can you become initiate without working within the undesirable, and the answer, my friends, is no. The undesirable will present itself to you time and time again until you can work with it and transmute its energies into its higher correspondence.

There is an interface of impression that you are required to add, the energy of love, too at this time; the impression from the lower worlds requires you to identify what this impression concerns, not from your intellect, as your intellect has not the capacity for love, or the capacity to see beyond the impression, as the capacity to love. Can you be touched by this love? Can you touch this love by giving over to it? Can you be impressed by love, as love is the access to impression?

There are many things you can touch with your hands which create sensations according to what is touched. Realise the sense of touch was the second sense developed and relates to the second plane, the astral; this you call now the emotional in relationship to your personal identity and other individual identities, but you must understand the astral plane itself, and all that resides there, is not a reality, it contains most of the past energies of humanity, and in a way the higher sense does not exist. This plane also relates to the second initiation and the energy consciousness of idealism and devotion. Can you see, my brothers, where your problems could be lying, and how difficult it is for those who have gone further than you to instruct you regarding this, as you possibly will not understand? Unless you give serious consideration to the Law of Attraction and elevate your consciousness away from the astral plane, and all the psychic phenomena that exists there, they will distort your reality.

If you want to know what the future holds and the effects of the past, ask the Spiritual Man, because then you will receive truth, and that is very hard for most people to face. *Truth*, I am not just referring to yourself, in fact it is better I don't, but the truth about everything you experience, what you hear, touch, and see. An analysis of this requires a detached viewpoint, in fact detached also from your personality, because the Spiritual Man can also hear, touch, and see. He is not beyond these senses, he is but a higher correspondence of them, and if you embody the consciousness of the Spiritual Man, then he will be aware of your personality senses, and bring his higher senses into your lower senses. Can you imagine the result of this higher sensory perception? But be not confused with the *psychic sensory perception* that these words are mainly allied with; it is nothing like them. As the lowest aspect of them has their consciousness with the sub-divisions of the physical consciousness, this is instinct; so I wish to tell you there is psychic instinct, and what is relayed through this is but the nature of fear. Be aware what you are told by these so-called spiritual people. I wish you not to be deceived and taken away from your purpose.

Can you remove your consciousness away from these things of phenomena? Can you let it go? You can through love and, of course, wisdom, as it relates to the higher plane of Buddhic; go one plane above to Atma, and then you will be aligned with the will and purpose of the plan. That will take you away from those things, and then any descent into those regions will be in full consciousness of them, you will then be safe. This plane of Buddhi is where your spiritual impressions should come from, so, my brothers, let us take the word *transformation* into your consciousness for you to ponder over, and then relate this to an elevation of consciousness. Therefore, I will transmit a meditation for you to use as frequently as is required; this meditation is an alignment to create a channel directly into your brain consciousness so that your thinking will be aware of the undesirable, and also be impressed by the transcendent consciousness.

Meditation

Place yourself in a comfortable position for meditation.

You are required now to render your lower three aspects into silence and you do this by experiencing the silence that surrounds you.

Place the light of the Spiritual Man above the head. There is a line of light from the Spiritual Man into your head centre, and its light is also within your heart centre.

Now sound the OM into the space to bring into resonance your physical body.

Sound another OM to quieten your emotional body.

And a third OM to remove all intellectual thought.

Now imagine, if you will, that you are travelling upon a line between past and future. Realise this line represents the Rainbow Bridge.

Your problems and the undesirable represent past.

Can you hear their sounds as you travel upwards on this line of light? Its composition is made up of seven colours, think of a rainbow and you will know what they are.

So, on one side of your line of light, which is also your path, (you choose which side of the path), you hear all the discordant sounds of the past, and on the other side of the path lies the future. What sounds can you hear from the future?

You may be struggling with this as the Past is firmly established in your consciousness, and if you do hear any sounds, they will probably be a distortion of the past that you think you are perceiving of the future.

Realise that your past needs to be transmuted by the future, but first the future needs to contain the energies for this transmutation. This is when you enquire up to the Spiritual Man for his help; request the energies to be present for the future.

The Spiritual Man floods your future with energy and then you will have a duality. You will hear the past in one ear and the future in the other.

It is important to retain the Spiritual Man as a centre of light above the head as this is the governing factor. If you cannot retain the Spiritual Man, discontinue the meditation.

As you walk the path, you can hear the sounds from the past and the future. Stop walking at this point.

The sounds of the past now need to be transmuted into the sounds of the future, so imagine a triangle. At the top - the centre of light which is the Spiritual Man, at the bottom on one side - the past, and on the other - the future. Each one is either the right or left ear.

From the centre of the light, see a line of energy coming down into the future point, and the physical ear that represents the future.

Then through the head and along the base line of the triangle to the physical ear that represents the past.

And then back up the triangle to the centre of light, which is the Spiritual Man.

Now continue to circulate this energy, and the sounds of the past will be transmuted. What will they be transmuted into? The sounds of the future. By this I mean that when you then think about the past, it will be from your understanding regarding the future.

To further this into an assimilation of energy consciousness, reverse the direction of the energy from the Spiritual Man above the head, to what you identified as past, through to the future, and then back to the Spiritual Man.

You now visualise, at the same time, a vortex of light is being created in the cave in the centre of the head, and finally, a spiral is created from this vortex up to above the head into the centre of light of the Spiritual Man.

Stop the circulation of the triangle, and as you do the spiral comes back down from the Spiritual Man, into the cave, and then back again.

Visualise this spiral going up and then back down several times.

Then focus onto the physical plane and the physical body with the sound of a single OM, completing this transmuting meditation.

Thank you for your determined effort, and dedicated service.

The Master K.H.

An addition to what the Master D.K. has presented, but only when you are comfortable, is to bring each spiral downwards through your centre system, down to the earth itself, and then back up. Do not attempt this too soon, as there will be a surge of energy and it is unwise if you are not ready, as it could over-stimulate your centre system, and certainly it is unwise to stimulate the Kundalini. This, for your understanding, happens as a natural process through the elevation of your consciousness through the centre system, and at some point, the combined consciousness of your centre system will call it forth through a certain tone and vibration that will be present.

A certain amount of this latent energy does rise in gradual stages and rates of vibration. Again, I will stipulate this is a natural process, because it removes the sheaths between the major centres of consciousness that, to analogise, separate them, not in the sense of your understanding of separation, which indicates a barrier exists between one thing and another, but these sheaths monitor the amount of energy that passes through, throughout the centre system. The Kundalini and its power surge of energy burns through these sheaths. Can you imagine the result if one is not ready, meaning the consciousness is not expanded enough, and through this elevation of consciousness, the centre system has increased its vibration and has opened its chambers into the higher fields of consciousness and living?

It is remarkable how many of you seek this higher consciousness and will do anything to obtain it, even to the extent of trying to raise the

Kundalini from its slumber, and yet, what is the need telling you? That it is an earthly need from the consciousness of the Earthly Man or, if you prefer it, the personality, therefore, it is of the ego and has a selfish intent for the personal 'I' identity, and if that is so, you will unleash this energy into a centre system that has only managed to incorporate mainly the energies of the lower planes. Can you imagine the burning through of the sheaths on the lower planes if you are not integrated with the Spiritual Man? Suddenly your physical, emotional and mental devas that make up the substance of your bodies will not know where they are, they will all confront each other as there will be no sheath separating them, and all this you will register in your brain consciousness, all manner of things will be experienced, and you could totally enter into madness, so do not even contemplate the rising of the Kundalini.

Fortunately, most people have not the power of mind to do this anyway, so these sheaths I have mentioned filter energies within the chakra system; they are etheric in nature, and the strength and quality of their substance is according to the consciousness and, as I have said, they filter energies, a bit like a sieve, so they react also according to your consciousness. They are not made up of the same consistency in everyone, and if they become concretised they inhibit the flow through the centres, because the centres themselves reveal the condition of the sheaths. They can filter the debris of thought and of emotion from affecting the centres directly, as they are processing energies into the physical body, then the condition of the sheaths is important for your well-being, as the centre system expands into, for example, the plane of the Spiritual Man, they become finer and light, they will therefore move through them more easily. You can look at them as protection for your brain consciousness and your physical body. If you think about a musical scale and take, for example, the key of F, they will represent the B flat, and the centre is F sharp, so they can, if you look at this analogy, ground and bring down in harmony the vibration of the centre system.

There is little known about these sheaths as it has been unwise to give any information regarding them, other than that they separate the centres of consciousness, and this particular information has been given in relationship to the Kundalini. So, what do these sheaths represent for your consciousness? They allow you to separate the real from the unreal and they carry Karma, they have a relationship to the spleen in the affect that they also transduce pranic energies within the etheric body; they are generally found in their alignment with the spinal column, hence the karmic relationship, and it is worth considering this also in relationship to the major centres, and their emotional and mental divisions. So, consider for one moment that there is a centre channel of energy and two other channels that criss-cross this this central channel down the spine. Our concern here is the central channel, which is etheric in nature, as a counterpart to the spine. This central channel has its inlet for energies within our highest, so to speak, 'bodily' centre, the crown, and then comes down the central etheric channel to the base centre. If you ponder a little on this, you will understand why I referred to the process and the raising of the Kundalini being a natural process, if you bring this instruction into your mind in a visual way.

Now, the amount of energy and the quality of energy that descends this channel is dependent upon your growth in consciousness, and also how you are using that growth in consciousness - is it for the self to acquire spiritual powers, or is it for the helping of others in many multi-dimensional ways, because all this will condition the energy's ascent, because it doesn't just descend, this is not how energy flows, this is not how energy moves through a centre, This channel does have a relationship to the centre system in the way it descends, but first think about its ascent also bearing in mind the sheaths. Now, if one is acquiring spiritual knowledge for one's own ends, and is mentally polarised there, the ascent of this energy will conceivably come to rest in the solar plexus and little of it will reach back to the crown, and further still (we will discuss this later on); the quality of energy that does reach the crown will be tinged with the colouring of the earthly man and his solar plexus. So think on this, if the ascent reaches the heart centre, and if the heart centre has a direct communication with the Spiritual Man, then the energy ascends very quickly, and look also that this energy is the communication of energy consciousness if it makes the heart centre, but the heart centre is but a reservoir for the sacral centre and the emotional nature, then it will congest there and so congest within the sacral. Now, the etheric, you will perceive for your understanding, is upon the fourth sub-plane counting upwards, and this sub-plane is the energy substance of the buddhic plane; here the love aspect has a perfection concerning your planetary life. There are other planes that are of love, maybe I could introduce some sort of information at some point regarding them.

So, imagine now this central channel, which is etheric in nature and is upon the fourth sub-plane, is also running counter with the third sub-plane, the super etheric, which is also buddhic in nature, but here we see the dilemma regarding the flow of energy, because this central channel incorporates both aspects of etheric which relate to consciousness - the ascent of the energies, and the condition of the sheaths in relationship to the centre system. With what aspect of consciousness does this flow of energy represent? Is it mental, emotional, or physical? There is a correspondence between the crown and base, and it depends whether their energy consciousness is in communication as to the energy flow of this channel, and this will depend upon your nature, because the sub-divisions below the etheric are of air, liquid and the last is dense in substance and if you are dense in your consciousness, your sheaths will reflect this and will function at a very low frequency, and their gateways will be all but closed. Fortunately, most people are beyond this stage. Consider the liquid state, and as I have said, if the ascent is based on your emotional nature, then you will understand the ascent is only within the sixth sub-plane, impossible to reach up to the Spiritual Man. It can slowly reach the crown on its own level, after pooling in the sacral centre, but understand, the crown is known as the thousand petalled lotus, and the sacral centre within this symbology has only six petals, the base has four petals. Can you see now, through this analogy, the level of the brain consciousness?

The state of air moves more rapidly, but there is an interchange also with emotion and the motivating power that is governing thought, hence, as I have quoted, the ascent and the pooling in the solar plexus, and this represents eight petals. Now think on this, the heart has twelve petals, and the Spiritual Man has twelve higher petals; let us multiply this and arrive at one hundred and forty four. Consider this in relationship to the Fibonacci sequence and the divine ratio, 1 to 1.618. Things are not so apparent until you delve into their inner meanings; this I am attempting to do. You can relate these petals, in a sense, to consciousness, so we see within the four of the base a representation of earth, this you can consider as four directions, four elements, and the square. Can you imagine when the crown links to the base, and the base links with the crown? Hence the central channel. Now, the throat has twenty petals; if you add the twelve of the heart to the eight of the solar plexus, you arrive at twenty, personality and soul in full expression.

Ponder, then, that if your consciousness is of the solar plexus, and do not be too linear with this, then there will only be eight petals functioning in the throat centre, and those eight will be the lower eight of the twenty, the remaining twelve will be dormant until the heart awakens. You can easily imagine what the expression will be.

I am relating these petals to each centre, but you also have to consider there is an overlapping of consciousness from one centre to the next, and also a free flow through the centre system on certain levels. The twelve of the heart are known as the bridge, and there is a very good reason for this as the heart lifts the consciousness to the higher sub-divisions, and there will then occur a reciprocal action with the Spiritual Man, which will activate the ninety-six petals of the Ajna centre; ninety-six aspects of consciousness, when fully opened, creates the illumined mind.

Let us consider the number nine; as with the heart and Spiritual Man, the one hundred and forty four reduces down to nine, and so adding up the petals of the six centres mentioned, they come to one hundred and twenty six, reducing down to a number nine, therefore you could say this is a central sphere of consciousness created by the centre of consciousness fully opened, as the number nine relates to the progress of the sphere and circle, and this is where you are required to consider the point at their centre in relationship to the radius, and notice how that word conjures up another word, *'radiatory'*, because the degrees of the circle and sphere from the centre point reduce down to a number nine; its full travel around the circle is 360°, reducing down to a number nine.

But there are many circles and spheres that overlap, each one has a centre point, and each one has a transition zone where the energies of both blend, so, are the sheaths transition zones relaying information from one centre to another? The centres of consciousness, as they expand into the higher spiritual bodies, naturally blend together and at some point, a continuity of consciousness occurs. The Earthly Man becomes the incarnated consciousness of the Spiritual Man; this is the descent of the Spiritual Man through the centres, but what about the ascent? This ascent occurs within the crown centre, which is known as the thousand petalled lotus. Can you start to understand the potential that exists when these petals come into resonance and are awakened? They hold within themselves the six that lie below, so there is a correspondence within the petals of the crown to the six centres below, and so, for your enquiring mind, the crown will then govern them in consciousness, and they will function according to the function of the crown, and so the energies from the crown will be permeating the brain consciousness directly, because there is nothing then that will inhibit the brain consciousness, as the centres below, as I have stated, are governed by the crown.

A momentous happening, but that happening does not just concern the crown and those centres below; you have to understand it also concerns the Spiritual Man, but there is much more. Before we move into that area, consider what inhibits the crown, and that is by the limitations of the consciousness of the centres below it, because that limitation of consciousness will be within the sub-divisions of the crown as represented by the petals. Enlightenment of these lower centres and the sub-divisions of them that reside within the higher centre, and their petal function, will enable the crown to open up more of the spiritual petals, and align more fully with the petals of the Spiritual Man. The more limited your consciousness is, the less active is the crown centre, and the dimmer will be the brow. It is a dilemma really, until that realisation occurs, that you can be far more than what you are, you will not even consider making the effort. But always there is a two-way flow, so how can mind conceive mind? The answer is not from present mind, but future mind, the mind of the Spiritual Man, from the mind itself that contains within it the wisdom, and do not conceive this over-shadowing mind and wisdom contains all past mind and wisdom. It may contain portions of it. Because those portions have not manifested as yet into the consciousness of humanity, the wisdom that has manifested is useful as a guide, but it is past wisdom related to the time.

A human being is far different now in mind, emotion, and appearance; this appearance also represents incarnation within this time. What better time to try to perceive this mind and wisdom? It is there to be translated, it is there to be communicated, it is there to be formulated into a plan. Can you conceive that your individual plan could be part of the greater plan? Each one of you has within yourself part of the plan for the fulfilment of the plan, latent creative abilities to be impressed by the wisdom which then activates this part of your nature that you have incarnated with, it is a part of your blueprint for life. So, lifting the activity of the lower centres, and I am referring to the consciousness of the lower centres, and not their natural physical function, which, on that level, needs to be kept in harmony and active so that the consciousness as a whole is governed by the crown centre.

I am wondering whether you could step aside from yourself long enough so that you can receive impressions from the Spiritual Man and bring about a further resonance with the crown centre. I say this because you have opened many petals already and have a good understanding of your lower centres, although this understanding tends to be mainly seen in others and not yourself, but nevertheless, you have an understanding so, to a degree, having this in mind, there are aspects of your thinking process that still relate to the 'I' identity and the 'I' consciousness, not relinquishing its imprisonment upon you. You may say, "I am not imprisoned." Well, that statement truly says you are, because imprisonment is limitation and to believe you are not imprisoned in some way is the consciousness of your individuality. You have individuality, and that fact you need to retain on a physical level as you cannot be absorbed by another person, or the environment, but individuality of consciousness circumscribes consciousness to your individuality, in short, to yourself, and that self makes the necessary alignment with the Spiritual Man, the crown, and others. In short, you have the understanding and can relay it to others, and you see in others where their limitations are, but you cannot see so clearly your own limitations, as there is a gap in communications between your centres, and within your centres lies the limitation, and this limitation is very clever at disguising itself. It diverts your consciousness to others rather than upon itself. You have to realise your substance is made up of devic life and this life responds to an ordered sequence of intelligent activity, so releasing your limitations and the activity of the limitation itself, via the deva substance, will cause a transformation of these limitations, but, as I say, they are very clever at directing the mind away from them.

So, what you do is focus on others and maybe what you see in others is a reflection of your limitations, but you could take that literally, because from your earthly consciousness within that limitation I have mentioned, you will begin to put yourself down and, of course, this is another play on the real limitation that is disguising itself from your consciousness. You may be registering other people's limitations of consciousness in relationship to what we have spoken of before, as illusion and glamour, because you have a need to. You cannot live and move within the physical manifest plane without some sort of protection and, of course, also this limitation likes you to work upon yourself; this, you will understand, is related to the aspect of reflection previously mentioned, and once again the limitation will cleverly present you with things other than itself. In general terms, this limitation is called the Ego. Yes, there are many subsidiary aspects of the ego, but as you peel them away, you will be getting to the ego itself, and what, for you, is a very powerful entity, and that is what holds you within the lower worlds.

So, all these aspects of ego you perceive are just its aspects, not its core of being; that is what you need to overcome, because it controls you. It controls you in so many ways and it uses the 'I' identity as its central focus so this ego has a relationship to the deva of appearance, the manifest builder of form, and within its consciousness, which is of form, lies the intellect of the ego, the desire of the ego, and the action of the ego. The deva, you could say, has more presence than the Spiritual Man if you ponder upon the fact that it represents all the manifestation of the physical plane, then it is easy to see that the Spiritual Man cannot be seen or touched in the same sense, whereas the physical world is only too apparent, so the question is: how is this dilemma overcome? It is through light; through the light of the Spiritual Man into the cave in the centre of the head, so we need to use the word recognition as a cornerstone for the quest for the lightened mind, and then you will start to realise what controls you. Is it the ego which likes to control, or is it the Spiritual Man who, I will say, governs you, but not in the form of government as you know it, with its rules? The Spiritual Man has rules, but they do not control, and you always have the choice, and then you will perceive that these rules I speak about are actually laws, and laws are just energy exchange; they are not decided upon, they just are, and as they are evolutionary, so they are not static, and the energies concerning these laws are transformational, and affect consciousness.

Inevitably you will have to confront your limitations, your ego, but do it sooner rather than later, because your growth in consciousness is all important for your evolution, and not just this lifetime. All through these transcripts, this is what I am trying to relay to you through stimulating your consciousness. So first consider, is your 'I' identity that of the Spiritual Man, or that of the ego? There is no question here where it should lie, because the ego can gain momentum if it does not lose its power; it has held you in control for many lifetimes. Now is the time for it to relinquish its control, because you have two parallel lines running here through time, one is the Spiritual Man, the immortal self who receives the energies and consciousness of the Divine Man in his three aspects; the other is the ego, who can dominate the form nature and then become abstracted into the sea of substance, to once more surface through the incarnation process, and underneath the surface mind will dwell the many states of ego from the past.

I wish now to present a series of meditations based upon the previous concepts presented, and the first concerns the centre system and the sheathes in correspondence with the higher consciousness, which, when invoked, will bring about a harmonic resonance.

Meditation

Bring into your state of mind the fact of invocation and evocation, this is the means for the precipitation of energy through the planes and into the world of manifestation. That which is evoked is called forth from the higher planes into the substance of the lower planes. To invoke creates a reciprocal action between the planes and the higher consciousness into matter, and then through the transformation of matter back into the centre of consciousness that was the source of invocation.

So, if you please, take your centre within the silence and the peace of the space in which you are sitting. Realise this is your sacred space whereby you can be at one without any interruption.

Here I am referring not only to the physical aspect of your sitting within the space, but your emotional attachment with that which lies beyond the space, and also your mental attachment. You need to be free of these, so abstract yourself totally from any environmental consciousness, and surround yourself in a cocoon of golden light.

This golden light you will invoke from the Spiritual Man above your head. Use whatever invocation you are inspired to use, and then initiate your creative imagination to achieve the cocoon of golden light.

Can you imagine this? Can you be sensitive to its energies?

Now evoke from this cocoon of golden light its conscious and healing energies to precipitate into your centre system for your upliftment of consciousness.

Realise this light contains consciousness, the higher consciousness, and so it enters your centre system. You do not need to be specific in the direction of energies into each part of your centre system. Just imagine the flow as an overall effect.

Now, turn your attention to the sheaths within the centre system, which lie in between each centre.

Is the transference of energy of a rhythmic nature?

Do not dwell too long on this, just receive a sense of their function.

Now, align the sheaths to the Spiritual Man via a column of light that travels from the Spiritual Man down the etheric counterpart of the spine. You may feel the need to move the physical spine as the energies travel down.

Imagine the energies imbuing each chakra, which you visualise as a vortex of energy going upwards for the crown, horizontal front and back for the brow. The same for the throat, heart, solar plexus, sacral, and then downwards into the earth centre, which is a reverse vortex of energy going into the earth.

In between these vortexes are the sheaths which you visualise as discs of energy.

Imagine now a complete integration and rhythmic energy circulation within the aura.

Through the cocoon of golden light, the energy traverses from the Spiritual Man into the earth through the centres and sheaths.

Be aware also that through this action, there will be healing and also regeneration.

When you have reached a point of equilibrium, everything will become still.

Come back to physical awareness when you are ready.

An important word I have mentioned in this particular part of this instruction, is the word 'communication'. You all understand that word and know from where the communication comes, for example, the mind or emotion activates the voice and sound then enters the atmosphere, the sound that forms words according to language, and is picked up and understood through the sense of hearing and the mind in relationship to the sense of hearing.

Now, communication relies very much upon your senses in relationship to mind; the mind formulates the communication according to its capacity to think, so one has to ponder how expansive and creative are your thinking processes. With a conversation there is a receiving and there is a response to what is received. Depending on what level of mind you perceive the communication will be your response, and response mainly is instant, so what you hear creates a response from you as in a conversation, your thoughts on this, first of all your instant response would be of a third ray expression, which dominates you. Does the server and, of course, the product give value for money? Can you sense where I am going with this?

I give you a few minutes to try to elevate your consciousness to the Spiritual Man to gain his understanding.

Let us focus upon the concept of 'the server'. What do you serve in this example? The customer, your employer, and so many of you become servers in everyday life in whatever walk of life. Now, when you sign up to the Spiritual Man, you also become a server, but in a very different way, because if you sign up to the Spiritual Man, you also start to embody the over-shadowing spiritual soul, the essences of the Spiritual Man and the Divine Man, and this starts to become part of your incarnate consciousness, then you will find, as a natural process of this, you will be working for the Divine Plan as it seeks to manifest. So what will you now serve? You will then serve humanity, and as I have said, you will be working for the Divine Plan as many others do, and your consciousness and soul will be part of the ashram. In this sense, there is what is known as the greater ashram, a combination of all the ashrams, and of this you will surely be a part, but also part of a specific ashram according to your means of service.

Now, what will be the substance used for your service? Yes, there is your energy consciousness, the light you will carry; it will be the substance of the plan, the thought currents of the plan, and all this through group alignment, and your co-workers will be upon many planes. Yes, they will be upon the physical plane, although you may not know them, but they will also be upon the inner planes. All will be in service of the plan in whatever field they will be working and they will be all in communication with the ashram and its sphere, and also the plan contained within it and to be able to work for the plan requires a listening ear, it requires you to be in communication and through this communication there will be manifestation and, I might add, the seventh ray, which is becoming stronger in its influence upon humanity consciousness, is almost magical in its manifestation and appearance. So, if you can take humanity as the customer, what is its demand? I will leave you a short time to ponder this. Thank you for giving your time to this.

Consider the demand is not for more money or goods, more comforts - that is not the demand. If you bring your attention to the soul of humanity, you will find out what that soul is crying out for. The soul demand is very different from the demand of the personality, and indeed the persona that has many demands. They are crying out for understanding, for love, and to be released from their imprisonment, and yet their personalities have created a concrete form around themselves, so many realise not their need. The Divine Plan, and this concerns humanity, knows what the next step should be, and this is the communication you enter into. How can you then work for the Divine Plan? And, yes, the first thing is that you will not be paid for it, not how you relate work, but you will be supplied with what you need, but you must not ascertain what you need, because this is not how it works. Remember the seventh ray is almost magical, use this magic with divine intent, throw away your sequenced mind, communicate with the ashram, lift your consciousness into the ashram and the ashram you are concerned with is synthetic in nature, it is not just one stream of divine consciousness, remember there are seven such streams that form centres of consciousness and energy known as an ashram on buddhic levels of existence. Now, this ashram is a combination of three streams and, of course, if I assign numbers to them, you will find they are one, two, and seven. This stream is made up of a condensation of these three streams into one centre, which produces, when blended, a new stream of energy.

Ponder on this and you realise why you can receive many abstract ways of thinking totally new, totally non-comprehensible in some ways, and yet your Spiritual Man interacting with the inner man, via the Earthly Man into the brain consciousness, will start to perceive the importance of these many abstract thoughts, and will eventually come to understand that they are going beyond existing thought, and then there is no need to understand these abstract ways of thinking, because you then identify with them and that is lifting of the consciousness into the energy consciousness of abstract thinking, and this is the higher mind. Can you conceive how versatile this higher mind can be? How many times have you been in the position of not having the answer to a problem? It is because you focus upon the problem from a third ray intellect, which means there is a yes and a no, a right and a wrong, a positive and a negative. When you conceive within your brain consciousness that you are right, you are also identifying with the opposite aspect, which is to be wrong, and, of course, vice versa, so therefore, you have instilled into your brain consciousness the concept of right and wrong. In fact, you don't have to instil it because it is always there; it is a product of the age humanity has gone through, so there it is upon the mental plane and everywhere you go in all aspect of life, you will encounter this concept of right and wrong, and you buy into it, not in money, well not directly, but in communication and mental activity.

How can there be a right or wrong? But what you have really is differentiations of an idea, a proposition, or whatever the subject is, and if you bring it down to a basic level, it can come down to morals and behaviour, but then they all conceive consciousness and the ability of the consciousness to portray spiritual values.

Enough of that for the moment, as there is a need for the transference of energy, back to the Master K.H.

Master K.H.

Greetings. I wish to proceed now with this instruction by projecting to you a meditation. We will take the theme, initially, of communication.

Please prepare for meditation in the way you are most comfortable with, but be concerned with an ability to become still within the space.

Meditation

Having now initiated that stillness, become focussed and aligned in consciousness via a third eye alignment, integrating your three lower aspects of consciousness into a combined unit that identifies with the Divine Plan.

Hold this focus to allow your lower bodies to resonate in harmony.

Realise they are communicating this concept of the Divine Plan, and so they are aligning themselves, via a devic communication. This is an automatic response to your request from the third eye Ajna centre identification.

Are you now resonating in harmony? Ask yourself this.

Are you prepared to make a further alignment with the head centre, via your withdrawal of energy from the Ajna centre into the cave in the centre of the head, then into the head, and then rapidly into centre of consciousness of the Spiritual Man?

You set up a brief two-way flow of communication, but remember to listen to the Spiritual Man. How does he view this earthly thought upon right and wrong? What does he wish to talk to you about? There is a need to be objective with the language you are using.

Lift your consciousness into the consciousness of the Spiritual Man.

Enter now into no-thinking to allow the Spiritual Man to communicate with you; have an attentive ear, but do not think. If you hear something, allow it to wash through your brain consciousness.

The idea behind this is to negate your intellect, allowing the intuitive aspect of your brain consciousness to intuit a response.

Now, communicate a seed thought towards the Spiritual Man.

What do you wish this seed thought to be? I will give an example, "I am light".

Project this seed thought into communication with the Spiritual Man and wait for a response. You will find it might be instantaneous.

Remember, this is thought - your thought, so when you receive an answer to your seed thought, ask a further question. A response will come and, therefore, you will be in communication.

I leave you with this. It will naturally come to a conclusions.

A record of this will be useful.

The seed thought I have given you is also an affirmation, because it starts with "I am", which is very powerful in its intent to embody that which it states, in this case, light, so this is something quite different in the use of seed thoughts, as you are stating that you *are* the seed thought. So, I will present to you more seed thoughts to be used with this meditation. The second is, "I am love", and the third is, "I am life". On the conclusion of these, you can then bring them into a synthesis by using the seed thought "I am Light, Love, and Life," and through the communication with the Spiritual Man, you will gain a higher understanding into those words. These I have presented before in the Point of Stillness work.

Now these three energetic impulses are from the higher consciousness and therefore they can break through your limitation, your gap in consciousness, and become an integrative way of illuminating your mind as to your hidden limitation. The inner man is aware of this, as he is in communication with your brain consciousness and your devic lives, as there is the key to your spiritual enfoldment through the illuminations of your limitation, and remember, this limitation has its own consciousness within the brain consciousness and the inner man. If you realise this, then you will seek to embody the Spiritual Man, to throw his light upon this subject, and also he can throw his love and his life upon this subject, therefore, you will become aware. You will become aware of yourself within circumstances, you will become aware of yourself within yourself. Only too often the self, or the limited self, diverts the consciousness away from itself onto others, analysing others, giving advice to them, all from your limitation.

So, it is well to ponder upon limitation and, of course, restriction; to be restricted holds you within a certain sphere and all too often this is not a sphere at all, it is confined within certain levels of consciousness that cannot be called a sphere, because a sphere is a perfect example of the divine nature. So, I seek now, through meditation, to create a condition whereby you can be aware of your limitation, and so create your sphere.

The first thing I wish to place in your consciousness is the aspect of pride. This is the energy of limitation, it congeals the consciousness, which then becomes concretised within existing mental thought patterns and, of course, pride is the energy consciousness of limitation.

Meditation

Take yourself now into the space, release yourself into the space, relegating all thought and feeling into the space, so there is nothing that can hinder the descent of the Spiritual Man.

You identify with the Spiritual Man on its own plane, with is causal. Realise this plane exists and enter into it, thus negating all aspects of time.

Now, this plane, which is causal, also exists on a certain level of your heart centre. So, you are focussed upon the causal plane that of the Spiritual Man which is identified above the head.

Now from this, identify the causal plane as an aspect of your heart centre. You may find a limitation here as your heart centre also has a relationship to the lower centres - thought, feeling, and action.

This causal plane you can identify within the heart centre, approximately twelve inches outside of the physical body

Now bring the energies of the causal plane through the levels of the heart centre into the physical body, and the brain consciousness.

First identify more fully with the Spiritual Man, you see him as a sphere of light and this sphere of light you create within your auric field, and imagine this sphere of light surrounding your auric field. This is on the causal plane and it will be a shade of blue.

Holding your focus with the Spiritual Man, and also upon the level of the causal plane of the heart centre, start to bring light, tinged with blue, inwards into the mental level of the heart centre.

This is where you will encounter an aspect of your limitation, and, at the same time, you flood this energy into the solar plexus.

What is the word that represents your mental limitation? Give this your due consideration, then replace this word with its opposite word, with the love of the Spiritual Man.

Move now the energies into the emotional, feeling aspect of the heart.

Visualise the blue-white light entering, and at the same time drop these energies into the sacral centre.

What word represents your limitation? Be honest with yourself, and let your pride go.

If you have this word, then ask the Spiritual Man for a word to replace it.

Bring now this light into the etheric physical of the heart centre. What do you now perceive as a limitation?

Remember, all words are an energetic form, so the opposite word will bring about a state of peace.

Register the word you need to alleviate your limitation upon the etheric and physical plane.

Finally, flood all these levels with the light of healing from the Spiritual Man.

Allow a few minutes for everything to settle and become harmonious.

You will probably have gained some realisations from this meditation. I wish that you use those constructively, and not in any way as a centre of focus for you to dwell upon; I am seeking to move your consciousness out of your limitation, not to bring your consciousness into the limitation as the results and realisations of this meditation, as that will only give your limitation the energy of your focus, leading your brain consciousness into confusion. So, as an addition to this meditation, I am going to project a healing meditation, which will work very nicely with the meditation you have just used, but first I wish to correct any thoughts you may have concerning your limitation. Whatever you perceive in relationship upon the physical planes, has a point of identification upon the causal plane. You may ask, "How can I have a limitation upon the causal plane?" Well, the limitation upon the causal plane concerns recognition. You can have an identification upon the causal plane, but do you recognise it? The receptivity of this recognition is not causal, it is upon the physical plane, therefore, the Spiritual Man, although complete in himself, is limited by the physical planes, because the Spiritual Man created your incarnate consciousness, therefore, his essence has descended into manifestation.

Prepare now for this meditation.

Meditation

Enter into the silence of the space, and also become aware of the point of stillness.

Lift your consciousness above the head to the Spiritual Man. Perceive a sphere of light, and then the inner man, via a line of light into the heart centre.

The Spiritual Man makes a request to the inner man and asks him to be prepared for healing.

The inner man then communicates this request to its devic life and form.

The Spiritual Man then abstracts from the divine consciousness the energy of love and healing.

The Spiritual Man then requests the inner man to release all pain.

The inner man then communicates, first with its mental deva, requesting all oppositional thought to be adjusted, and to be in alignment with the Spiritual Man in divine order; light and healing from the Spiritual Man is then projected into the mental body.

The inner man now communicates with its emotional, or astral deva, to release any harmful feelings and glamours, and to bring the emotional body into an alignment with the Spiritual Man in divine order; light and healing is then projected into the emotional astral body.

Once this is aligned, communicate to the deva of appearance that governs the physical body; affirm the line of communication as being the Spiritual Man, the inner man, and then the deva, for the healing of the physical body, according to divine law.

Visualise your etheric body as golden light, which then moves inward and impregnates all the substance of the physical body.

When you have the sense of stability, bring this mediation to a close, and then become physically present.

Can you now evaluate the results of these two meditations as an observer, which requires your consciousness to be with the Spiritual Man, and in doing so, you personally are not required to dwell upon your limitation, as it has been realised, and there will have been some sort of recognition.

Now, the key to this is to develop all those potentialities present which the limitation has restricted you from experiencing and, of course, do not mentally try to abstract these potentialities from your inner man, as he will not cope with your demands; just go with whatever tendencies wish to change, but not those that represent your limitation. You may ask, "How will I know the difference?" That is quite easy, really. If it is the limitation, then those aspects of yourself that you are familiar with will escalate in their expression, if they are allowed to do so. You will know these as they do not serve you, and you will have already ascertained what they are, or you might not have realised this. When there is any sort of realisation, then there will be an opposition occur to counter this realisation. Now, with many of your realisations, it is just a matter of moving this realisation into the waking consciousness and life circumstances; not a lot of opposition will occur there, unless your life circumstances has many attachments. By that, I mean you are - on the three levels of the mental, emotional, and physical - involved, and cannot function freely due to this involvement.

Now, it is wise to seek counsel regarding this. I wish to present seven aspects of this for your consideration. These seven aspects represent seven streams of energy, which I have mentioned to you before.

So, the proposition to function freely is related to your work concerning the divine plan, not your work concerning making others happy, or fitting in with whatever others find agreeable. What do you want to function freely as (this is worth taking into meditation)? Freely as the Spiritual Man, or freely as the Earthly Man? Two very different ways of living, and by now you will be familiar with both, although there may be some confusion between the two, so, if I relay to you some information concerning these seven aspects in relationship to the Spiritual Man and the Earthly Man, you will gain some understanding that will be of use to you.

The first stream to consider for your identification is will and power, relating to purpose. Can you see the dynamic use of this energy in service, which is really your work concerning the Divine Plan? It cuts through the veils of illusion and glamour, and enables you to discriminate the essentials and non-essentials, and it enables you to implement the plan as you have perceived it. But it is also regarding the Earthly Man who then seeks to control, to build a fortress of isolation, to be always right. Now, to function freely, you require the second stream of love and wisdom, and to blend it with the first, as the Spiritual Man.

Can you feel and experience from your higher aspect, that of the Spiritual Man, what this might mean? Take this also into meditation to gain insight into your Earthly Man. Regarding the Earthly Man, will and love are something quite different, and you can relate them to the three lower centres of consciousness, the base, sacral, and solar plexus. But you could add the third stream of active intelligence also to these three centres, and there you will find the horizontal life, and their combined activity upon the physical plane. Now, if active intelligence governs will and love upon those lower planes, then the activity upon those planes will reflect this within the Earthly Man for his own ends, as in chaos; one aspect governing the other according to the circumstances, resulting in a confused brain consciousness.

These three streams, if received from the Spiritual Man, will have quite a different result, as they affect the brain consciousness, so it is quite reasonable to assume the brain consciousness has two aspects, one of the Spiritual Man and the second of the Earthly Man, with, in general, the Earthly Man's brain consciousness being more dominant. So, as you aspire to function more freely, you will wield these three streams of energies from the consciousness of the Earthly Man, although it will be from the higher aspects of the Earthly Man, and this, you will understand, is a natural progression, until the higher understanding from the Spiritual Man enters. Then, as you progress through consciousness, you will see the difference and so you will fluctuate between the two, and until you fully understand this process of fluctuation and enter into it, you will be in conflict with it.

That is not necessary, so the fourth stream gives you the resolution for this, as it relates to harmony through conflict. Such a versatile stream of energy and, yes, it will create conflict until harmony is achieved through your embodiment of the previous three streams, and creativity used and expressed in harmony with the Divine Plan, and this is the answer to the proposition of how to function freely. You must understand that humanity has been functioning within its overall consciousness from the aspect of the third stream. Now, with the transition we see coming rapidly in the fourth stream, with the seventh stream as an overall governing consciousness as against the existing third stream, the right and the wrong, the good and the bad, which is so ingrained that humanity automatically responds to these suggestions and many others that limit its ability to function freely. But, this has to be a gradual process, and this is the same for you, although the seventh stream can produce instant manifestations, the fifth energy stream is also a governing factor as it relates to science, and what awesome progress has been made over the last one hundred years.

Now, the question I ask you is, can you function on the fifth stream and the fourth at the same time, as in all appearances, they are very different qualities, and can you shift your third stream consciousness onto the seventh stream, incorporating both? What I am trying to say is that you can become all the streams in consciousness and in expressions, and this is the ability to function freely, so with this in mind, consider the sixth stream, which has been a dominant energy for a long time, and has influenced humanity to work more with the third stream, so if you are moving towards the future, you will be moving away from idealism and the direction of the sixth stream. Can you see this sixth stream working out in groups of all description? This could all seem confusing as to what you should be, and the answer is - be yourself, your spiritual self, your divine self. You might now ask, "How do I do that?" You become the Thinker, and you think in seven directions, and upon seven streams of energy consciousness, not one or two, and you are then thinking upon the lower aspects of duality that the streams give when they enter the physical planes. You lift your consciousness away from the mundane, from the normal, from the conformity, so you then will have the ability to jump consciousness from one stream to another, as I might point out, what will govern your thinking at any particular time and circumstance; all this in line with the Divine Plan and that aspect I am mentioning all the time, again might seem other than your consciousness, so I will say to you, your Divine Plan and purpose for your life, because there is no difference between both, and the reason is you are a microcosm within the macrocosm, both are one and the same thing.

Now, let us consider how to become the Thinker and first, a meditation in preparation for this. You can assume the Thinker is upon a certain plane of consciousness and upon a vertical line, but the consciousness of the Thinker is on a circle and contained within a spiral.

Meditation

Prepare for meditation with the concept of the Thinker within your consciousness, and swiftly reach a point of stillness.

Now, because you are at the point of stillness, your auric field is clear, you are receptive.

Bring into your mind the concept of the Thinker, just hold the words *the Thinker*.

Now identify and imagine the Thinker as a centre just above your head; imagine this centre is a centre of receptivity, and what lies over-shadowing the centre of the Thinker is the over-shadowing spiritual wisdom, and all the Thinker has to do is become receptive to this wisdom.

Reaffirm your state of meditation, the silence, the Thinker above the head, a clear auric field, with only the words *the Thinker* moving through it, and the over-shadowing wisdom.

Hold now this state of meditation, this is creating a point of tension for receptivity.

Now bring into your mind the seed thought *'the Weaver is the light'*. Where does the Weaver lie? Is it within the sphere of the Thinker?

No, it is the result of the Thinker, the Weaver is the spiritual soul of man.

What is this light you are meant to weave? Think about this.

Where does this light come from? Think about this.

For this meditation, it will come from the over-shadowing wisdom. Imagine lines of light from this source entering the sphere of the Thinker, but also the Thinker above the head is also within the head, and it is from that place, through the vertical alignment, that you can start to really think. It is from that place that you can weave the thought of the Thinker into a pattern, and trust the pattern will emerge and become a tangible reality.

So, now ask the question as the Thinker, "How can I become a weaver of light for the Divine Plan? What is my job concerning the Divine Plan?"

At this point thoughts may well enter. Try to weave them into a pattern. Realise this you are doing as a part of the One Life.

Anything of significance for humanity, place into a geometric sphere of lines of light and send out it onto the etheric network into the consciousness of humanity.

Then bring everything to silence, retaining only the Thinker above the head and within the head, and then bring the meditation to a close.

A record at this point of your experience would be invaluable to you for the future, as what you record could open more doorways of consciousness, and further activate the Thinker.

You will notice that I am presenting the Thinker as something apart, to a degree, from yourself. There is a reason for this, because your consciousness identifies things in that way, this is the Law of Economy that keeps things separate, and this is the Law concerning the dense physical plane, so to start with, see the Thinker as that sphere of consciousness and identify as the Thinker, and so you will be bridging the gap in consciousness between yourself within the physical worlds, to then bring about an identification with yourself within the higher worlds. You must remember this higher self, (and this terminology is quite familiar with a lot of people), is a totally different self than yourself within the physical worlds.

So, is this higher self then the Thinker? It is part of the Thinker, but the true Thinker is yourself within mind upon the physical plane of mind, integrated within time and space with the higher mind through the ability to bridge the gap in consciousness, via the aspiration to do so within the true reality, forging across this gap, producing lines of light and this is the Rainbow Bridge, and so the form also weaves in the light. What the Thinker then does is outpour the results of his thinking, the results of his realisations, and his consequent awareness. As you then become the Thinker, and that doesn't mean you are the Thinker all the time, not as in abstracting from the over-shadowing wisdom that which is intangible to the world of knowledge, but you can become the Thinker when it is necessary, and this necessity corresponds with the work you are doing for the Divine Plan, so there can be no complacency here whereby you decide to become the Thinker once a week. Who is doing the deciding in this case? Certainly not the Thinker, because the Thinker decides when to enter into the state of receptivity, and it will be more than once a week, because if you become the Thinker, you will set a rhythm, and be assured you will be drawn to this rhythm, so do not try to decide what it will be according to your circumstances. As the Thinker, you will also be testing yourself, your physical self, regarding your commitment; this the Thinker requires from you, and if you ignore the Thinker, then he will disappear until you sow the seeds once more for his appearance.

Think very carefully on what I have said. The Thinker comes when you decide to think, then both aspects begin to resonate, resulting in manifestation. Now, there is a process for manifestation, so if you have understood how the Thinker works, and remember it is abstract moving in seven different ways, what do you do to start the manifestation process? First, you need to want to do it, to see the benefits of doing it, to see it as a worthwhile process, and not only to see, but to understand and feel it is a worthwhile process.

Very few people are committed or dedicated to enter this process, it requires too much from them, specifically time, and that is a major mind problem which needs to be overcome, because you base your effort on physical time and a third ray understanding whereby it will take up a lot of your time. Far from it, that is a misconception, because as you become the Thinker, then you are capable of rhythmic continuous thought that overcomes the time element that you all suffer from. What your intellect or mind would conceive as something that would require many hours to achieve, would be achieved in probably one-tenth of that time. So, this element of time you need to forget, and every time it enters your thoughts, dismiss it and tell your mind this is not a reality, but always the existing mind will say these thing to you. That is what happens, as you possess a physical brain consciousness, but the more you become the Thinker, the more you realise this duality, and you give those thoughts as little energy as possible. So, the Thinker becomes your inner voice, the voice from out of the silence, and if it is not out of the silence, then it is the sound of your existing thought that will tell you many things.

I now wish to present a concept: that your senses have an intelligence, which you might say is the functioning of the brain in relationship to the senses, and the brain controls the senses, so in that proposition, the senses are the product of the brain. Could the senses function without the brain? In this context, you would say they couldn't because there would be nothing to register what they are receiving, so also one can assume the senses are receiving stations for the functioning of the man within the brain to then analyse and formulate a sensation.

The reason I am now bringing your awareness to the senses is because the Thinker utilises the senses. He also utilises the centres of consciousness, a triangle of head centres and the corresponding endocrine glands, and the brain itself. The senses become an extension of the Thinker; he is aware of the many levels that they can be activated upon, and, at some point, they become a synthesis producing further senses that, for your understanding, expand into higher realms of consciousness, so it is this synthesis of senses which occurs upon the higher sub-divisions of the buddhic plane that has a relationship to the synthesis of the seven rays of consciousness that I have mentioned regarding the Thinker, and his ability to switch from one mode of thinking to another.

It is worth me reiterating that each mode of thinking is not just one ray and one stream of consciousness; it is a mixture of more than one with just one stream being dominant, for that time, concerning the aspect of thinking in relationship to yourself, to your environment, and to the materialisation of the Divine Plan. As long as the Thinker is aligned with the Divine Plan, then he is aligned with its purpose and your purpose within it. Come to this realisation of yourself and your purpose; stop running around, and that is not just physically, but mentally. Through the Thinker you will pick up the signals from the Divine Plan that is held in substance upon the buddhic plane, and, yes, that might be an aspect of the plan for humanity as a whole concerning the many aspects of humanity and how it functions, for example, education. But also, you will pick up that aspect of the Divine Plan that is for you to develop. "But I am not important enough," you might say. Everyone is important to the Divine Plan, it misses no one out; it's just that your thinking concerning the Divine Plan is somewhat distorted, you separate the planes, you understand the lower planes which are physical, even the mental is considered to be physical, and this is because they are tangible to you, which means, basically, everyone is aware of their existence, they do not necessarily understand them, but they recognise the three concepts concerning them: thoughts, feelings, and actions, the very basis of *interrelations*, and this word is very important.

Now, the other planes that are spoken of are regarded as intangible and also spiritual, and there the separation is seen by most of you. Because they are intangible and spiritual, they can seem beyond your reach until you apply many spiritual practices, for example, meditation, mantrums, affirmations, rituals, and also seek purification to invoke the spiritual worlds into your consciousness, or another way is to '*chase the rainbow*' so to speak, and wish your life and consciousness to be upon those spiritual planes, abdicating the physical plane as a place not to be. Can you see all this separation? If you think your life would be easier and full of love and light upon those planes, think again. It is not like that, because, to be upon those levels, the aspect of desire does not exist, nor does this aspect of separation, and for you wishing to be on those planes contains both these aspects. Also, what is required is the sacrifice of these wishes and desires and so you will take on a responsibility such as you have never known before, the responsibility to the plan, to your group, to the One Life, and in many instances, humanity, and the lower kingdoms. So, this sacrifice is the sacrifice of the personal self and one word connected to this is '*gain*', because you will not gain anything, you will function without any expectation of results, as this is not the way of enlightenment, so put away any concepts that enlightenment is a wonderful, serene and peaceful state. Far from it, but there are other things that can outweigh the sacrifice that is made.

Now, if you realise the physical is only separate in your mind from the spiritual because of your over-identification with the physical, you can start to realise they are not so intangible or separate. If you can understand this, then you will not seek outside of yourself for the answer. Any so called initiations or attunements which are offered, all the mantrums in the world, will not do this, nor the affirmations, and anything else that is acclaimed to transform you into a spiritual, enlightened person; they will not do this - you have to initiate your own growth. You have to become the Thinker; the Thinker bridges from the tangible into the intangible, and then the intangible becomes the tangible, and many interrelations are formed; a channel is created between the tangible and the intangible and you will become the Thinker. When you wish to become the Thinker, the senses will become more intelligent concerning receptivity, and all these aspects I have mentioned form an interrelation, and the brain consciousness is able to discriminate what is real and what in unreal. The realities of this will become only too apparent, and this is also a sacrifice, the sacrifice of your personal self within interrelations, and, of course, the Thinker functions freely within interrelations, but the Thinker also discriminates these relationships.

Meditation

So, let us use the concept of interrelations as a seed thought for meditation, and initiate the weaver of light. Prepare yourself for meditation, we will use the concept of motion.

Bring yourself, via an identification of your total earthly self, within the silence of the space.

You realise there is a point of silence within the heart centre, and you realise the Spiritual Man above the head, and then bring about a fusion of the Spiritual Man and the Earthly Man into the centre of the head. The Earthly Man is fused via the point of stillness within the heart.

Now, from this centre within the head, you enact a further expansion upwards to a centre of consciousness. You do this via an act of the will.

Imagine this centre full of vibrant life and within the centre is the Divine Man.

Imagine also this centre is in constant motion. It is attracting into it from an even higher sphere and radiating energy downwards into the lower spheres.

Pause now to meditate upon the seed thought '*interrelations*'

Now this sphere of consciousness that is of the Divine Man, is your place of identification for this seed thought.

Be creative, try to conceive what the relationships are to this sphere of consciousness from above and beyond it; then the relationship to that which lies below, and realise all this is related to each other.

See these interrelations expanding out into the cosmos via a triple interrelation with the Great Bear, Pleiades, and Sirius.

Attempt to perceive the lines of energy, realise the interrelation of yourself with these, this greater whole, this universal conception.

Be inventive with your thought processes by dropping your surface mind below the level of your awareness of it.

I leave you now to proceed with these ideas.

Pause

I will ask you now, have you any ideas concerning interrelations? Can you perceive the energy of these ideas?

Place these ideas into the centre of consciousness of the Divine Man, see the words enter into its sphere of consciousness.

Now clear the mind, because within this sphere of consciousness lies the Divine Plan.

Enter a waiting stage. You are ready now to receive back your ideas from the centre of consciousness of the Divine Man, and these ideas will be impregnated by the Divine Plan.

They may be totally different from what you projected - well, in your mind anyway.

Also realise your ideas have stimulated a response. You imagine the reciprocal ideas entering the Spiritual Man.

Now, the Spiritual Man is group consciousness, so perceive the Spiritual Man as a group - many Spiritual Men connected together.

You imagine yourself as a part of this group consciousness.

You may register more interrelations and ideas from this identification.

See many lines of light from the highest point of your meditation into the cosmic spheres, the Great Bear, the Pleiades, and Sirius, into the centre of the Divine Man and then the Spiritual Man.

See these lines interrelating, not just of a vertical nature, but an outward nature, in motion and circular.

Bring a focus upon three of these lines of energy. Realise first the stream of will and purpose from the Divine Man, then the stream of love and wisdom, then the divine intelligence.

Identify them amongst the many streams and become the weaver of light. Blend these together into a synthesis within the centre of the Spiritual Man, then down into your instrumentality, realising the interrelations of all your parts.

You experience total integration.

Now, bring your attention to the Ajna centre, approximately six inches outside your physical brow, and project the combined energies out upon the etheric network, into the consciousness of humanity.

Imagine will, love, and intellect precipitating into the totality of human consciousness.

Relax your attention.

So, now ask yourself: can you function freely within interrelations? Can you exhibit the qualities and expressions of the seven streams of consciousness?

Quite a task, you might think, and that is the key word *'think'*, and the proposition of the Thinker, as I have presented, and all of this without any expectation, because expectation will not achieve any results, not if you think about it. If you have any expectation of yourself, that expectation becomes a limitation, according to the expectation, but you also have to have no expectation from a place of expectation! Quite a dilemma, which means you can expect the unexpected, but you cannot mentally formulate what to expect. That is the limitation I have mentioned, and, of course, you have to let go of physical time, because you might expect a period of rapid spiritual growth, according to your understanding of time, and your place within your lifetime.

What I will say is that when you do become the Thinker, and there are various degrees associated with the Thinker so you cannot just say, "I am the Thinker", although you can if you are using this statement as an affirmation. (I have spoken about the *'I AM'* principle in other works, so I will not expand upon it here.)

Now these degrees I have mentioned have an interrelationship to the initiation process. Technically, the cosmic physical plane, as represented by the planetary ring pass not. offers nine initiations, with initiation six opening the door onto seven paths, the choice is there - which path will be taken? Nine relates to the circle and the sum of its parts, but if you take the circle as a whole, then the nine become the one, with nine sub-divisions, but they are essentially a one, so there is but one initiation. You might find this confusing, but if you have expanded yourself as the Thinker, this abstract presentation will ring a truth, and sometimes all that is necessary for your understanding is that it rings a truth, so you can embody this truth that sounds out without having to intellectually understand the concept from that level of consciousness, because that level of consciousness will limit the truth. Now, here you will find one of the major battles of your personality; the personality needs to know, but how can it know, because it can only understand that limited band of consciousness within which it functions. Now, the Thinker also requires to know, and the more the Thinker expands his thinking, then the Thinker becomes the Knower and with this proposition, he has no need to break down the truth into its parts to gain an intellectual understanding, because he knows the truth. But, he will break down and intellectualise the parts, when it is necessary for him to do so for the benefit of others, and to give them an understanding of the truth; all the time the Thinker is trying to initiate within others to also become the Thinker.

Back to the concept of time, for you to gain an understanding, the early stages of the Thinker can seem very slow, with little reward for your effort, but realise this - as you become more and more the Thinker, then things will speed up quite considerably, so it is worth understanding this. You have spent five years trying to expand your consciousness, and you have tried many ways, going here and there. You may have found a method, but still you have little reward, so you gravitate towards more methods that promise you instant results, and at some point you may believe you have expanded your consciousness because of your experiences, and there is the trap of glamour and illusion because your experiences are all outside of yourself; they are just experiences, they are not consciousness. This is the danger of the early initiations, the early stages of the Thinker, or, I should say, the aspiring Thinker, who looks for his thinking outside of himself, from other people.

So, contemplate the use of knowledge to the Thinker, if the knowledge reveals truth, then it is worth acquiring, but do not be trapped within knowledge and also do not be trapped in what some people regard as the intuition. A common statement by those who are starting to adjust to the intuition is to ask "What does that mean?" They want to know and gain an interpretation of a spiritual experience, and so the aspiring Thinker will be seeking outside of themselves for an answer, and the more people who are asked, the more answers they will receive, all different, so as far as the Thinker is concerned, it is better to seek your own answers, then at least it will be your truth.

Now, if the Thinker, through a spark of enlightenment, suddenly realises that results will come if he perseveres, if he keeps on meditating and trying to reach out for the over-shadowing wisdom, then the glamour and illusion will start to be seen and realised, and you will have the power of discrimination. There is a danger here of seeing too much and focussing your attention on all these things that you have realised, and consequently be more critical of what you perceive as being in opposition to the Spiritual Man. I have covered some of this, but it is well worth revisiting to get the point home. If you criticise something with the intent to criticise, then you are giving over a certain amount of your energy to it, therefore, you will be identifying with it and limiting yourself to everything of similarity of energy consciousness, and hence you will be separating yourself from the One Life. Observation is different as certain aspects need to be discussed. An observation states the truth and that can be a stark reality, but observation does not criticise, it relays the truth of the observation, and the more the Thinker enters into higher states of thinking, the more real and concise will be the observation.

Now, as this happens, and the Thinker penetrates into these higher states of consciousness, then things speed up and the Thinker becomes the Probationer. He knows where he is going, he has found the way, and what he should be identifying, although there may be certain things that may attract his attention and try to steer him off the path - those of an exterior nature through environment, and then there are those, and I shall call them 'tests of thinking', that will require what I will call 'decisions of truth', and these may be of a more personal nature. Where is the Thinker leading you in consciousness, what revelations are you receiving, and what will you do with them? These are all questions that the Probationer is required to sort out, so this stage of the Thinker is a sorting out stage. Things have speeded up, a higher consciousness is revealing itself, and yet there appears, at this point, so much to be sorted within yourself and your environment.

The Master D.K.

Thank you for your attention to this subject. If this was not so, then I would not be relaying to you more insight at this time.

This particular stage of development will focus your energies midway between your emotional and mental aspects, and it is this cross-over between the two states; although you may perceive this as automatic. It is not. This particular zone and cross-over occurs within certain, and I will use the terminology of these instructions, sub- divisions, if you cross over from the level of the solar plexus, then you will realise a condition of limitation, and your gateway of consciousness will be self-centred. The Thinker will also be self-centred, but also the Thinker will not understand anything else: self-centred, self-contained. You may think this condition is one step below the aspiring Thinker - not so, my Brethren, it is the result of the aspiring

Thinker believing he knows what is better or not better, according to his consciousness and the cross-over of energy between the emotional and mental states, and this occurs within your brain consciousness via the surrounding sheaths of the brain itself. What you are lacking here is love.

The personal will is developed and you have aspired your thinking towards a goal, but this goal is self-centred; for want of a better phrase, it is what you can get from it. Here the aspiring Thinker is using the material thinking methods of manifestation and that does not work, because how can the Law of Economy accommodate any spiritual enterprise, whether that is an externalisation of a plan, or an expansion of consciousness? You have used the Law of Attraction with your aspiring thinking, then you have dropped it down to a material method of manifestation by using the cross-over between emotional and mental functioning from the level of the solar plexus. This, as a Probationer, you are confronted with, you are receiving many ideas and you are killing them off, so to speak. This is why the term *probationer* is used. Can the Thinker, at this point, be trusted with any higher revelations and ideas?

So, the cross-over, and this just does not exist between the emotional and mental, needs to be from the level of Buddhi, so I am talking about an interface between the heart centre, the causal plane, and the consciousness of Buddhi. You will note a continuity of consciousness here regarding the second aspect of love, and the penetrating energy of the second ray. In its lower aspect, you will identify with the sacral centre. It is worth drawing a diagram to appreciate this flow, to also realise where this interface lies, where the cross-over point is regarding the Thinker. Can you find your cross-over point? Can you lift your consciousness above the solar plexus? Can you cross-over on the level of Buddhi pure love, and into the centres of consciousness and their ring pass, not to then become an accepted thinker? So then ponder upon yourself within the ashram, and realise you then will be under the influence of its central consciousness that is, in its turn, a recipient of monadic consciousness. Can you be influenced by monadic consciousness, the will and purpose of the One Life, as it identifies itself within the consciousness known as Shamballa; this is where the will of the One Life lives.

So, I wish to leave you with an alignment.

Considering what I have said, align yourself with your heart centre.

Bring your lower centres into alignment with your heart centre.

Sound the OM from the heart into the lower centres, bringing about a complete alignment.

Project a golden line of light towards the soul; remember the soul is causal.

Sound the OM into the causal plane, activating the love aspect of the soul within the causal body, which you identify as being a specific distance outside of the physical, which fills with blue light, and which then moves inwards through the lower bodies into the physical.

Stay focussed upon the soul, then project the golden line of light into the Buddhic plane and the central ashram.

Experience this level of consciousness and place yourself as the Thinker within it.

Ponder and meditate on the seed thought '*I am the Thinker within the central consciousness of Buddhi*'.

Meditate upon what this means for five minutes, seeking to extract the wisdom from the Buddhic plane.

Now, as the Thinker, you become aware of the essence of the central consciousness, which, on this level, is pure love.

Bring this energy of pure love down through the levels, the soul, the heart, and the sacral; this is the line of least resistance.

Now bring into your brain awareness, and as you do this, you become aware that pure love leads to will and purpose.

Sound the OM and blend these two aspects together into the brain consciousness.

Now, whilst doing the Great Invocation, send energy via the Thinker out into the consciousness of humanity.

From the point of light within the Mind of God,
Let light stream forth into the minds of men.
Let light descend on Earth.

From the point of Love within the Heart of God,
Let love stream forth into the hearts of men.
May Christ return to Earth.

From the centre where the Will of God is known,
Let purpose guide the little wills of men -
The purpose which the Masers know and serve.

From the centre which we call the race of men,
Let the Plan of Love and Light work out,
And may it seal the door where evil dwells.

Let Light and Love and Power restore the Plan on Earth.

Sound three Oms

Thank you for your participation.

The Master Jupiter.

It is most irregular that I participate in any communication, but I have been called for the purpose of illuminating you concerning the last line of the invocation - "Let Light and Love and Power restore the Plan on Earth", so I wish to take you way back into the past, back further than your education permits you to go. That matters not, for I have no inclination towards your receptivity; I am here just to project what I have been called forth to do. If you can grasp at this moment that what is happening now has happened in the past, and the past I am talking about predates your history.

It was a very unusual time, the civilisation was in three parts, other than what lay outside of the civilisation. These three sections of society integrated the heaven and earth through their principles; these principles were projected by the Enlightened Man, who walked the earth at that time, and the plan, the Divine Plan, was in operation. If I said to you the third group, which now you would call the workers and labourers, were the group that was in full identification with the earth, they lived side by side with the animals, communicated with the flowers and plants, and also the crystals, they were aware of the devas of these realms, so all was in balance. Some workers had the task of building, so they were aware of the divine geometry. I am telling you this so you will understand what needs to be restored, because although on an evolutionary level you have advanced beyond the time I am talking about, you have lost something along the way, so these workers communicated and the crops grew, but not only that, the elements also worked with them - it rained when it needed to. Are you getting the picture?

It was not a utopia, far from it, but the consciousness of the time was balanced with nature. They had very little personal desire and so you will realise there was no separation between the human kingdom and those below it, the intelligence of the civilisation was influenced by the Enlightened Ones, but as the intelligence started to identify with personal desire, personal power, a very simple method of exchange entered into number, also the desire for gold as a means of power. Gold is the symbol of the sun and its three aspects that related to the three groups, and revealed to man the alchemical process of transformation. So the word 'wealth;' entered into the consciousness, and as the consciousness was very young compared to today, it only took the consciousness of opposition to enter for man to be in conflict with man, because of the desire for wealth, pleasure and power. The intelligence became corrupt and the Enlightened Ones gradually withdrew from the physical plane. Psychic powers were developed and the balance was disturbed, and the elements responded, and humanity entered into darkness.

So, where do you stand regarding all this now? I bring your attention to the word 'light'; this is the light of mind, an Enlightened One is the bringer of this light, it is the light of mind whereby you will receive the truth. I bring your attention also to the word 'love'; this energy will connect the mind to the heart. And then there is 'power'. Such a word for you to think about. Does this word give you strength? Does this word give you the strength for your desire, and enable you to gain wealth and control? If so, you are required to think again. Power is life, it is will, and it is the motivating power of the Divine Plan. You are far beyond the consciousness, in some ways, of the civilisation I have spoken of, and in other respects you are not, because they accepted they were part of the One Life, until it all went into retrograde. Now your consciousness has entered more into the mental plane; the science and the technology are incredible, but remember, many of you are recapitulating your growth from that previous civilisation and have arrived at the same place on a higher turn of the spiral, so you were part of the One Life before. You can be again; this is the time of resurrection, and for your growth.

I have entered into your consciousness for the language I have needed to use, so I leave you with the last line of the invocation, with a modern definition of a word of power. Use it wisely.

Let Light, Love and Power restore the Plan on Earth. *So mote it be.*

The Master K.H.

I now wish to bring together those previous projections. The cross-over point the Master D.K. was talking about indicates a level of awareness and love that the consciousness has risen to within the One Life. The previous civilisation was at a lower cross-over point, but was more balanced within the One Life regarding the kingdoms below the human, and had developed, through that, the love aspect of the Spiritual Man whereby the intelligence was developing. The intelligence aspect of the Spiritual Man and the building were in line with the will and purpose of the Spiritual Man, but they still could not comprehend that they themselves were the Divine Plan; they could see themselves as part of the One Life, but not the Divine Plan, and, to them, the Divine Plan was represented by deity. This situation still exists, but it has changed from the many idols that represented deity, so the cross-over point was upon the astral plane and, as you know, the astral plane is governed by Ray Six - idealism and devotion - hence the major religions of the worlds, but again, all religion sees the ideal of the religion as being outside of itself. I will explain this. They see what represents the religion as being an object of worship, and that worship will open the gates of heaven for them, and also, and this is the folly, the ideal is then presented as the perfection of the religion, and needs to be followed. Re-read these words, and then understand that the object of devotion is something beyond them, they are not it, and it is not them, and if you worship it, you can enter into the realm of heaven. How can you do this if you cannot aspire towards the greater prospects?

So, the concept is that you have to become an Enlightened One, and when you finally get there, and that is the purpose for your evolution, you will not wish to be worshipped. So, for example, the Christ. He wished not to be worshipped, so that being the case, what then do people worship, if it is not the Christ, as he wishes that not to be? Ponder upon the mass thought forms of religion regarding the Christ. What have you arrived at? And that is the same in any religion, no matter what its name. The mass thought form created upon the mental plane creates the image of what the mass thought form wishes it to be, and gives it life and form, and then those who have created the mass thought form are then influenced by their creation. You could say the thought form is a life within itself, but it is not only created upon the mental plane, it is at the cross-over with the astral plane, and enters into feeling and psychic impression. This is what the civilisation did, and so if the mass thought forms were corrupt and distorted, then so would be the information received from this living form.

So, the many visions of deity were not deities at all, they were, and are, what humanity has created by the power of their thought and emotion. Taking this concept further, they are whatever you desire and will experience, if they have already been created or you have the power to create, so be aware of your glamour and your illusion, because this is the danger, and the danger is everywhere. Let us take this further. You have a spiritual experience, so called; now if this experience is from the astral and lower mental planes, then the experience will be of a human nature, either from a mass thought form, for example Archangel Michael, or your own wish to invoke Archangel Michael, for, in most cases, personal reasons. Nothing of this type can be for personal reasons, so the image that you may see will further verify your terrific psychic powers, and yet all it is, is a creation of your own imagination. Can you see how the Law of Attraction works regarding your desire?

You have to turn the word *desire* into '*aspire*'. To aspire is something very different, aspiration starts to cross over on the causal plane. I have mentioned this aspiration regarding the Thinker and I will not pursue it any further; I will shift the focus towards a higher perspective. How can humanity embody the divine principles when it sees itself as master of its own universe? How can it appreciate the need to think and to transform itself with right relationships? What will initiate a further striving forward towards the light? I am asking all these questions to stimulate your thinking. What will cause you to up your speed and spiritual growth? No effort, no results, so is your effort based upon the need of others? This is a duality that I present to you, it has two meanings, one is of the personality, and the other is of the Spiritual Man.

Let me deal with the personality aspect first; the concept was, "*is your effort based upon the need of others?*" Or, in this case, I should say "*is your effort based upon the free time you have from others?*" Believe me, many people require your time, and they have a need for your time in many ways. Ask yourself, "Do I postpone my spiritual growth because of the demand of others?" Their demand might well be of an emotional nature, and, to all intent, quite reasonable; a balanced perspective will see the right use of time. In this first instance concerning the personality, your effort is based upon what time you have available according to you commitments and responsibilities, and if your spiritual growth depends upon these, then you will be in trouble, because you will have contacted the Spiritual Man and he will be entering into your consciousness. Then the demands of others will be entering into your consciousness, and the third factor will be coming from your own inner consciousness regarding the truth of yourself and, of course, your wish not to hurt others, and to live up to your responsibilities, but also you may have come to a realisation regarding your responsibilities, and wondered how you ended up with them all.

There comes a point when decisions are required to be made based upon the second proposition from the Spiritual Man. There is much need in the world other than those around you, although they will be displaying some of the need of the world. So, through self-consciousness to what is known as group consciousness, reality becomes the pinnacle for your endeavour; your endeavour to move your consciousness towards the Spiritual Man, and then you become the Spiritual Man, you are his reflection. You may ask, "Why bother to change? It all seems too much, and things are just the same as they have ever been. It's not so bad." That one statement says it all. In the first instance, you are fixed upon a timeline, you would find it hard and too much effort to change this, and the last bit, "*it's not so bad*", your reference is the word *bad* and not the word *good*, so you have accepted your situation.

A transference of consciousness will tell you what will be the result of this attitude, and there are many who think this way, and will not try to understand the Spiritual Man. "That's a load of rubbish", "I don't understand that", and many other ridiculous comments, and what constitutes a load of rubbish is a large amount of unwanted things that have no use, or are the remnants of something which was useful and now is deteriorating. That last word is very appropriate, because the word gives you a very good reason for trying to transfer your consciousness from the environmental to the self-consciousness, to the consciousness of the Spiritual Man, because that is exactly what will happen upon the timeline I have mentioned - you will slow down, and your belief system will do this because you cannot expand out of it, so it will restrict you more and more until you become totally imprisoned within in. The moment you stop trying to think and expand your concepts on life is the moment you will have informed the deva substance of your bodies to stop creating, this you will understand, because the consciousness of the Spiritual Man stimulates the activity of the devas, and they respond according to the consciousness that is the governing factor.

So, think on this: as time goes by within this imprisonment with no change in consciousness, the motivating power of your consciousness starts to wane and what you will become, from our perspective, is very sad. All this potential that you possess, lost in time, so to speak, until another opportunity arises. You understand opportunity only from the aspect of gain so I will use this, then, to give you some understanding: what you will gain from the Spiritual Man far outweighs the effort that is required. I could use the word *sacrifice*; can you sacrifice yourself within time into the timeless place of the Spiritual Man? Can you gain a continuity of consciousness from that place? All this is possible if you strive towards that which you do not possess, and realise you can embody what, at this moment in time, is beyond your comprehension. You are required to enter into a forcing process. Yes, you may perceive this is coming from the Spiritual Man, and that may well be the case as you have invoked a response from him, but also you, the Earthly Man, have initiated this forcing process which is a process of transmutation on the level of the Earthly Man, and a transformation encompassing the Earthly Man and the Spiritual Man. Not everything concerning this occurs upon the physical plane; there is also a reciprocal action upon the higher planes. You see, the higher planes are not separate, if you initiate an enterprise that is in line with the Divine Plan, then you can expect support for your enterprise from the higher planes, this is the Law of Response. Another way of putting it is if you meet the demand that lies within humanity, then your effort to meet this demand requires, according to Law, a similar effort from the higher planes. The problem here is to support the enterprise energetically, many ideas come to nothing because they become grand ideas, and the philosophy of existing manifestation govern them.

All the constitutions and laws can destroy an idea before it even starts to manifest; do not clothe an idea with existing conformity - it will not work, there will be too much mental control over the idea, and then the idea will change its simplicity and the method will become complicated to the point of dissolution. What needs to be realised is where the idea came from, and because the idea, for example, has come into the mind and brain of an individual or group, they believe the idea is theirs. Can you see what problems will then occur if an individual believes the idea is his? He will turn his energy towards the idea and embody it as his own, he will circumscribe the idea with his own personal energy, and so the carry-through of the idea will be according to the personal desires of the idea. He will believe he is the creator of the idea, to an extent this is true as there are certain requirements for receiving ideas, the wiring has to be connected, so to speak, and there has to be some, although vague, memory that the idea has to attach itself to. Do not think linearly with this statement, because then you may believe you cannot receive an idea because of it. What you need to realise and overcome, as this instruction has stated many times, and I will put it another way: most of the time you are working and using the surface mind because it is necessary to employ this aspect of your mind, and mostly that is what you are aware of, therefore, you are conditioned by it, believing what you are thinking, or are capable of thinking, belongs to the surface mind. Now you are all starting to, or have been for some time receiving, intuitive insight. The surface mind will see this as separate until its expression and thinking changes, whereby the surface mind will automatically, when required, relay intuitive insight as a part of its conditions.

Below this surface mind, although *below* is not the correct word, lies the sub-conscious mind. If I relate the surface mind to the size of a pea, in relationship the sub-conscious mind is the complete plant containing the peas, each pea representative of a lifetime and the many experiences that the surface mind has encountered, but not retained within the living memory; the sub-conscious mind registers everything that is experienced. By comparison, the higher mind represents the field where the plant grows; I am using an analogy here, so in reality it is vast and immeasurable, it is not the higher mind itself, it is what the higher mind is in contact with. What I am trying to tell you is you are more than the surface mind, and are capable of receiving from the higher mind, and retrieving from the sub-conscious mind, so if you think you can do nothing with an idea that has descended into the consciousness mind from the Divine Plan, because it requires some sort of existing memory that the idea can latch on to, it is worth thinking again and understanding that this is a possibility.

Now, it is so easy to dismiss this idea as nebulous thought, especially if the surface mind has been very active with emotional and mental thought of a personal nature. Now the trick is to know that, and because you know this can happen, you reserve a space within your brain consciousness and the surface mind, as an area of receptivity for a divine idea. Now understand that also this space will receive realisations concerning your surface mind and the mental in which you live, which then filters into the sub-conscious, this then makes way for an idea, as the areas of the sub-conscious that are restricting the surface mind from expanding and capturing an idea from the over-shadowing wisdom, via the higher mind, and in this instance, realise you are not separate from the higher mind, meaning you can access it when required, but the higher mind is not inactive to the surface mind.

So, you access an idea, but also be prepared to recognise an idea sent to you from the higher mind, as you will be creating a two-way flow incorporating the sub-conscious mind. Recognition is the key word, and this requires action; as I have mentioned before, the surface mind will not retain intuitive suggestion, therefore, it needs to be manifested, the sub-conscious mind will receive this suggestion, but the surface mind may never retrieve it, and from this level, it is wise not to. So, this space you have reserved within your brain consciousness allows you to have a vertical alignment, it doesn't mean you will be problem-free. You may ask, "How do I create this space?" Well, that last word is the answer; to know and have the ability to be at one within the silence of the space, that will create the space within the brain consciousness. I will again reiterate, this does not have to be free from noise or people, although that's what most of you strive towards, the silence of the space with an absence of noise, and in this modern world, it is nigh impossible, you will find nature very noisy.

You see, the problem here is that you are relating the silence of the space on a physical level, yes, to a degree; with this though one has to be wise and create certain conditions for group work, but if you really want to climb Jacob's Ladder, you must develop the ability to be present within the spiritual space whilst in the physical space, and to understand this is to realise that when in the spiritual space, your higher senses are active and awake, and the physical senses then are receptive to them, and not to the goings on of your surrounding environment. It is the personality that requires everything to be in a perfect state for the personality to achieve spiritual awareness; it is not like that. Can you understand what I am saying? To embody the Spiritual Man means you discard personality preferences, quite a difficult task, as you could be put out, which means it is not agreeable to you.

You could be given many challenges regarding what I have said, until you are able to function as the Spiritual Man, whatever the situation. If you are contemplating a spiritual concept and creating an idea from it, if you wish all to be quiet to enable you to do this, I can tell you now - it will not happen. Is this not one of the challenges? The frustration sets in and you create a separatist attitude to what is disturbing your quiet. Can you see how problems develop, especially if you get together with others experiencing the same thing? That will be a topic of all your conversations, you may become aloof to others within your group spirituality, so called.

The last part of this instruction is probably not what you were expecting, but the importance of it is paramount, if you wish to climb the ladder, and you understand what that means. To climb the first rung you have to have a foundation upon the earth, so, I will continue. I will give you an example. Have you ever noticed when you go to meditate how noise can suddenly happen, whether it is from the family or outside noise that is reaching your senses? You then look at the subject of the noise and become frustrated. You could try living in a monastery, or at the top of a mountain, but you have to climb the mountain on the ladder, and this is not to place yourself physically upon it to achieve the perfect physical state for your meditation or contemplative thought. This is not the way - not now.

Many still pursue this, and those who do this that are of a higher spiritual nature are working, what I will call, *subjectively*. Many, in these circumstances, are not, they are avoiding their karma. Do you wish to do this? It might be easier for you, but you will not climb the ladder. But the ladder will be there next time, it is worth doing it now. As you climb the ladder, your personality desire will be recognition note; the same word I am using, a completely different concept, you will wish to receive recognition. There are many clever people who attain recognition and have all that goes with that, but that is a physical recognition, it is of human origin. As you climb the ladder you will receive recognition, but from more than the physical plane, so you can expect your physical recognition will not be fame of fortune, but the spiritual recognition will provide all your needs so, therefore, come to terms with the aspect of money as an economy necessary to expand your service capacity and develop the spiritual ideas that the higher mind is giving you. The Divine Plan, if you are working for it, will not leave you destitute because it needs you not to worry about economy, it will provide in just the right proportion for the work you are doing, and sometimes you may feel it is not providing at all. But then, if that is the case, you will have an over-emphasis upon your economy and will be thinking about it from the aspect of the personality and a Third Ray approach, you will be trying to work it out and, therefore, your service activity will be based upon economy and it will not work. How can the Plan provide you with economy if you are working out your economy from materialistic levels of consciousness? There needs to be a transference here from the intellect to trust, and with this, the Seven Ray of Magic can intervene and manifest spontaneously.

You have to sow the seed, then the Divine Plan can water the seed so that it can grow. This is within your consciousness, the seed has to be present, you need to assign a space within the brain consciousness for the seed to be planted. There is already a seed that every human being has, and that is the pineal gland, but you have to create the space so that the pineal gland can be activated, it will not activate if your consciousness is of the surface mind; the Thinker activates the pineal gland by the sheer fact of thinking beyond ordinary thought and as you know, the glands condition the person in many ways. They are affected by the centres of consciousness, the chakras; a balanced endocrine system is important for the health of a human being, so by the analogy that the higher governs the lower, one can understand that the pituitary gland related to the brow centre is called The Master Controller of the other glands.

What do you suppose will happen if the pineal gland came into a conscious activation in esoteric science, this is related to the crown centre? It will affect most definitely the pituitary gland, which then will have an effect upon all the others, and then the related consciousness from the pineal gland will bring into alignment the others, particularly below the diaphragm, and change their expression, this, of course, is energetic, which will consummate creative expression of a divine nature. How will you perceive this expression? Well, it will manifest in many abstract ways, a total turning of the spiral. And what is the gland that governs the soul? Well, this is not physical at all, but from a reverse context, it is known as the Jewel in the Lotus, and the centre of consciousness that activates this jewel is the nomadic consciousness that is the highest chakra centre possible. I am using the context of a chakra in this instance so that you can gain some sort of continuity of thinking regarding the many levels of consciousness. It will also enable you to understand the concept of the One Life and the Greater Life.

Yes, it would be easy to relate this also to number, but the circle and the sphere are also worth thinking about in this context. A chakra centre, or centre of consciousness, is a place of focus for a specific quality and vibration of energy, and this reflects the consciousness concerned. They are individual in this aspect only, so your seven major chakras are part of your One Life, and yet, as they develop, they become part of other lives, and yet they are a multitude of lives within themselves. So, the One Life contains within it all that is influenced by its consciousness, the One Life which we are discussing, has seven major chakra centres. It depends, at this point, whether you regard the One Life as planetary, solar, or cosmic.

Just some food for thought, the cosmic One Life of which there are seven, contains within that, for example, seven solar lines; these can be regarded as chakra centres for the cosmic One Life, and so on down to humanity itself as a whole, with all it contains, is a chakra centre of the planetary One Life, and this planetary One Life is approaching a major initiation, so everything within its sphere of consciousness is undergoing a forcing process, humanity as a whole and every individual human being. The light of this One Life is penetrating into the light that is already present within humanity, and stimulating it; also, it is penetrating into the dark and dissipating the forms present there. It is this light I am seeking to deal with, to bring about the light of understanding to you so you will find your own relationship with the One Life and move into the rhythm of the One Life, and this is why the Buddhic plane is so important for this process.

So, this light comes from the same source as that which you understand as light, the sun, but the light of consciousness that is the planetary One Life, also comes into the planetary life from other sources than the sun and the central solar life, it comes from the sun, Sirius, and two other major constellations, the Great Bear and the Pleiades. So at this point, if you can imagine yourself as a One Life, this may be difficult considering what I have spoken of, but you are the centre of consciousness for all the lives that make up your existence on the physical level, and also the energetic levels, so realise you are a One

Life and you have a responsibility for the lives that you govern. The Spiritual Man understands that many of these lives are impressed by your consciousness, as, for many, it only needs environmental and subsequent internal stimuli.

So we will do a meditation to bring the planetary One Life into your own One Life through your seven major gateways. How can we do this? Only by alignment and your creative imagination on that which, to you, is intangible.

Meditation

So, present your brain consciousness to the consciousness of the Spiritual Man.

The space within your brain consciousness that you have kept receptive, is filled with light. This light is from the Spiritual Man.

Ponder now on the fact that you are a One Life. Try to gain a deeper meaning into that statement.

Recognise the fact that your One Life is presented to you as seven major aspects, each of these is related to your One Life, and also the planetary One Life, therefore, each of these seven is related to a Kingdom within the planetary One Life.

Remember the seven is the one, so your lowest centre at the bottom of the spine has a relationship to the crystals and minerals of this planetary One Life, but also to the highest centres of logoic consciousness.

You send a line of light from the lighted space within the head, six levels above the crown. For this process I will not name them, because your intellect already possesses knowledge of them, and this would limit your experience of them.

Have you now revealed this sixth level above the crown? If you have, just hover your mind there, the energy builds and then descends down your line of light into the crown and head, and then rapidly down the spine into the base centre, and then into the earth and vitalise the crystals and minerals, all in line with the Divine Plan.

You will now continue this process of transference and integration by identifying that your lower creative centre relates to the plants and flowers and all that grows out of the earth.

Can you experience the beauty of this kingdom?

Focus back to your line of light from the space within the head, and travel back up this line of light, five levels above the crown.

This place in the Monadic consciousness. Here you are dealing with will and love. Allow the energies to build as you hover there.

At the appropriate time, they will descend down your lighted line into the head, down the spine into the centre above the base, your interrelationship centre.

The energies also move to the front of the body.

Use your imagination to see these energies entering this Kingdom, imbuing it will life and love.

Your next centre above the last one is identified with the animal kingdom. It possesses instinct and has social orientations.

Find your line of light and travel four levels above the crown to the Plane of Atma will in relationship to life.

When the energies have gathered they will descend, (you will not have to imagine this, it will just happen), into the head and down the spine, into the solar centre, they go also to the front of the body, and then into the animal kingdom, giving them life.

The next centre is the heart centre - this is a major gateway into the kingdom of souls and humanity itself.

From the head, go to the centre above the crown - you are so familiar with this now.

The energy builds and travels into the head and heart centres.

You realise your group soul relationship, and then link this relationship to other group souls incarnate within humanity via the heart centre.

Become aware of the throat centre, humanity represents this centre within the One Life, but also from the head.

Go two levels above the crown, this is a sub-division of the sixth kingdom.

The energies of divine mind accumulate and transfer down the lighted line and pass into the throat centre, and into the front.

You spontaneously sound the OM, transferring these energies into the mists of humanity, via the etheric network.

Become conscious of the Ajna centre. Take that line three levels above the crown where you will find Buddhi, the kingdom of Enlightened Masters.

At this point you are within an Ashram.

You see yourself within the sphere and transfer the energies down the line into the Ajna, and out into the consciousness of humanity.

This is the energy of Divine love.

Go back to the sphere within the head, link into crown, and from this place, your lighted line you project into the solar One Life.

Become conscious of this and finish by linking your One Life with the solar One Life.

At this point, you may well experience the energies of the three aspects of the sun.

Relax your focus.

Thank you.

Finish, third book of Transcripts from the Master KH

10th June 2015

Thanks

I wish to thank the following who have contributed to this book making it into manifestation:

> Sue Trudgian – for her typing support and sense of humour.

> Clare Carter – for her dedication and perseverance, and for living with me – not an easy thing!

Andy.

About the Author

Andrew Carter's life is dedicated to his work. His Destiny is to bring illumination to people's minds and to alleviate as much pain and suffering as possible. This he does through his healing, teaching and writing, helping to raise consciousness so there is more compassion and integration with the methods of dealing with disease and the approach to health.

He has been healing since 1996 and runs crystal and healing courses at The Rose School in Northamptonshire.

Other books by Andrew Carter:

The Third Floor – Part one - Johns awakening
Part two – Johns Challenge
Part Three – The last word
Part Four – The word
Part Five – The Dark night of the Soul
24 steps to your Destiny
Crystal Destiny
Healing Destiny
Destiny the Point of Stillness
Transcripts from the Master K. H.

Andrew can be contacted via his websites:
www.crystaltherapycourses.com

Or www.thecrystalbarn.co.uk

Printed in the United States
By Bookmasters